IN MEMORY OF:

Mr. Lemuel J. "L.J." Mosier

PRESENTED BY:

Mr. & Mrs. John J. Carr
& Son

An Illustrated Guide to
MAPLES

Antoine le Hardÿ de Beaulieu

Translated by André L. Mechelynck

Photography by

Michel Timacheff
Philippe de Spoelberch
J. R. P. van Hoey Smith

TIMBER PRESS

Portland · Cambridge

Published in 2003 by

Timber Press, Inc.

The Haseltine Building

133 S.W. Second Avenue, Suite 450

Portland, Oregon 97204, U.S.A.

Timber Press

2 Station Road

Swavesey

Cambridge CB4 5QJ, U.K.

Printed in Hong Kong

Library of Congress Cataloging-in-Publication Data

Le Hardÿ de Beaulieu, Antoine.
    [Guide illustré des érables. English]
    An illustrated guide to maples / Antoine le Hardÿ de Beaulieu ; translated by André L.
Mechelynck ; photography by Michel Timacheff, Philippe de Spoelberch, J. R. P. van Hoey Smith.
        p.   cm.
    Includes bibliographical references and index.
    ISBN 0-88192-601-9
    1. Maple—Identification. 2. Maple—Pictorial works. I. Title.

QK495.A17L4 2003
583'.78—dc21

2003053704

A catalogue record for this book is available from the British Library.

CONTENTS

FOREWORD

Maples! These trees have awakened huge interest among passionate gardeners. The incredible variety of their foliage shape and color and the great elegance of their habit justify this widespread enthusiasm of botanists and horticulturists alike. A great diversity of species and subspecies may be admired in private collections as well as in parks and gardens. Maples, however, are temperamental trees, and three must be planted so that two may prosper. But, my, what a person won't do to be able to admire them, in all seasons, those magnificent *Acer* trees with their palmate leaves and resplendent colors!

In your hands, you hold the largest illustrated reference on maples. The author, Antoine le Hardÿ de Beaulieu, with the aid of photographer Michel Timacheff, has assembled a complete inventory of the hardy species currently cultivated in Europe. The descriptions of these species are precise and compact and include, insofar as possible, where each maple grows, be it in nature or in a botanical garden. The information is priceless for anyone who wants to plant or transplant a maple on a given site. Of course, a site's microclimate should be considered to confirm the hardiness of any of the 250 species and varieties mentioned in this book.

In this volume the author has resisted the temptation to modify maple taxonomy and nomenclature, a decision I applaud. He was right to adopt the systematics of Piet de Jong, the most recent author on this subject.

This book will no doubt find a well-earned place in the libraries of amateur or professional maple fans. It is easy to use and it provides an exhaustive survey of the hardy maples.

PHILIPPE DE SPOELBERCH
Herkenrode, Belgium
16 September 1998

PREFACE

As a landscape designer and nurseryman, I am often asked to describe the plants I propose to use. It is especially difficult to describe them in winter when branches are bare, and it becomes even more problematic given how few abundantly illustrated sources exist in French, the language I use in my business. This lack of information prompted me to begin preparing a fully documented work on all the maple species cultivated in Europe, whatever their origins, including both Asian and American species. My goal is to provide gardeners with a wide sample of plants from which they can make the best choice for their garden.

Although I have covered maple species as thoroughly as possible, I have chosen to mention only those cultivars that are widely represented. A complete and permanent list of maple cultivars is not possible, since new plants are constantly being offered while others cease to be available.

The numerous photographs in this book are an ideal source of information for selecting a particular form. This is why I have taken special care to show each maple at different stages of growth, thus emphasizing its particular features.

I have used Piet de Jong's classification of maples, as it is the most complete and the most recent work to my knowledge. The geographical and historical information included here is, I think, also useful.

My hope is that this book will introduce more variety to our gardens and that the magnificent plants we know as maples will not just remain arboretum specimens. Landscape designers play a significant role in creating appropriate settings for the lesser-known maples in their projects. Nurseries will then start growing these maples and thus satisfy the ever-increasing demand.

ACKNOWLEDGMENTS

This book would not have been completed without the help of Philippe de Spoelberch, who has kindly given me access to his transparencies and provided thoughtful advice. I particularly thank him for the time he has spent in preparing this work.

I also extend my thanks to the following:

Jelena de Belder, for her gracious welcome and for her invaluable advice and information. Many photographs herein were taken in the magnificent Hemelrijk arboretum in Essen, Belgium.

Benoît Choteau, for his detailed information on propagation by grafting, his specialty.

Dominique Duhaut, for his advice and experience with propagation by seed.

André Charlier, for much information about his rare tree collection and for the time he has devoted to this book.

Charles Snyers d'Attenhove, for the welcome he extended us at Beaulieu arboretum and the detailed information he gave about the maples inherited from his grandfather, Robert Lenoir, founder of the arboretum.

Jean-Claude Baudouin, co-author of the book *Les Plantes ligneuses* (Ligneous Plants), for sharing useful information as well as some excellent photographs reproduced in this book.

Allen Coombes, botanist at the Sir Harold Hillier Gardens and Arboretum in England, for his professional advice.

Michel Timacheff, for the quality of his photographs and his many labors for this book. I had the opportunity to enjoy his agreeable company during numerous photographic expeditions.

The Belgian National Botanical Garden, for the documents it supplied.

INTRODUCTION

Maples comprise a diversified genus of woody plants, with more than two hundred species and subspecies, some of which have given rise to numerous cultivars through horticultural selection. They offer a wide choice of shapes, sizes, and colors. Coming from the four corners of the Northern Hemisphere, maples are well suited to temperate climates and are an essential element in the landscape.

DESCRIPTION

Acer is a large genus of mainly deciduous species. Most of these are medium sized, but some reach great heights and a few are shrublike. Other species are evergreen. All members of the genus have similarly shaped fruit and opposite leaf arrangement. The fruits, known as samaras, are joined at the base. Each samara consists of a nutlet attached to a long, slim wing. The nutlet contains one or two seeds. The typical maple leaf is large, flat, fan-shaped (palmate), and divided into 5 lobes, but many variations are found within the genus. The leaves of some species have 9 to 13 lobes, others no more than 3. The leaves of section *Negundo* are compound with 3 to 5 leaflets; those of section *Indivisa* are undivided.

GEOGRAPHICAL DISTRIBUTION

Maples are found throughout temperate regions of the Northern Hemisphere, especially in areas where the average annual rainfall reaches 1000 mm (39 in.). The habitat of individual species can, of course, vary greatly. *Acer pectinatum* is native in the mountain forests of Nepal, at altitudes ranging between 2700 and 3800 m (8,900 and 12,500 ft.), while *A. rubrum* grows on the edge of swamps in the United States. Some species grow in tropical climates, in Thailand and Malaya. Geographical and climatic influences have a strong effect on the overall shape of the plants.

HISTORY

Plentiful plant fossil material has enabled paleobotanists to find traces of trees resembling our maples dating back to the beginning of the Tertiary period (70 million years ago). The fossilized leaf of a palmate maple growing 9 million years ago is very similar to that of a present-day *Acer palmatum*.

During subsequent periods, maples colonized the Northern Hemisphere with the help of a favorably humid climate. Their progression throughout Europe was hindered in some countries by the glacial periods, but was maintained in Asia, where three-quarters of the world's known plant species are growing.

The earlier works of European literature contain few references to maples, but by the 6th century Japanese authors were praising the marvelous shapes of maples. The lack of diversity characteristic of European flora resulted in maples being used for timber and carpentry, and it was only during the 19th century, when an enormous botanical exchange took place between East and West, that ornamental plants began to attract attention. During that period, many new cultivars were selected and propagated in Europe. At the beginning of the 20th century, almost all species of maples were being grown in arboreta.

Today, maples are still grown for their timber but in smaller quantities than oaks, beeches, ashes, or conifers. The production of plants for landscaping is expanding in Europe, and maples are part of this trend.

ETYMOLOGY AND NOMENCLATURE

The Latin name for the maple genus, *Acer* (sharp, pointed), was chosen by Carl Linnaeus and appears in his work *Species Plantarum* (1753), in which nine maples are described.

Latin has remained the language of dendrology, a custom that, for international purposes, is practical. Moreover, some of the more exotic maples do not have a common name or the one they have cannot be easily translated.

Species are defined by an epithet, which refers to various distinguishing features of the plant, such as

- the place of origin, as in *A. pensylvanicum, A. tataricum*
- the shape of the leaf, as in *A. acuminatum, A. macrophyllum, A. truncatum*
- the name of the person who discovered or first described the plant, as in *A. maximowiczii, A. davidii, A. paxii, A. sieboldianum*
- a feature of the fruit, as in *A. diabolicum* (horned)
- a resemblance to another plant, as in *A. carpinifolium, A. crataegifolium, A. platanoides*

Each epithet is also linked to the name of the person who named the plant, followed by the year the description was published.

LEAF COLOR

The leaf color of trees in their natural surroundings depends on the type of soil and the climate. When trees are cultivated or grown under other conditions, their coloring can undergo a complete change. Other factors in determining leaf color are related to the plant itself. Generally speaking, a young, healthy plant in full growth will display little fall color, while a plant under stress will grow less vigorously, will flower and set fruit more abundantly, and will display more pronounced leaf colors. Stress may be due to environmental (wind, frost, drought, sunburn, excess water, lack of nutritive elements) or biological causes (overpopulation, damage by insects and other fauna, rot, disease). Lastly, human activity remains sometimes important, as for instance in the case of acid rains or wounds inflicted on trees.

Fall colors are the result of a chemical process. A pigment present in chlorophyll, which captures solar energy, gives leaves their green color. When chlorophyll disappears, other, secondary pigments take its place to harvest sunlight using other wavelengths. Thus carotenes are orange, yellow, or red; xanthophylls are yellow; and anthocyanins are purple, scarlet, and blue. The color transformations that leaves undergo in the fall are due to changes in the amounts of these pigments before the leaves fall. Research has also shown the relationship between sugar levels and xanthophylls, which explains why sugar maple (*Acer saccharum*) takes on such wonderful colors.

BARK

The snake bark maples (section *Macrantha*) are justly renowned for their beauty. No less than twenty maples, cultivars included, have striated trunks. The bark is reddish or greenish, overlaid with vertical whitish lines. This aspect is evident on young trees but tends to decrease on mature trees.

A few maples display seasonal color variation on their branches. *Acer argutum, A. circinatum,* and *A. pensylvanicum* are examples. Noteworthy cultivars show even stronger marking, as is the case with *A. pensylvanicum* 'Erythrocladum'.

The most spectacular bark is that of *Acer griseum,* a coppery orange-brown color; it peels away. The other species have less singular bark, varying between the completely smooth trunk of *A. mono* and the almost corky bark of *A. miyabei*.

FLOWERS

Maples bear flowers that differ greatly in size and shape according to the various species. The male flowers have 8 stamens as a rule (the number can vary between 4 and 10) situated on the inside or the outside of the nectar-bearing disc. Female flowers have a short style divided into two distinctly separate stigmas. Hermaphroditic flowers bear male and female sexual parts, but the organs of one of the sexes are often shrunken. These flowers thus behave either as male flowers or as female flowers. Some species have shrunken flower parts, such as *Acer saccharinum,* which lacks petals. In contrast, the flower of *A. negundo* has hyper-developed filaments.

Assigning sexual status to maples is a complex subject. Dioecious species are a simple case, as male and female flowers are carried on separate trees; examples are *Acer argutum* and *A. barbinerve.* The remaining species bear, on the same tree, inflorescences with male and hermaphroditic flowers, as well as female flowers, but in lesser numbers. This polygamous form is frequently found in maples. Moreover, the ratio of male to female flowers on a given inflorescence may vary strongly from one tree to the next and from one season to the next. In the same way, male and hermaphroditic flowers may appear at different times and in variable quantities. This feature, shared by several plant families, is called dichogamy. Because the genus *Acer* consists of numerous species, it also exhibits a large number of sexual combinations.

Flowering times differ also according to species. The earliest maples to flower are species of section *Rubra,* where the flowers appear well before the leaves. In other species flowering takes place simultaneously with the unfolding of leaves. During this period, most maples are at their maximum ornamental potential. Examples are *Acer ×dieckii, A. monspessulanum,* and *A. opalus.* Other maples, such as *A. campbellii, A. nipponicum,* and *A. oliverianum,* flower much later.

Finally, the flowers of some species, such as *Acer pseudoplatanus,* produce nectar.

INFLORESCENCES

Maple inflorescences can be grouped into six basic types: clusters, spikes, panicles, racemes, corymbs, and umbels (see the schematic botanical drawings on p. 452).

Inflorescences may be more than 20 cm (8 in.) long, as in *Acer pseudoplatanus* and *A. macrophyllum.* The inflorescences of *A. diabolicum* and *A. sinopurpurascens* are very spectacular, whereas those of *A. sieboldianum* are quite inconspicuous. Some inflorescences, such as those of *A. rufinerve* and *A. erianthum,* are covered with a light down.

The number of flowers carried on an inflorescence varies between three on *Acer triflorum* to several hundreds on *A. nipponicum.* The latter species bears fruit only after reaching the age of 20, but *A. sinopurpurascens* may start flowering in its 3rd or 4th year.

FRUITS

The samara is made up of a winged part and a nutlet that contains the seed. The nutlets vary in form and the angle at which the wings are attached may vary between 180 and 0 degrees (perfectly parallel). In the case of *Acer heldreichii* subsp. *trautvetteri,* the wings cross over each other. The angle at which the wings are spread is one of the most important criteria in identifying the various species. Alfred Rehder, when describing the different seeds, considered even the cotyledons.

The samaras may be carried by the wind for several dozens of kilometers. The fruits fall as they ripen, at different times of the year, according to the species. Generally, they ripen in September. Fruits of section *Rubra* ripen in May and germinate immediately, since the pericarp is not woody. In contrast, fruits of section *Trifoliata* are very hard and require two to three years of stratification before they germinate.

Fertilization of fruits by wind is not always effective for dioecious species, where male and female flowers are on separate trees. Non-fertilized seeds are sterile but identical in appearance to viable (or fertile) seed; the difference can only be seen by opening the nutlet. This tendency to parthenocarpy (to reproduce without being pollinated) is one of the criteria used to determine the degree of specialization of a given species, the most evolved species producing the least amount of sterile seed. Broadly speaking, fruits presenting only one fully developed samara (one winged part and one seed) tend to be less parthenocarpic than fruits made up of two samaras with the winged parts forming an acute angle.

Some fruits are bright red, hence a cultivar of *Acer pseudoplatanus* and another of *A. tataricum* have been named 'Erythrocarpum'.

Pubescence (or its absence) is another noteworthy distinguishing feature of maple fruits. Fruits of *Acer macrophyllum, A. maximowiczianum,* and *A. heldreichii* subsp. *trautvetteri* are known for their hairy surfaces.

PROPAGATION

Four methods are used to propagate maples.

Sowing of seeds. In this method, the samaras are usually collected after they fall (in the autumn), the wings are removed, and the seed is stratified and sown in the spring. The seeds may be sown in specially prepared seedbeds or in pots. Seed germination is very rapid, of the order of a few days. The seedlings require special care and attention.

Cuttings. Before taking softwood cuttings, a substrate is prepared containing two parts humus and one part sand. The cuttings should be dipped in a growth hormone before being inserted into the substrate. Rooting time varies according to the species.

Layering. In this method, branches are pinned down into the soil after a small piece of their bark has been removed. Once layered, branches can be severed after a couple of years. *Acer cappadocicum, A. japonicum, A. negundo,* and *A. palmatum* may be propagated by layering. This method has not been generally used more recently.

Grafting. When seed propagation is not feasible, maples may be propagated by grafting. In the case of species, the rootstock must be selected from within the same section. If such a rootstock is not available, *Acer pseudoplatanus* may sometimes be used, since it is the only rootstock known to be compatible with maples from other sections. In the case of maple cultivars, the rootstock is generally a seedling of the species to which the cultivar belongs.

GROWTH AND HARDINESS

Few trees grow as easily as maples do. They require in general a fertile, moist soil and a moderate amount of sun. A key to successful planting lies in knowing as much as possible about the plant and its needs, its aesthetic characteristics, and its soil and climatic requirements. Plant hardiness is another important factor. Hardiness is not merely a question of temperature. For instance, *Acer pensylvanicum* withstands very low temperatures (–35°C or –31°F) in the United States, but may perish in Europe at –15°C (5°F) for lack of sufficient warmth in autumn to ensure its ripening. Species originating in different parts of the Northern Hemisphere will vary in their capacity to resist low temperatures. Botanical observations have yielded empirical data for each region, showing the minimum temperature that a tree will withstand. Maps (pp. 456–457) show hardiness zones for the plants. Gardeners will want to also consider important climatic variations of a given site, such as microclimates, late frosts, and so forth.

HYBRIDIZATION

Natural hybridization occurs frequently in cultivation between species of the same section. *Acer davidii* in section *Macrantha* shows a strong tendency to hybridize, as does *A. palmatum* in section *Palmatum*. In fact, the latter is so prone to hybridize that it is extremely difficult to distinguish between the species and subspecies of its section.

Artificially obtained hybrids appear each year. About fifteen well-known hybrids are described in this book, including *Acer ×conspicuum* and *A. ×zoeschense*. These hybrids are always propagated by vegetative means, since seedlings will exhibit characteristics of the parent plant to varying degrees.

TAXONOMY

The Aceraceae is a family containing only two genera, one of which, *Dipteronia,* is represented by only two species. (Aceraceae is subsumed into the family Sapindaceae in newer classifications.)

The other genus, *Acer,* includes 124 species, 95 subspecies, and 8 varieties. This classification was proposed by Piet C. de Jong and is based on recent and sensitive scientific techniques (for example, chemitaxonomy), as well as two centuries of research and classification, starting with Carl Linnaeus in the early 18th century. Some questions naturally remain unanswered, however, and others are still open to debate.

Building on the classification used by Yves Desmarais and Edward Murray, de Jong made further connections between species sharing similar morphological features and distributions. His work has resulted in 14 new groupings.

The regrouping of some maple species as subspecies allows for a more global approach and an even easier comparative analysis. Desmarais, for instance, grouped the maples of series *Saccharodendron,* all of them American, under *Acer saccharum,* which thus includes six subspecies and three varieties.

Comparative analysis of sections and of their geographical origins has led to several observations. The first is that maple species geographically confined to a limited area show little difference from each other. They are easily classified into homogeneous sections, as is the case with section *Macrantha.* In contrast, the species belonging to section *Platanoidea* are clearly different from each other, since they are found over a large area from Europe to Japan.

More surprisingly, species belonging to the same section may be geographically separated from each other. Such is the case of *Acer circinatum* and its relatives. *Acer circinatum* thrives in North America, while all its relatives, the other members of section *Palmata,* grow in Asia. This type of link leads to important questions: When did these species become separated? Which were the original plants? What are the evolutionary properties of these maples? Like all life forms, maples evolve and the criteria for measuring their level of evolution are related to reproduction and flower structure (reduced corolla, flowering expression, wind pollination, and parthenocarpy).

Maples can be divided into different sections based on the characteristics of their parts (leaf, flower, and fruit) and the degree of relationship. The sixteen resulting sections are listed below in order of their degree of reproductive specialization, starting with the most primitive species in section 1.

A few isolated species are difficult to classify and the subject of much controversy. Among these are *Acer carpinifolium, A. nipponicum,* and *A. wardii.*

1. Section *Parviflora*

This section represents the primitive maple type. It comprises deciduous trees and shrubs that are dissimilar except for sharing a primitive type of pollen. The large inflorescences are in corymbs or spikes, terminal and axillary, bearing 35 to 400 flowers. Moderate parthenocarpic tendency. Species belonging to this section include *Acer caudatum, A. distylum,* and *A. nipponicum.* Sections *Glabra* and *Macrantha* show affinities with *Parviflora.*

2. Section *Palmata*

Unquestionably, *Palmata* is the most representative section of maples, both in number of species and in diversity. It includes deciduous and semi-evergreen trees and shrubs. Leaves are entire or have from 3 to 13 lobes. The inflorescences are in corymbs. The buds have four pairs of scales. Slight to moderate parthenocarpic tendency. The pollen is primitive in nature, similar to that of section *Parviflora,* and typical of the other primitive sections. With the exception of *Acer circinatum,* which thrives on the West Coast of North America, all the species of this section come from temperate areas in the Far East.

3. Section *Wardiana*

This section has one species, *Acer wardii,* the subject of much controversy.

4. Section *Macrantha*

The section comprises 14 species of trees and shrubs with entire, deciduous, five- or seven-lobed leaves. Axillary buds are borne on peduncles, and the terminal buds have two pairs of scales that touch but do not overlap. The inflorescences are in racemes, rarely in corymbs, terminal and axillary, bearing 10 to 25 flowers. The nutlets are convex on one or both sides, or flat. This section includes all maples with a very thin bark, striped like snakeskin (snake bark maples); all are of medium size and similar habit. They are distributed over a large area, from the Himalayas to Japan, with the exception of *Acer pensylvanicum,* which comes from the U.S. East Coast. Some of the species, such as *A. capillipes* and *A. rufinerve,* display fine fall colors.

5. Section *Glabra*

The section is divided into two series. Series *Glabra* is North American and comprises a single member, *Acer glabrum,* and its subspecies, while series *Arguta* includes several dioecious, more evolved species from eastern Asia. The small inflorescences are in racemes or corymbs, terminal or axillary, bearing 10 to 25 flowers. Fruits are flat and glabrous, with very distinct veining. Strong parthenocarpic tendency.

6. Section *Negundo*

This section is divided into two closely related series, both with compound primitive leaves and few bud scales. The inflorescences are in simple or compound racemes, carrying 15 to 20 flowers with large terminal stamens. The American series, *Negundo,* has only *Acer negundo* and its subspecies, a dioecious species with large compound leaves. The Asian series, *Cissifolia,* has two smaller species, *A. cissifolium* and *A. henryi;* both of these are also dioecious with compound leaves; they are highly ornamental.

7. Section *Indivisa*

Acer carpinifolium is the only member of this taxonomically isolated section. The leaf is entire, with parallel lateral veins, and withers but does not immediately fall from the tree. The pollen structure is very different from that of other maples.

8. Section *Acer*

This section is divided into three series. Series *Acer* comprises *Acer pseudoplatanus* as well as four other species and subspecies. All are large deciduous trees, with large, broad, three- to five-lobed leaves. They are native from Europe to western Asia.

Series *Monspessulana* consists of five species and subspecies. All are small trees or large shrubs bearing small to medium-sized leaves, either deciduous or evergreen.

Series *Saccharodendron* has one member, *Acer saccharum* and its subspecies and varieties, distributed throughout America, from Canada to Guatemala. Tree size varies and the five-lobed deciduous leaves are very polymorphic.

9. Section *Pentaphylla*

The section is divided into two series. Series *Pentaphylla* has one very distinct species, *Acer pentaphylla,* whose palmate leaves have five to seven lobes. Series *Trifida* comprises 10 species, all of Chinese origin, growing in warm-temperate and subtropical climates. Their leaves are generally evergreen, entire or three-lobed. Among these species are *A. buergerianum, A. oblongum,* and *A. paxii.* Section *Pentaphylla* is similar to sections *Trifoliata, Acer, Ginnala,* and *Lithocarpa.*

10. Section *Trifoliata*

Although the members of this section have reached an advanced stage of evolution, they have a primitive trifoliate leaf. They are native to Asia and are closely related, as evident in the shape of the flower perianth, to members of section *Lithocarpa.* Some of the species have peeling bark. The leaves are deciduous, and the buds bear 11 to 15 pairs of scales. The inflorescences are in racemes or in corymbs, terminal or axillary. The pericarp of the seed is thick and woody.

Series *Grisea* includes three species: *Acer griseum, A. maximowiczianum,* and *A. triflorum.* All three bear abundant fruits. Series *Mandshurica* comprises a single species, *A. mandshuricum.* Native to central China, this small tree or large shrub has leaves with three leaflets, the center one on a longer petiole, and glabrous fruits and leaves. Strong parthenocarpic tendency.

11. Section *Lithocarpa*

This section consists of two series. Series *Macrophylla* is more primitive and has one species, *Acer macrophyllum* from North America. The large inflorescences are in panicles and corymbs, terminal and axillary, bearing 30 to 80 flowers. The leaves are the largest among the maples. The petiole contains a latexlike substance, as do the leaves of section *Platanoidea,* thus suggesting a remote relationship.

Series *Lithocarpa* comprises *Acer diabolicum, A. sinopurpurascens,* and *A. sterculiaceum.* These are native to Asia, from Nepal to China. All are large deciduous trees with thick branches and large three- to five-lobed leaves. The buds have 5, 8, or 12 pairs of scales. The inflorescences are in racemes or corymbs. The woody fruits are generally covered with stiff hairs. Strong parthenocarpic tendency.

12. Section *Platanoidea*

Native from Europe to Japan, the maples of this section are medium to large trees with three-, five-, or seven-lobed leaves. The inflorescences are in corymbs, terminal and axillary. Moderate parthenocarpic tendency. All 10 species and 10 subspecies of this section have petioles that produce a milky sap when damaged or severed.

13. Section *Pubescentia*

Two very rare and little-known species from China and western Asia belong to this section. *Acer pentapomicum* and *A. pilosum* are small trees or large shrubs. Their leaves are three-lobed and tough, with a glaucous underside.

14. Section *Ginnala*

Acer tataricum and its subspecies are the only members of this section. Native to Asia and eastern Europe, the trees and shrubs have deciduous, entire or three-lobed leaves. The inflorescences are in corymbs, terminal and axillary.

15. Section *Rubra*

This section includes three species of large deciduous trees. *Acer rubrum* and *A. saccharinum* come from North America and *A. pycnanthum* from Japan. All are considered very advanced in terms of evolution, because of the clusters of axillary inflorescences in umbels. Flowering occurs very early, before the leaves unfold. Fruits have a stunted samara. The seed germinates immediately. Slight parthenocarpic tendency.

16. Section *Hyptiocarpa*

This section from Southeast Asia is probably the most evolved. It comprises two species, *Acer garrettii* and *A. laurinum*. Both are evergreen, sometimes deciduous, trees distributed from China to Vietnam. They bear tough leaves, glaucous below, with entire margins. The inflorescences are in corymbs or racemes, axillary. The nutlets are large. Very slight parthenocarpic tendency.

SYSTEMATICS

Classification of the major species according to P. C. de Jong. Minor species and those not described in this text are not included in this list.

1. Section *Parviflora* Koidzumi
Series *Parviflora*
Acer nipponicum Hara
Series *Distyla* (Ogata) Murray
Acer distylum Siebold & Zuccarini
Series *Caudata* Pax
Acer caudatum Wallich
Acer caudatum subsp. *ukuruduense* (Trautvetter &
Meyer) Murray
Acer spicatum Lamarck

2. Section *Palmata* Pax
Series *Palmata*
Acer ceriferum Rehder
Acer circinatum Pursh
Acer japonicum Thunberg ex Murray
Acer palmatum Thunberg ex Murray
Acer pauciflorum Fang
Acer pseudosieboldianum (Pax) Komarov
Acer pseudosieboldianum subsp. *takesimense* (Nakai)
de Jong
Acer pubipalmatum Fang
Acer robustum Pax
Acer shirasawanum Koidzumi
Acer sieboldianum Miquel
Series *Sinensia* Pojárkova
Acer campbellii Hooker f. & Thomson ex Hiern
Acer campbellii subsp. *flabellatum* (Rehder) Murray
Acer campbellii subsp. *wilsonii* (Rehder) de Jong
Acer elegantulum Fang & Chiu
Acer erianthum Schwerin
Acer oliverianum Pax
Acer oliverianum subsp. *formosanum* (Koidzumi)
Murray
Series *Penninervia* Metcalf
Acer fabri Hance
Acer laevigatum Wallich

3. Section *Wardiana* de Jong
Acer wardii W. W. Smith

4. Section *Macrantha* Pax
Acer capillipes Maximowicz
Acer caudatifolium Hayata
Acer crataegifolium Siebold & Zuccarini
Acer davidii Franchet

Acer davidii subsp. *grosseri* (Pax) de Jong
Acer laisuense Fang & Hu
Acer micranthum Siebold & Zuccarini
Acer morifolium Koidzumi
Acer pectinatum Wallich ex Nicholson
Acer pectinatum subsp. *forrestii* (Diels) Murray
Acer pectinatum subsp. *laxiflorum* (Pax) Murray
Acer pectinatum subsp. *maximowiczii* (Pax) Murray
Acer pectinatum subsp. *taronense* (Handel-Mazzetti)
Murray
Acer pensylvanicum Linnaeus
Acer rubescens Hayata
Acer rufinerve Siebold & Zuccarini
Acer sikkimense Miquel
Acer sikkimense subsp. *metcalfii* (Rehder) de Jong
Acer tegmentosum Maximowicz
Acer tschonoskii Maximowicz
Acer tschonoskii subsp. *koreanum* Murray

5. Section *Glabra* Pax
Series *Glabra*
Acer glabrum (Hooker) Wesmael
Acer glabrum subsp. *douglasii* (Hooker) Wesmael
Series *Arguta* (Rehder) Rehder
Acer acuminatum Wallich ex D. Don
Acer argutum Maximowicz
Acer barbinerve Maximowicz
Acer stachyophyllum Hiern
Acer stachyophyllum subsp. *betulifolium* (Maximowicz)
de Jong

6. Section *Negundo* (Böhmer) Maximowicz
Series *Negundo*
Acer negundo Linnaeus
Acer negundo subsp. *californicum* (Torrey & Gray)
Wesmael
Series *Cissifolia* (Koidzumi) Momotani
Acer cissifolium (Siebold & Zuccarini) K. Koch
Acer henryi Pax

7. Section *Indivisa* Pax
Acer carpinifolium Siebold & Zuccarini

8. Section *Acer*
Series *Acer*
Acer caesium Wallich ex Brandis

Acer caesium subsp. *giraldii* (Pax) Murray
Acer heldreichii Orphanides ex Boissier
Acer heldreichii subsp. *trautvetteri* (Medvedev) Murray
Acer pseudoplatanus Linnaeus
Acer velutinum Boissier
Series *Monspessulana* Pojárkova
Acer hyrcanum Fischer & Meyer
Acer hyrcanum subsp. *keckianum* (Pax) Yaltirik
Acer hyrcanum subsp. *stevenii* (Pojárkova) Murray
Acer hyrcanum subsp. *tauricolum* (Boissier & Balansa) Yaltirik
Acer monspessulanum Linnaeus
Acer monspessulanum subsp. *turcomanicum* (Pojárkova) Murray
Acer obtusifolium Sibthorp & Smith
Acer opalus Miller
Acer opalus subsp. *obtusatum* (Willdenow) Gams
Acer sempervirens Linnaeus
Series *Saccharodendron* (Rafinesque) Murray
Acer saccharum Marshall
Acer saccharum subsp. *floridanum* (Chapman) Desmarais
Acer saccharum subsp. *grandidentatum* (Torrey & Gray) Desmarais
Acer saccharum subsp. *leucoderme* (Small) Desmarais
Acer saccharum subsp. *nigrum* (Michaux f.) Desmarais

9. Section *Pentaphylla* (Hu & Cheng)
Series *Pentaphylla*
Acer pentaphyllum Diels
Series *Trifida* Pax
Acer buergerianum Miquel
Acer buergerianum subsp. *formosanum* (Hayata) Murray
Acer buergerianum subsp. *ningpoense* (Hance) Murray
Acer coriaceifolium Léveillé
Acer discolor Maximowicz
Acer fengii Murray
Acer oblongum Wallich ex de Candolle
Acer paxii Franchet

10. Section *Trifoliata* Pax
Series *Grisea* Pojárkova
Acer griseum (Franchet) Pax
Acer maximowiczianum Miquel
Acer triflorum Komarov
Series *Mandshurica* Pojárkova
Acer mandshuricum Maximowicz

11. Section *Lithocarpa* Pax
Series *Lithocarpa*
Acer diabolicum Blume ex Koch
Acer sinopurpurascens Cheng
Acer sterculiaceum Wallich
Acer sterculiaceum subsp. *franchetii* (Pax) Murray
Series *Macrophylla* Pojárkova ex Momotani
Acer macrophyllum Pursh

12. Section *Platanoidea* Pax
Acer campestre Linnaeus
Acer cappadocicum Gleditsch
Acer cappadocicum subsp. *divergens* (Pax) Murray
Acer cappadocicum subsp. *lobelii* (Tenore) Murray
Acer cappadocicum subsp. *sinicum* (Rehder) Handel-Mazzetti
Acer longipes Franchet ex Rehder
Acer longipes subsp. *amplum* (Rehder) de Jong
Acer miyabei Maximowicz
Acer mono Maximowicz
Acer mono subsp. *okamotoanum* (Nakai) de Jong
Acer platanoides Linnaeus
Acer platanoides subsp. *turkestanicum* (Pax) de Jong
Acer tenellum Pax
Acer truncatum Bunge

13. Section *Pubescentia* de Jong
Acer pentapomicum Stewart ex Brandis
Acer pilosum Maximowicz

14. Section *Ginnala* Nakai
Acer tataricum Linnaeus
Acer tataricum subsp. *aidzuense* (Franchet) de Jong
Acer tataricum subsp. *ginnala* (Maximowicz) Wesmael
Acer tataricum subsp. *semenovii* (Regel & Herder) Murray

15. Section *Rubra* Pax
Acer pycnanthum K. Koch
Acer rubrum Linnaeus
Acer saccharinum Linnaeus

16. Section *Hyptiocarpa* Fang
Acer garrettii Craib
Acer laurinum Hasskarl

PHOTO CREDITS

Permission to use their pictures has been kindly granted by the following:

Philippe de Spoelberch*
Jean-Claude Baudouin+
J. R. P. van Hoey Smith°

In the photo captions, each photographer is indicated by a symbol, as shown above. All unmarked photographs are by **Michel Timacheff**.

In the leaf photographs with a white background, scale is indicated by three small lines, which together represent 5 cm (2 in.), as shown below.

DESCRIPTIONS OF THE SPECIES

Acer acuminatum
in spring (Kew)

Acer acuminatum
Wallich ex D. Don (1825)

Section: *Glabra.*

Epithet: *Acuminatus,* pointed, referring to the leaf tip, which tapers to a narrow, elongated point.

Origin: Western Himalayas, from Kashmir to Nepal. Introduced in 1845.

General appearance: A small tree, 6 to 7 m (20–23 ft.) tall, or a large shrub, 4 to 6 m (13–20 ft.). Upright habit, often multitrunked. Branch tips downward-pointing.

Trunk: Very light gray-green at the base.

Branches: Becoming browner and rougher with age. Young shoots have light orange-green tips.

Buds: With pairs of bud scales.

Leaves: Three- to five-lobed, 10 to 18 cm (4–7 in.) long. Lobes triangular, center lobe very pointed and slightly pendent, the two basal lobes very small or insignificant. Margins very denticulate, often biserrate, the teeth forward-pointing. Main veins on the leaf underside covered with yellowish white hairs initially, becoming glabrous with age, except at the base of the leaf. Young leaves very red and even more pointed than mature leaves.

Flowers: Dioecious species. Male flowers in corymbs. Female flowers in small umbels.

Fruits: In racemes 10 to 20 cm (4–8 in.) long. Samaras 3 to 4 cm (1–1.5 in.) long, the wings forming a right angle.

Propagation: Difficult, given the paucity of viable seeds. Few rootstocks are suitable for grafting; one is *Acer pseudoplatanus.*

The habit of *Acer acuminatum* is typical of maples in section *Glabra*. The short, narrow trunk gives rise to numerous upright branches, which grow into a large, rounded crown. This vigorous plant is suitable for all soil types and is very robust, as the flourishing growth of its numerous young branches shows. Leaf color is not spectacular, even in the fall. Only young plants have ornamental interest, the juvenile brown-yellow trunks contrasting well with crimson-red new growth. *Acer acuminatum* is suitable for large gardens, positioned where the knotted shape of its mature trunk may be fully admired. Hardy to zone 5.

young shoots in summer	female flower
leaves in summer	fruits*
trunk (Westonbirt)	in autumn
	young trunk (Hillier)

Acer argutum

Maximowicz (1867)

Section: *Glabra.*

Epithet: *Argutus,* sharp toothed, referring to the margins of the leaves.

Origin: China and Japan. Introduced in Europe in 1881 by Charles Maries.

General appearance: An elegant small tree, with an erect, shrubby habit, reaching 8 to 10 m (26–33 ft.) tall and spreading with age.

Trunk: Light gray-brown.

Branches: Young branches turn bright red in winter. Branches fork easily.

Buds: Turning bright red in winter.

Leaves: Five-lobed, 5 to 10 cm (2–4 in.) long and wide. Lobes very pointed. Margins biserrate. Leaf underside downy, especially along the whitish veins.

Flowers: Dioecious species. Male flowers in upright spikes, appearing before the leaves. Female flowers on racemes in the leaf axils.

Fruits: Samaras small, purple-red, and very ornamental, with horizontal wings.

Propagation: By seed. Collect it in the fall and stratify it before sowing the following spring. Most seed is sterile, but viable seed germinates quickly.

This large shrub takes on a lovely golden color in the fall and remains attention-deserving throughout winter. The young branches turn bright red as early as September, a trait shared by other maples in section *Glabra,* such as *Acer glabrum* subsp. *douglasii.* Flowers and fruits of *A. argutum* are also very ornamental. The shape and the dense growth of the branches make this a plant to grow both alone and in groups, with other round-headed shrubs. It prefers a slightly acid soil. Avoid dry and very sunny sites. Hardy to zone 4.

leaves in autumn	leaves
flowers	fruits
habit (Hillier)	in autumn (BMP)

Acer barbinerve
Maximowicz (1867)

Section: *Glabra.*

Epithet: *Barbinervis,* having bristles on the veins, referring to the underside of the leaf.

Common name: Pointed-leaf maple.

Origin: Northwestern China (Shaanxi province) and southwestern Manchuria, where it grows sporadically in forest. Introduced in Europe in 1890.

General appearance: A small tree or a large suckering shrub, 7 to 10 m (23–33 ft.) tall. Upright habit, multitrunked, with curved branches like maples in section *Macrantha.*

Trunk: Greenish, with reddish suckers.

Branches: Brownish. Young shoots are green, pubescent.

Leaves: Five-lobed with a broad base, rounded to ovate, 6 to 10 cm (2.4–4 in.) long, dark green above, pubescent below with noticeable whitish tufts along the veins (thus the epithet). Lobes separated by a very small sinus, the center lobe shortened at the base, tips slightly pendent, base cordate. Margins strongly and coarsely serrate. Petiole bright red, pendent, as long as the leaf and also covered in fine hairs. Leaves of young plants larger and slightly pubescent.

Flowers: Dioecious species. Yellowish. Male flowers in small clusters of four to six. Female flowers on terminal racemes, 5 cm (2 in.) long. Appearing in April.

Fruits: Hanging from hairy petioles in drooping clusters. Samaras 3 to 3.5 cm (ca. 1.25 in.) long, the wings forming an angle of 120 degrees.

This maple becomes a tree in China. In cultivation it remains an upright shrub and its trunk is covered with suckers and young shoots at the base. These turn red in the fall, as the foliage turns yellow. It is a fast grower. Hardy to zone 5. Suited to background uses, with its quietly ornamental presence. The species is prone to verticillium wilt.

young leaves	branches in autumn
downy leaf underside	in autumn (Herkenrode),
male flowers*	collected on Shanghai Hill, China
fruits	suckers*

Acer ×bornmuelleri

Borbás (1891)

Acer ×bornmuelleri,
leaves in summer

Epithet: *Bornmuelleri,* after German botanist Joseph F. Bornmüller (1862–1948).

Origin: Bosnia-Herzegovina, the Balkans, and northern Greece, in mountains. A hybrid of *A. campestre* × *A. monspessulanum.*

General appearance: A small tree, 15 m (50 ft.) tall, with a very dense, broad habit.

Trunk: Gray-brown, like the branches and twigs.

Branches: Branches and twigs are covered with young side-shoots, which are short and crowded with leaves.

Leaves: Usually three-lobed, 4 to 7 cm (1.5–2.75 in.) long, 5 to 6 cm (2–2.4 in.) wide, dark green, glabrous, glossy. Veins yellow. Petiole light green, 2 to 5 cm (0.75–2 in.) long.

Flowers: Yellowish, in umbels.

Fruits: Samaras 2.5 to 3 cm (ca. 1 in.) long, the wings horizontal like those of *A. campestre.*

Propagation: By grafting on *A. campestre.*

The search continues for the exact parentage of this hybrid growing at Hillier Arboretum in England. The morphological characters that this hybrid shares with *Acer ×coriaceum* could indicate that this maple should be called *A. ×coriaceum* 'Bornmuelleri'. *Acer ×bornmuelleri* also resembles *A. opalus,* whereas distinctive features of *A. campestre* (such as a latexlike sap in the petioles) are not found. Further research will be required to identify the parents of this small tree, which has all the appearance of *A. monspessulanum,* including abundant flowers in spring and a densely branched crown. Furthermore, this fine hybrid seems to be a fast-grower and would be of interest for further reproduction.

flowers	
fruit	in spring
in early autumn	

Acer buergerianum

Miquel (1865)

Section: *Pentaphylla.*

Epithet: *Buergerianus,* after J. Buerger (1804–1858), who discovered this maple.

Common name: Three-toothed maple, trident maple.

Origin: Asia. Introduced at the Royal Botanic Gardens, Kew, in 1896.

General appearance: A medium-sized tree, reaching 20 to 25 m (66–82 ft.) tall, densely branched, branches drooping downwards at their tips. It may also form a shrub.

Trunk: Gray-brown. Bark peels off in flakes. Young specimens are a lighter gray-brown.

Branches: Very thin, easily breakable, tending to split at the fork.

Leaves: Three-lobed, pendent, 3 to 7 cm (1.1–2.75 in.) long, very variable in shape, thick, smooth, glossy. Lobes triangular, forward-pointing. Margins irregular.

Flowers: Small, whitish, numerous, surrounded by down. Appearing in May.

Fruits: Samaras closely spaced, the wings parallel, the seeds small and plentiful.

Propagation: By cuttings, which give good results when grown under the right conditions. By seed, which needs plenty of heat to ripen. Seed sown in spring after it has been stratified for a few weeks germinates well.

This tree will stand up to severe drought as well as to intense cold, such as that experienced in Europe during the winter of 1985–1986, but without sufficient heat during the autumn, the wood ripens badly and the tree then suffers from frost. It is well suited to shady sites, except in maritime climates where it does better in a sunny location. Unfortunately, it does not tolerate heavy soils and is prone to verticillium wilt. The marvelous fall colors make it an ideal specimen tree or member of a shrubby group. It is often used for bonsai. The leaves are strongly polymorphic.

CULTIVARS

About twenty cultivars are known, the majority growing in China and Japan. Some are pictured in the following pages, while others are only mentioned.

flowers and young shoots in summer°	flowers
bonsai*	fruits
in autumn	large trunk (Morris Arboretum,
in autumn	Philadelphia)*

Acer buergerianum in spring
(Les Barres)

A. buergerianum 'Jōroku aka me' (BMP)	*A. buergerianum* 'Jōroku aka me' (BMP)
A. buergerianum 'Goshiki kaede'	*A. buergerianum* 'Kifu nishiki' (BMP)

Acer buergerianum in autumn
(Herkenrode)

Only very recently imported from the Far East, where they are widely cultivated, some cultivars are interesting for the diversity they offer. Their hardiness has yet to be fully checked, but generally these maples prefer a sunny, dry location where their wood stands the best chance of hardening-off, thus enabling the plants to survive the coldest winters.

Acer buergerianum 'Jōroku aka me'

Imported from Japan in the 1990s. A fine-looking shrub, 4 to 5 m (13–16 ft.) tall, with remarkable spring foliage. The young reddish, glossy leaves slowly turn green, starting around the veins, and then become dark green. They are glabrous underneath. Fall color is red.

Acer buergerianum 'Kifu nishiki'

Yokoi (1989). Japan.

A dwarf shrub, hardly 1 m (3 ft.) tall. Densely branched, bearing very irregularly shaped leaves: some are entire, some lobed to varying degrees. In Japanese, *nishiki* means variegated, and some leaves do sporadically show variegation. Suitable for small gardens, but should be planted in a sheltered site.

A. *buergerianum* 'Koshi miyasama', young shoot in summer	A. *buergerianum* 'Koshi miyasama' (BMP)
A. *buergerianum* 'Mitsubatō kaede' (BMP)	A. *buergerianum* 'Mitsubatō kaede' (Savill)

Acer buergerianum 'Koshi miyasama'

Shibamichi Honten Company (1975). Japan.

A small, shrubby, semi-evergreen tree with a very dense crown. It is very vigorous in growth, reaching 5 to 6 m (16–20 ft.) tall. The three-lobed leaves are rounded at the base and are regularly shaped. The leaves are 4 to 5 cm (1.5–2 in.) long, becoming even larger on young shoots, which are often reddish. The leaves are also rough in texture. This cultivar is hardy to zones 6 and 7, which means it should be planted in a sheltered position.

Acer buergerianum 'Naruto' (BMP)

Acer buergerianum 'Subintegrum' (BMP)

Acer buergerianum 'Mitsubatō kaede'

A shrub with a dark trunk and a dense crown of many narrow branches. The trunk becomes slightly corky with time. The three-lobed leaves, 5 to 7 cm (2–2.75 in.) in size, are light green on both sides. The green leaves of summer never turn bright colors in autumn. Suitable in the landscape for its spring display of yellow-green foliage. Hardy to zone 7.

Acer buergerianum 'Naruto'

A small tree or a medium-sized, vigorous bush between 3 and 4 m (10–13 ft.) tall. The branches are fairly narrow. The three-lobed leaf is T-shaped with a long, triangular center lobe flanked by two lateral lobes set at a perpendicular angle. The leaf margins are very distinctive; they curve inwards, making the leaves look narrower than they are. The leaf upper side is a glossy green color, tinged with red. In the fall, the leaves turn a lovely shade of yellow. Hardy to zone 7.

Acer buergerianum 'Subintegrum'

A large shrub, occasionally bushlike. The tough, three-lobed leaves are 5 to 7 cm (2–2.75 in.) long and wide. They are glossy green above, blue-green below. They have no special fall color, but drop late in the season. This cultivar is widely planted in southeastern China. Hardy to zones 6 and 7.

Acer buergerianum subsp. *ningpoense*

(Hance) Murray (1982)

Section: *Pentaphylla.*

Epithet: *Ningpoense,* from Ningpo, a district in Zhejiang province, China.

Origin: China (central Ningpo and Zhejiang provinces).

General appearance: A small tree, 12 to 15 m (39–50 ft.) tall, or an even smaller shrub.

Trunk: Dark colored, smooth in texture.

Branches: Brown. The young shoots are a lighter brown and are covered with small brown hairs.

Leaves: Two-lobed, borne on the branches, glossy, resembling those of subsp. *buergerianum* but smaller. On the young shoots, the young, red leaves are in groups of three, with a larger leaf in the middle, two smaller ones on the sides. Petioles red.

Flowers: Similar to those of the type, but with longer stamens.

Fruits: Samaras small, the wings forming an angle between 30 and 60 degrees, the nutlets round and flat.

This subspecies has good ornamental value in spring, when the young shoots are very colorful. It is also very attractive in the fall. Hardy to zones 6 and 7. It needs a site in full sun.

Acer buergerianum subsp. *ningpoense,*
young shoot (Hergest Croft)

Acer buergerianum subsp. *ningpoense,*
leaves in summer

Acer caesium flowering in spring (Hillier)

Acer caesium
Wallich ex Brandis (1874)

Section: *Acer.*

Epithet: *Caesius,* bluish, referring to the bloom on young shoots.

Origin: Northwestern Himalayas, from India to Nepal, China, and Pakistan, at high altitudes, in damp, shady valleys.

General appearance: A large tree, reaching 25 m (82 ft.) tall, with sturdy, dense, upright branches.

Trunk: Light gray-brown bark with vertical, dark brown stripes. With age the bark tends to peel away and forms fissures where the branches fork.

Branches: Light brown. Young shoots are light green.

Buds: With scales covered in grayish down.

Leaves: Five-lobed, large, 18 to 20 cm (7–8 in.) long, 20 to 25 cm (8–10 in.) wide, grouped in clusters at the end of the shoot. The three main lobes have well-defined veins on the underside, the remaining lobes are smaller and ovate, all with pointed tips and a cordate base. Margins finely toothed. Petiole red, thick, up to 30 cm (12 in.) long. Young leaves open bronze-brown, turning dark green and glabrous above, blue-green and downy below.

Flowers: Monoecious, yellow-green, in upright clusters.

Fruits: Samaras reddish brown, 4 to 5 cm (1.5–2 in.) long, the wings at a right angle, the nutlets large, 1 cm (0.4 in.) in diameter, round, hard, and bright green.

Propagation: Easy, by seed, but seedlings must be protected from strong sun during the first summer. By grafting on *Acer pseudoplatanus,* in summer.

*A*cer caesium is a tree for large gardens and parks where its height will show to best effect this maple's spring colors: a fine show of flowers against young coppery red leaves. Its other ornamental feature is its large, glossy green foliage. Fall colors are not especially noticeable. Although it grows well in cultivation, this maple needs a partly shady site and damp soil. It is threatened in the wild, because of the overexploitation of forests for commercial and local needs.

young shoots and flowers in spring	fruits
A. caesium (Les Barres)	trunk (Hillier)

Acer caesium subsp. *giraldii*

(Pax) Murray (1969)

Section: *Acer.*

Epithet: *Giraldii,* after Italian missionary and botanist Father Giuseppe Giraldi.

Origin: China (Shaanxi and Yunnan provinces).

General appearance: A deciduous tree, 10 to 15 m (33–50 ft.) tall, with upright, open, relaxed branching.

Trunk: Dark brown, with vertical, gray stripes, as on the branches. The bark flakes.

Branches: Young branches are covered with a whitish bloom.

Leaves: Three- or five-lobed, large, 20 cm (8 in.) long, up to 30 cm (12 in.) wide, blue-green above with yellow veins, downy below with ribbed veining. The center lobe large and triangular, the lateral lobes shorter; tips end in a short point. Base cordate. Margins sparsely dentate, with gaps between teeth. Petiole red, 15 to 20 cm (6–8 in.) long.

Flowers: Monoecious, whitish, in upright corymbs.

Fruits: Samaras longer than those of the type, 6 cm (2.4 in.) long, the wings almost parallel to each other, the nutlets small and rounded.

All the beauty of this tree lies in the contrast between the whitish branches and the large blue-green leaves carried on bright red petioles. Still called *Acer giraldii* in the English-speaking world, this maple was classified as a subspecies of *A. caesium* by Murray in 1969, who also established its parentage. It is easy to distinguish this subspecies from the species: the subspecies has pruinose branches in an open crown and a less-vigorous rate of growth.

 Acer caesium subsp. *giraldii* is rare in cultivation, although it is perfectly hardy (zone 5). It is much used as a street tree in the Chinese provinces where it originated.

leaves	habit (Hergest Croft)
trunk	twigs

Acer campbellii

Hooker f. & Thomson ex Hiern (1875)

Section: *Palmata.*

Epithet: *Campbellii,* after English explorer and botanist Archibald Campbell (1805–1874).

Origin: Himalayas in Sikkim, Bhutan, and Nepal, at altitudes up to 3000 m (9900 ft.).

General appearance: A vigorous-growing tree, reaching 25 to 30 m (82–100 ft.) tall in habitat, half that size in cultivation. Upright habit with dense branching, often remaining shrubby.

Trunk: Dark olive green.

Branches: Green, glabrous. Young shoots are reddish.

Leaves: Five- or seven-lobed, 10 to 16 cm (4–6.4 in.) long, 15 to 20 cm (6–8 in.) wide, dark green and glabrous on both sides. Lobes ovate, cut to half the leaf length and ending in a drooping, very acuminate tip. Base cordate to truncate. The two small basal leaves are curled backwards, the central lobe is longer and larger than the others. Margins very serrate. Yellow veins are slightly hairy, particularly at the juncture with the red petiole. The young foliage is generally red.

Flowers: Terminal, with white petals, yellow sepals, and eight stamens. Inflorescences pendent panicles, 15 to 18 cm (6–7 in.) long. Appearing in May, after the leaves. Small hairs on the floral disc (visible in the photographs on the opposite page) distinguish the type from *A. campbellii* subsp. *flabellatum* var. *yunnanense.*

Fruits: Glabrous. Samaras 3.5 to 5 cm (1.4–2 in.) long, the wings forming an angle of 150 degrees, almost horizontal.

Propagation: By seed, or by grafting on *A. palmatum.*

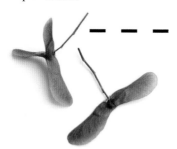

Although it survived Britain's harsh winters of 1984–1985 and 1985–1986, this lovely maple is not sufficiently hardy (zones 7 and 8) to be planted throughout Europe. It requires more care in the garden, but should nonetheless be tried in maritime climates where its elegant habit and foliage bring an exotic touch to the garden.

The leaves are reminiscent of those of *Acer erianthum,* with the pendent tips revealing the bright red petiole. In the fall, the foliage turns yellow, sometimes orange-yellow, before showing a fine, dark green trunk in winter.

Acer campbellii closely resembles its Chinese cousin *A. flabellatum,* found on Mount Emei in Sichuan province; both have seven-lobed leaves. *Acer campbellii,* however, differs from *A. campbellii* subsp. *flabellatum* var. *yunnanense,* which has a smaller, five-lobed leaf (see photograph on middle of p. 46).

leaf upper side	leaf underside
leaves	flower details
habit (Hillier)	flowers
	fruits

Acer campbellii subsp. *flabellatum*

(Rehder) Murray (1977)

Section: *Palmata.*

Epithet: *Flabellatus,* fan shaped, referring to the leaves.

Origin: China (Sichuan province), on Mount Emei. Introduced by Ernest H. Wilson in 1907.

General appearance: A tree, 10 to 15 m (33–50 ft.) tall.

Leaves: Seven-lobed, 8 to 12 cm (3–4.75 in.) long, rounded, green and glabrous above, with hairy veins below. Lobes rounded at the base, bearing distinct markings on their lower third, very acuminate. Margins very serrate. Petiole red.

This maple is the Chinese equivalent of the Himalayan *Acer campbellii*. The difference lies in the leaf base and margins as well as in the leaf tip, which is less acuminate in subsp. *flabellatum* than in the species. This tree is rare in cultivation. Its variety *yunnanense* (see below) is planted more often.

Acer campbellii subsp. *flabellatum* var. *yunnanense*

(Rehder) Fang (1939)

Section: *Palmata.*

Epithet: *Yunnanense,* from Yunnan province, China.

Acer campbellii subsp. *flabellatum* var. *yunnanense* at left, *A. campbellii* subsp. *campbellii* at right (Hillier)

Origin: China.

General appearance: A small tree, 10 m (33 ft.) tall, occasionally a smaller shrub. Habit very upright.

Trunk: Green, with vertical stripes. Branches are dark green with a slight reddish tinge. Young shoots are red.

Leaves: Seven-lobed, thick, somewhat tough, 9 to 12 cm (3.5–4.75 in.) long, dark green, glossy, prostrate. Lobes ovate to lanceolate, base slightly cordate. Margins widely dentate, the teeth forward-pointing. Petiole narrow, red, 3 to 6 cm (1–2.4 in.) long.

Fruits: Reddish, in terminal panicles, 10 to 15 cm (4–6 in.) long. Samaras 2 cm (0.75 in.) long.

The seven-lobed leaves distinguish var. *yunnanense* from *Acer campbellii* and *A. campbellii* subsp. *flabellatum*.

young leaves (Westonbirt)	leaves (Hillier)
flowers (Hillier)	fruits (BMP)
trunk (Westonbirt)	*A. campbellii* subsp. *flabellatum* var. *yunnanense* in spring (Hillier)

Acer campbellii subsp. *wilsonii*
(Rehder) de Jong (1996)

Section: *Palmata.*

Epithet: *Wilsonii,* after English botanist Ernest H. Wilson.

Origin: China (Hubei, Yunnan, Zhejiang, and Guangdong provinces). Discovered by Augustine Henry in Yunnan and by Wilson in Hubei. Wilson introduced it in the West as early as 1907.

General appearance: A deciduous tree, 10 to 12 m (33–39 ft.) tall, sometimes a large shrub. Branches pendulous.

Trunk: Greenish.

Branches: Young shoots green-yellow, glabrous, drooping, and slender.

Leaves: Three-lobed, dark green, glabrous, and glossy above, with small tufts of whitish downy hairs sprinkled below. Lobes ovate, curved, drooping, forward-pointing, measuring half the size of the leaf. The lobes of young leaves are more deeply cut than are those of mature leaves. Base rounded. Margins more or less serrate on young leaves, entire on mature leaves. Petiole red, 3 to 5 cm (1.1–2 in.) long.

Flowers: Very small, whitish green with violet sepals, on pendent panicles, 5 to 8 cm (2–3 in.) long. The peduncle is glabrous. Flowers appear in May, with the leaves.

Fruits: Samaras 2.5 to 3 cm (ca. 1 in.) long, red turning brown-yellow, the wings almost horizontal, the nutlets small, rounded, and egg-shaped.

The largest individuals of *Acer campbellii* subsp. *wilsonii* came from the first seedlings collected and brought back from China in 1907. Since then, the trees have not reached the heights observed in their country of origin. Slow to grow or badly adapted in Europe, they are at least sufficiently hardy in very temperate zones (zone 7). In spring, the bronze-green young foliage is particularly striking. Fall color is scarlet red.

young shoot and flowers*	leaves and flowers*
fruits (Hillier)	in autumn*
young tree (Westonbirt)*	

Acer campestre

Linnaeus (1753)

Section: *Platanoidea.*

Epithet: *Campestris,* of fields or plains.

Common names: Field maple, common maple, hedge maple.

Origin: Continental Europe, England, and North Africa. Now grows throughout Europe, except Scandinavia and Finland.

General appearance: A medium-sized deciduous tree, 15 to 20 m (50–66 ft.) tall. Forms a large, conelike, rounded crown. Can also remain shrublike.

Trunk: Light or dark gray-brown. Bark has pronounced vertical fissures, slightly corky in texture and clearly visible on young specimens. The trunk is rarely very thick.

Branches: Red-brown, glabrous.

Buds: Small, red-brown, gray and downy at the tip, with overlapping scales.

Leaves: Usually five-lobed, sometimes three-lobed, shape and size varying with habitat, 5 to 10 cm (2–4 in.), dark green, dull above, glabrous and pubescent below. Lobes obtuse, lobulate, large, and entire. Base cordate. Young foliage is a striking red-brown shade in spring. Petiole yellowish, the same length as the leaf, containing a milky sap.

Flowers: Small, yellowish, hermaphroditic, in clusters of 10 on upright corymbs.

Fruits: Samaras 2.5 to 3 cm (ca. 1 in.) long, sometimes reddish early in the season, the wings horizontal, the nutlets generally pubescent and flattened.

Propagation: By seed.

young shoot	leaves from Belgium (left) and Romania (right)
flowers (Hemelrijk)	trunk (Lanhydrock)
fruits°	in autumn (Hemelrijk)
leaves in autumn	hedge (Wakehurst)

*A*cer campestre self-seeds from Russia to North Africa and is the true European maple. It varies in shape and size, according to its geographical setting. The field maple prefers chalky soils, although it tolerates moderately acid soils. Described long ago and grown for hundreds of years, it has many uses in the landscape; it is grown as a trimmed hedge in England, along a road, or as a windbreak in Denmark. It may also be grown in containers or as a stand-alone tree in large gardens or parks. It is slow growing with a life span of approximately 150 years. Sometimes its fine-grained, hard wood is used, but the slender trunk and the slow rate of growth make this maple of limited commercial use.

From far off, *Acer campestre* looks like the very distant *A. miyabei* and *A. hyrcanum*. The latter two, however, do not have petioles containing a latexlike substance.

In the fall, bright golden foliage makes *Acer campestre* highly noticeable. The tree then loses its leaves from the top down.

Numerous cultivars are described in the following pages.

*Acer campestre**

in autumn (Aywiers, Belgium)

trunk (Sohier, Belgium) | trunks°

Most cultivars date back to the 19th century. Among the best of these are 'Austriacum' (1824), 'Macrophyllum' (1836), 'Maculatum' (1862), 'Nanum' (1839), 'Pulverulentum' (1859), 'Schwerinii' (1897), and 'Tauricum' (1842).

The cultivars of *Acer campestre* are generally stable, although they may revert occasionally. Like the species, the cultivars are all hardy to zone 5.

Because the native European flora is relatively limited, botanically speaking, it had to be diversified by using the few species available at the time, including those of American origin. The beautiful Asiatic maples were only introduced and cultivated in the West at the end of the 19th century, as indicated by the dates in the descriptions that follow.

Except for the best of them, most of the old cultivars are no longer available. Thankfully, however, Dutch nurserymen have continued to select new varieties since the end of World War II.

Acer campestre 'Austriacum'
De Candolle (1824). Switzerland.

A very large shrub, 8 to 10 m (26–33 ft.) tall, many branched, with few twigs or no twigs. The leaves (see photograph on opposite page) are 5 to 8 cm (2–3 in.) long, 8 to 12 cm (3–4.75 in.) wide, and are larger than those of the species. They are dark green above, light green below, and slightly pubescent. The margins are entire.

Acer campestre 'Carnival'
Van Nijnatten (1989). Netherlands.

A large, dense shrub of medium height, reaching 3 m (10 ft.). The leaf has five deeply cut lobes and is variegated green, pink, and white.

Acer campestre 'Elsrijk'
Broerse (1953). Netherlands.

A medium-sized tree, 10 to 12 m (33–39 ft.) tall, with a dense, conical, rounded crown. The five-lobed leaves are 4 to 6 cm (1.5–2.4 in.) in size and have a brilliant green-gold tint when they unfurl, becoming dark green later.

Acer campestre 'Nanum'
Loudon (1839). England.

Synonyms, 'Compactum', 'Compactum Nanum', and 'Globosum'. A small, very bushy shrub, 2 to 3 m (6.5–10 ft.) tall, very rounded, with upright, vigorous young shoots that must be trimmed to maintain the rounded silhouette. The leaves are smaller than those of the type and a lighter shade of green, with a red tint on the margins of the young leaves. Produces very few flowers and therefore very little seed.

A. *campestre* 'Austriacum', leaves | A. *campestre* 'Austriacum', flowers

A. *campestre* 'Austriacum', fruits | A. *campestre* 'Austriacum', fruits

A. *campestre* 'Compactum'° | A. *campestre* 'Compactum', trunk°

Acer campestre 'Postelense'

Lauche (1896). Germany.

A shrub 3 to 6 m (10–20 ft.) tall or a spreading tree 6 to 10 m (20–33 ft.) tall. The leaves are smaller than those of the species and carried on a red petiole. They open golden yellow but burn in strong spring sunshine. In summer, the leaves are greener. This cultivar is easily propagated by grafting.

Acer campestre 'Pulverulentum'

Booth ex Kirchner (1859). Germany.

A large shrub between 4 and 5 m (13–16 ft.) tall or a small tree with a spreading crown. The leaves are the same size as those of the species, but almost entirely spattered with white flecks. Occasionally some leaves have fewer markings and some have none at all (see photograph on opposite page). This phenomenon of reverting to type may be seen on all the cultivars of all the species, and especially on *A. negundo*.

Acer campestre 'Red Shine'

Van den Oever (1980). Netherlands.

A large, vigorous shrub, fairly upright, with well-fissured branches. The foliage is a light purple-red as it unfurls in spring, becoming darker in summer. The leaves on the oldest branches are very dark green with purple highlights. Fruits are numerous and blood red in summer.

Acer campestre 'Royal Ruby'

Van Nijnatten (1980). Netherlands.

A large, rapid-growing shrub, reaching up to 5 m (16 ft.) tall. The young leaves are purple in spring, like those of 'Red Shine', but are less glossy.

Acer campestre 'Schwerinii'

Hesse ex Purpus (1897). Germany.

A small tree, 6 to 10 m (20–33 ft.) tall, wider than tall, with upright, dense branches. The young leaves are a light purple color, becoming darker with time. Summer foliage is a dark, purple-green shade. The fruits are also purple.

Acer campestre 'Tauricum'

Loudon (1842). England.

A small tree, 5 to 6 m (16–20 ft.) tall, wider than tall. The leaves are green, like those of the species, but slightly more acuminate.

A. campestre 'Marsicum' (Kew)	
A. campestre 'Marsicum', leaf	*A. campestre* 'Elsrijk'
A. campestre 'Globosum' (CECE)	*A. campestre* 'Nanum' (Savill)

A. *campestre* 'Postelense', leaves unfurling | A. *campestre* 'Postelense' (Savill)

A. *campestre* 'Postelense' (Kew)

A. *campestre* 'Postelense' (CECE) | A. *campestre* 'Pulverulentum' (Hillier)

A. *campestre* 'Red Shine' (BMP) | A. *campestre* 'Red Shine' (CECE)

A. *campestre* 'Pulverulentum' (Hillier)

A. campestre 'Schwerinii' in spring (Hillier) | *A. campestre* 'Schwerinii', summer growth*
A. campestre 'Tauricum'
A. campestre 'Tauricum' (Hergest Croft)

Acer campestre 'Schwerinii' (Hillier)

Acer capillipes
Maximowicz (1867)

Section: *Macrantha.*

Epithet: *Capillaris,* capillary, hairlike, referring to the very slender stalk of the samara, as narrow as a single hair.

Common names: Hair-foot maple, red-shoot maple, red snake bark maple

Origin: Southern Japan (mainly Honshu and Shikoku). Introduced in Europe and the United States by Charles S. Sargent in 1892.

General appearance: A deciduous tree, 12 to 15 m (39–50 ft.) tall, or a multistemmed shrub, with a dense, wide-spreading crown. Young shoots are pendulous.

Trunk: Brownish red, with white vertical stripes, becoming greener on old trees.

Branches: Purple-red, becoming brown striated. Glabrous.

Buds: Purple, sometimes gray, with ovoid scales 7 to 8 mm (ca. 0.3 in) long.

Leaves: Usually three-lobed, sometimes five-lobed, 8 to 12 cm (3–4.75 in.) long and wide, dark green with red veins, glabrous even when opening. The center lobe is perfectly triangular, with prominent parallel veins and an acuminate tip. Margins biserrate. Petiole always bright red. Young leaves scarlet red, glossy, and completely glabrous.

Flowers: Yellowish, with five petals, in racemes, 8 to 12 cm (3–4.75 in.) long, upright and then drooping. Male and female flowers are produced on different branches.

Fruits: Samaras 2 to 3 cm (0.75–1 in.) long, the wings forming an obtuse angle or almost horizontal, the seeds very small.

Propagation: Easy, by seed, but the species tends to hybridize with *Acer davidii* and *A. davidii* subsp. *grosseri;* seed collected in autumn and sown immediately germinates well. Equally easy, by cuttings taken in July.

Acer capillipes in autumn

young shoots	buds unfurling
flowers*	fruits°
dried fruits	trunk (Hillier)
branch (BMP)	

in spring (Hillier) | in autumn (Herkenrode)*
covered with fruit in autumn | habit (Savill)

Among the many snake bark trees, *Acer capillipes* stands out in summer when its contrasting colors are most striking. The glossy foliage, borne on scarlet petioles, contrasts well against the brown-red branches covered with green and white stripes. The abundant fruiting, also most attractive, is followed by remarkable fall color late in the season. This maple prefers damp but free-draining, fertile soil, but it is otherwise undemanding. It does not tolerate chalky soil. Despite putting on good growth in season, it does not always mature well; this may lead to trouble in winter although the species is hardy to zone 5. It is a short-lived tree. In the landscape it should be used as a solitary plant or in a border of small plants.

No cultivars are known. A fastigiate form (see photo below), selected by the author, has not yet been named.

Acer capillipes, an interesting fastigiate form, found in our nursery (BMP)

Acer 'Robert Lenoir' (Rond-Chêne)

Acer 'Robert Lenoir'
(A. capillipes × A. rufinerve)

First found in the arboretum at Rendeux-sur-Ourthe in the Ardennes, this hybrid is named for the arboretum's founder, Robert Lenoir. The plant, now about 40 years old, is propagated and sold by specialized nurseries. It has the upright, outward-branching habit of *Acer rufinerve*. The red bark of young plants is a distinguishing feature of *A. capillipes* as are the red petiole and the long red buds. The leaf is also elongated although rounded in shape. Fall color is orange-red.

This hybrid of section *Macrantha* is without question an interesting plant, although it exhibits a toned-down version of the distinctive and appealing characteristics of each parent. Hardy to zone 5. Propagation is by grafting on *Acer capillipes* or *A. rufinerve*.

Acer cappadocicum

Gleditsch (1785)

Section: *Platanoidea.*

Epithet: *Cappadocicus,* from Cappadocia, a region in ancient Turkey.

Common name: Caucasian maple.

Origin: Caucasus and Asia Minor. Introduced in Europe (mainly in Italy) in 1838.

General appearance: A medium to large deciduous tree, 25 m (82 ft.) tall in mild climates, shorter in colder climates (zone 5).

Trunk: Gray-white, lightly striped.

Branches: Yellow-brown, slender stripes. Twigs of the current year's growth are green, glaucous, and slightly pruinose.

Leaves: Five- to seven-lobed, 8 to 15 cm (3–6 in.) wide, dark green when mature, bright purple-scarlet when young, very thin. Lobes triangular, very acuminate. Base cordate. Petiole 5 to 10 cm (2–4 in.) long, containing a milky sap.

Flowers: Dioecious species. Yellow, in corymbs 5 cm (2 in.).

Fruits: Samaras flat, with wings 3 to 5 cm (1–2 in.) long, the wings forming an obtuse angle.

Propagation: By seed, which is abundant and has a high rate of germination. By grafting, on *A. platanoides.*

*A*cer cappadocicum resembles *A. mono* and *A. platanoides.* Furthermore, its natural habitat is between that of those two species. It is a very hardy tree. When young, it is vigorous growing throughout Europe. It prefers well-drained soils and is prone to verticillium wilt when growing in heavy soils.

Although suitable for parks, this tree is too often ignored. In spring, the crimson-red young shoots bring interest to the landscape. Fall color is a beautiful golden yellow. This maple is best used as a solitary specimen in a large park or lining a road.

The numerous forms of this species are remarkable despite their modest dimension. Non-grafted individuals produce abundant suckers, a distinguishing feature of the species. Cultivars are grafted on *A. platanoides* and do not sucker.

flowers	shoots in summer
suckers	in autumn

A. cappadocicum subsp. *sinicum* (left) in spring flowering with *A. cissifolium* (right)

Acer cappadocicum 'Aureum'

(Hesse) Rehder (1914). Germany.

A medium-sized tree, reaching 12 to 15 m (39–50 ft.) tall, having the same overall appearance as *Acer cappadocicum* but slower growing. Young specimens have highly ornamental trunks. The leaves are smaller than those of the species but the same bright purple-red color as they unfurl. They turn yellow, the dominant color in spring, becoming greener during the summer. Spring shows the tree to its best advantage, as the numerous flower clusters turn into yellowish-white fruits. Throughout most of the summer, the purple-shaded new foliage contrasts with the green-yellow mature leaves. In fall the foliage becomes completely yellow again but of a much duller shade.

Acer cappadocicum 'Rubrum'

Booth Nurseries (1842). Germany.

A large tree of the same shape and aspect as *Acer cappadocicum* but slightly shorter. The young leaves are a coppery red color with glaucous tinges. For the most part, the foliage retains these colors throughout summer and fall.

A. cappadocicum (Howick, UK)*

A. cappadocicum, trunk circumference of 2.6 m (8.5 ft., near the Citadel of Namur, Belgium)

Acer cappadocicum in autumn (Taviet, Belgium)

A. cappadocicum 'Aureum', leaves unfurling	*A. cappadocicum* 'Aureum', summer leaves
A. cappadocicum 'Aureum', new leaves	*A. cappadocicum* 'Aureum', flowers
A. cappadocicum 'Aureum', young summer shoot	*A. cappadocicum* 'Aureum', fruits
	A. cappadocicum 'Aureum', trunk in winter

Acer cappadocicum 'Aureum' (Hergest Croft)

Acer cappadocicum 'Aureum' (Kew)

Acer cappadocicum subsp. *divergens*

(Pax) Murray (1978)

Section: *Platanoidea.*

Epithet: *Divergens,* divergent, referring to the widely spreading samaras.

Synonyms: *Acer divergens* Pax (1869), *A. quinquelobum* Koch (1869).

Origin: Eastern Turkey and the Transcaucasus. Introduced at the Royal Botanic Gardens, Kew, in 1923.

General appearance: A small tree, to 10 m (33 ft.) tall, or a large multitrunked shrub, with upright branches.

Trunk: Brownish yellow, lightly grooved.

Branches: Vigorous, thick, often forked.

Leaves: Three- to five-lobed, 8 to 12 cm (3–4.75 in.) long, dark green above, paler below, glabrous on both sides. Ribs prominent on leaf underside. Lobes broad, ovate with a blunted point. Base truncate or cordate. Margins entire.

Flowers: Yellow, sparsely produced, in small upright panicles.

Fruits: Samaras 3 cm (ca. 1 in.) long, the wings forming a very wide angle, the nuts flattened on both sides.

Propagation: By seed, or by grafting on *A. platanoides.*

Arare tree, this maple was previously thought to be a distinct species but is now considered a subspecies of *Acer cappadocicum* and with good reason: both bear similar flower clusters and leaves. The leaves of *A. cappadocicum* subsp. *divergens* are small and glossy above, a typical adaptation to intense sunlight that enables the plant to reflect much of the light received. The tree is well suited to most warmer areas of southern Europe. Ideal in size and as adaptable as the species, this very attractive maple turns bright to golden yellow in the fall. Hardy to zone 5.

leaves (Hillier)	spring (Hillier)
trunk	
flowers	fruit

75

Acer cappadocicum subsp. *lobelii*
(Tenore) Murray (1978)

Section: *Platanoidea.*

Epithet: *Lobelii,* after Belgian botanist Matthias de l'Obel (1538–1616).

Origin: Southern Italy, Calabria.

General appearance: A columnar tree, 20 m (66 ft.) tall.

Trunk: Greenish brown, with fine brown vertical stripes.

Branches: Green, glabrous, sometimes glaucous or pruinose.

Leaves: Five-lobed, 12 to 15 cm (4.75–6 in.) long and wide, dark green and smooth above, covered with tufts of hair on the axils of the veins below. Lobes broad, acuminate, base cordate. Margins entire and wavy. Petiole 5 to 10 cm (2–4 in.) long.

∾

This maple is a very fast-growing fastigiate tree with golden yellow fall color. It prefers cool, free-draining soil. Although subsp. *lobelii* is very similar to the species, it bears only five-lobed leaves while leaves of the species are five- or seven-lobed. Furthermore, the margin of leaves of the subspecies are more undulate and tree habit is more upright.

leaf	leaf in autumn
flowers (Hemelrijk)	fruits
trunk (Hillier)	habit (Hillier)

Acer cappadocicum subsp. *lobelii* (Westonbirt)

Acer cappadocicum subsp. *lobelii* (Hemelrijk)

Acer cappadocicum subsp. *sinicum*

(Rehder) Handel-Mazzetti (1933)

Section: *Platanoidea.*

Epithet: *Sinensis,* from China.

Origin: Himalayas and China (Yunnan, Hubei, and Sichuan provinces).

General appearance: A medium-sized tree, 12 to 15 m (39–50 ft.) tall, with a short trunk and a broad, dense, well-rounded crown. Branches slightly pendulous.

Trunk: Brown-green, with vertical fissures.

Branches: Brown to red-brown. Young shoots red, glabrous.

Leaves: Five-lobed, sometimes seven-lobed, broader than long at 7 to 10 cm (2.75–4 in.) wide, bright green with a red rib. Lobes acuminate with long points, slightly hanging. Margins entire. Petiole red, 6 to 10 cm (2.4–4 in.) long. Young leaves coppery red.

Flowers: Yellow, numerous, on small racemes.

Fruits: Glabrous, rose-red turning brownish. Samaras rounded, 2 to 3 cm (0.75–1 in.) long.

Propagation: By grafting on *A. platanoides.*

As its name shows, this maple is the Chinese form of the Caucasian maple. Compared to the species, the subspecies is more compact in size, has smaller leaves, and has more markings on the trunk and branches. It is one of the most beautiful maples, especially in spring when the young coppery red leaves appear. The flowers are quickly followed by bright reddish-pink clusters of fruits, which stand out against the young foliage still at the soft green stage. The attractive appearance is carried through to the fall when the foliage turns lovely yellow to red shades.

Young plants are vigorous and put on good growth, which slows with age. Hardy to zone 6. This maple does not tolerate chalky soils or exposure to northerly winds.

leaves unfurling	young shoots (Hillier)
flowers	fruits
in spring (Hillier)	trunk

Acer cappadocicum subsp. *sinicum* var. *tricaudatum*

(Veitch ex Rehder) Rehder (1914)

Section: *Platanoidea.*

Epithet: *Tricaudatus,* three tailed, referring to the three lobes each with a long tip.

Synonym: *Acer mono* var. *tricuspides* Rehder (1913).

Origin: China (Hubei province).

General appearance: A broad, medium-sized tree, 12 to 15 m (39–50 ft.) tall.

Trunk: Green-brown.

Branches: Young shoots dark red.

Leaves: Usually five-lobed, sometimes three-lobed, 6 to 12 cm (2.4–4.75 in.) long, 8 to 15 cm (3–6 in.) wide, green above with red veins, lighter green below with prominent veins, glabrous on both sides, terminal leaves large with long tips. Lobes ovate. Margins entire, slightly wavy. Petiole dark red, 4 to 6 cm (1.5–2.4 in.) long. Leaves on young trees are polymorphic.

Flowers and fruits: Similar to those of *A. cappadocicum.*

The splendid spring colors of this variety are due to the contrasting purple-red shades and brilliant green hue of the young leaves. The foliage becomes entirely deep green in summer and turns yellow and red in the fall. This rare and handsome tree grows better in a sheltered site.

The difference between subsp. *sinicum* and subsp. *sinicum* var. *tricaudatum* is in the polymorphic leaf of the latter (leaves identical to those of *Acer sinicum* may also be found).

young shoot in summer	flowers

in spring (Hemelrijk)

Acer carpinifolium

Siebold & Zuccarini (1845)

Section: *Indivisa.*

Epithet: *Carpinifolius,* having leaves like *Carpinus,* hornbeam.

Common name: Hornbeam maple.

Origin: Japan (Honshu and Kyushu islands), in mountains. Introduced in 1879 by Charles Maries for Veitch Nursery.

General appearance: A small tree, 10 to 15 m (33–50 ft.) tall, with a broad, rounded crown and dense branching.

Trunk: Generally grayish dark brown, smooth.

Branches: Dark brown, glabrous.

Buds: Small, bright red.

Leaves: Simple, entire, oblong, 8 to 12 cm (3–4.75 in.) long, 4 to 6 cm (1.5–2.4 in.) wide, with approximately 20 prominent, parallel veins per leaf. Leaf tip acuminate. Margins biserrate, sharply pointed. Petiole 0.5 to 1.5 cm (0.2–0.5 in.) long. Young foliage covered in silky gray hairs, becoming almost glabrous by autumn. The leaves do not drop immediately after withering.

Flowers: Dioecious, but becoming monoecious with age. Soft green, with five or six stamens, in umbels or racemes, on a pendent peduncle.

Fruits: Samaras 1.5 to 2 cm (ca. 0.75 in.) long, 0.5 cm (0.2 in.) wide, the wings bow-shaped.

Propagation: Difficult by seed due to strong parthenocarpic tendency which results in mostly sterile seed. Viable seed germinates very quickly, especially when it has been well preserved at a low temperature. Easy, by cuttings.

Acer carpinifolium is very hardy (–25°C or –13°F, zone 3) and grows well on all soils and in shade. It is often mistaken for hornbeam, but the opposite bud arrangement proves that it belongs to the genus *Acer*. It has a remarkable feature: brown leaves that remain on the tree throughout the winter, only falling in spring. The tree is ornamental in spring, when flowers and leaves appear simultaneously: the pink-red buds contrast well with the young yellow-green flowers.

leaves	flowers
trunk (Westonbirt)*	fruits
	buds in winter
in autumn+	leaves in winter

Acer carpinifolium, as the leaves unfurl (Westonbirt)

Acer carpinifolium, in spring (Westonbirt)*

Acer carpinifolium 'Esveld Select'°

Acer carpinifolium 'Esveld Select'

Esveld (1978). Netherlands.

A dwarf form, bushier and more upright than the species, growing to only 2 m (6.5 ft.) in 20 years. The leaves are also smaller, 4 to 6 cm (1.5–2.4 in.) long and 3 to 4 cm (1–1.5 in.) wide. They turn golden in autumn. As hardy as the species, to zone 3. Well suited to very small gardens.

Acer caudatifolium

Hayata (1911)

Section: *Macrantha.*

Epithet: *Caudatifolium,* having sharply pointed leaves.

Synonyms: *Acer kawakami* Koidzumi (1911), *A. morrisonense* Hayata (1911).

Origin: Japan, in mountain forests.

General appearance: A small deciduous tree, 10 to 12 m (33–39 ft.) tall, with an upright, open-branched habit.

Trunk: Green, with vertical stripes of green, white, and brown. Covered with lenticels. Brownish folds at branching and around the forks.

Branches: Reddish brown with green stripes, the young wood even redder.

Buds: With scales that touch but do not overlap.

Leaves: Three-lobed, or five-lobed if the two small teeth at the base of the leaf are included, 10 cm long (4 in.), 7 cm (2.75 in.) wide, green with a reddish edge, glossy above, glabrous below. Lobes ovate, very acuminate, base slightly cordate. Margins serrate, teeth forward-facing. Petioles red, 5 to 10 cm (2–4 in.) long. Young leaves open reddish brown.

Flowers: Small, yellowish, in upright reddish racemes.

Fruits: Samaras 2 to 3 cm (0.75–1 in.) long, the wings forming an obtuse angle, the nuts small and flat.

Propagation: By grafting on any other maple of section *Macrantha.*

Geographically separated from the other maples of section *Macrantha, Acer caudatifolium* grows in mountain forests on the island of Taiwan, as does *A. oliverianum* subsp. *formosanum.* It is easy to tell the difference between the two, the former having a very acuminate leaf tip and bronze-red leaves in the spring. *Acer pectinatum* subsp. *forrestii* alone resembles it, with the same-colored petiole.

Acer caudatifolium is highly ornamental, not just for its yellow fall color but also for its shape and the distinctive color of its trunk. More fragile than the other maples of the section, it should be planted in a sheltered and slightly shady site. Hardy to zone 8.

leaves unfurling with the flowers	young shoot in summer
flowers	fruits
in spring (Hillier)	

Acer caudatum subsp. *ukuruduense*

(Trautvetter & Meyer) Murray (1966)

Section: *Parviflora.*

Epithet: *Ukuruduensis,* from the Ukurundu region, in China.

Origin: China (Ukurundu region), Manchuria, and Japan (Honshu island).

General appearance: A small tree or large shrub, often multistemmed, with upright growth, sparsely branched.

Trunk: Gray-brown with light green stripes.

Branches: Green-brown to orange-red in winter.

Leaves: Five- to seven-lobed, 7 to 13 cm (2.75–5 in.) long, often as broad as long, covered with yellow hair below. Lobes tapering to a sharp point. Base cordate. Margins very serrate.

Flowers: Whitish yellow, on spikes closely resembling those of *A. spicatum.*

Fruits: On upright racemes. Samaras 2.5 to 4 cm (1–1.5 in.) long.

Propagation: By seed, or by grafting on *A. spicatum.*

❧

Acer caudatum subsp. *ukuruduense* looks very much like its American equivalent, *A. spicatum,* which yielded the former synonym of *A. spicatum* subsp. *ukuruduense* (Trautvetter & Meyer) Pax (1889). In winter, the young wood of both species is reddish, but the color is brighter and a more attractive shade on *A. caudatum* subsp. *ukuruduense* than on *A. spicatum.* Subsp. *ukuruduense* is rare in parks and gardens. It is however hardy to zone 4, grows rapidly, especially in the shade, and prospers in all soils and all sites. In difficult growing conditions, such as those found on the Kuril Islands and on the island of Sakhalin, it takes on a prostrate shrubby form. The attractive blooming provides major landscaping interest especially in small gardens.

flowers (Lenoir)	leaves (Hillier)
fruits°	trunk
in flower (Herkenrode)	

Acer circinatum

Pursh (1814)

Section: *Palmata.*

Epithet: *Circinatus,* rounded, referring to the leaves.

Common name: Vine maple.

Origin: Northwestern North America (California to southern British Colombia), at altitudes up to 2000 m (6600 ft.).

General appearance: A very large shrub, sometimes reaching 8 to 10 m (26–33 ft.) tall, with a wide-spreading, impressive habit. Very densely branched. Forms impenetrable thickets when planted in groups.

Trunk: Short, with branching starting at the base, brown-red to light gray.

Branches: Always forking. Terminal wood is bright orange-red in winter, brown-red and thick in summer. Young shoots are redder and sometimes sticky.

Leaves: Seven- or nine-lobed, 7 to 13 cm (2.75–5 in.) long, dark green, glabrous. Lobes rounded, equal. Base cordate. Margins irregularly toothed or biserrate. Petiole 8 to 10 cm (3–4 in.) long. Young leaves yellowish or orange, hairy.

Flowers: Sepals red, petals and pistils white, in panicles, in very attractive clusters. Appearing as the leaves unfold.

Fruits: Samaras 3 to 6 cm (1–2.4 in.) long, the wings horizontal, the seeds large, round, red initially.

Propagation: Easy, by seed, which germinates freely but must be stratified for 2 years; the seedlings are all very similar. By grafting on *Acer palmatum* and vice versa.

The leaf shape of *Acer circinatum* is well known in the United States, where it is used as the insignia for the ranks of major and lieutenant colonel in the U.S. Army. The species is sadly not so well known in cultivation, despite being interesting almost throughout the year. In spring, the bicolored flowers contrast well with the soft green young leaves. In summer, the new red and yellow leaves break up the monotony of the surrounding green, while in the fall, the purple, red, and orange colors are a treat, even if the color change is less spectacular in Europe than in the United States. In winter, the tips of the branches are reddish orange.

Acer circinatum,
in autumn
(Tervueren)

leaves unfurling	flowers
branches in winter	fruit
in spring (Savill)	

Hardy to zone 5, this large shrub prefers a site in part shade and one with damp soil where its branching, rather stiff growth will prosper. The plant is prone to mildew at the end of summer. It is well suited to planting on the edge of groups of bigger trees, on the outer fringes of large humid areas, or as a specimen in flower beds. It looks very much like *Acer japonicum* and *A. pseudosieboldianum,* owing to the shape of its leaves, but it differs from the former by it seeds and from the latter by the structure of its branches (which in the case of *A. circinatum* are always forked).

CULTIVARS

Acer circinatum 'Little Gem' Cook (1970). Canada.

A dwarf form, densely branched, and slowly reaching 1 m (3 ft.) tall. The leaves are smaller than those of the species and display a greater variety of shapes. They are green in summer and attractive against the dense red shoots of the young growth. (The same ornamental young shoots may be admired on the species.) The cultivar is well suited to small gardens providing the soil is kept damp.

Acer circinatum, early autumn (Tervueren)*

A. circinatum 'Monroe' Mulligan (1974). United States.

A large shrub, 3 to 4 m (10–13 ft.) tall, taller than wide. The branches are quite thick, stiff, long, and often curved. The young shoots are pure green and slightly sticky. The five- or seven-lobed leaves are deeply incised, right down to the base of the leaf, even more so than those of *Acer japonicum* 'Aconitifolium'. The leaves are 6 to 10 cm (2.4–4 in.) long and light green to yellow. In the fall, the yellow tint becomes stronger, sometimes turning orange. This shrub is often attacked by mildew, especially at the end of a damp summer.

| A. circinatum 'Monroe' (Savill) | A. circinatum 'Monroe', early autumn |
| A. circinatum 'Little Gem' (Esveld) | A. circinatum 'Little Gem' (Esveld)° |

Acer circinatum × *A. japonicum* 'Aconitifolium', flowers and fruit (Hillier)

Acer cissifolium
(Siebold & Zuccarini) K. Koch (1864)

Section: *Negundo.*

Epithet: *Cissifolius,* having leaves like *Cissus,* grape ivy.

Common name: Vine-leaf maple.

Origin: Japan (Honshu and Hokkaido islands). Introduced in Europe around 1865.

General appearance: A small deciduous tree, 10 to 12 m (33–39 ft.) tall, as broad as tall, with a compact, rounded shape.

Trunk: Light gray, smooth.

Branches: Dark brown. The current year's growth is tomentose.

Buds: With two pairs of scales.

Leaves: Consist of three leaflets, each 5 to 10 cm (2–4 in.) long, oval or ovate, with reddish-brown veins, bright green above, lighter below. Margins densely serrate at the tips, teeth forward-pointing. Petiole 5 to 8 cm (2–3 in.) long, brown-red, covered in small white hairs. Young foliage reddish, with red veins, upper leaf surface covered in tiny white hairs.

Flowers: Dioecious species. Petals long, yellow; inflorescences very long, up to 25 cm (10 in.); pedicels thick, recumbent.

Fruits: Abundant, on female plants, on pendent clusters in pairs. Samaras 2 to 3 cm (0.75–1 in.) long, turning soft reddish pink by summer.

Propagation: Easy, by cuttings, but preferable by seed. Has a noticeable parthenocarpic tendency.

Acer cissifolium, in autumn, with fruits*

flowers	fruits (Lenoir)
glabrous petiole	autumn (Batsford)
in spring (Westonbirt)	

*A*cer cissifolium is a very attractive small tree with a rounded, stocky, flat-topped silhouette reminiscent of *Parrotia persica.* It grows in the wild on a short trunk or on several stems. The abundant fruits hang in colorful clusters until the end of summer. Fall color, which appears early in the season and is very typical of maples, is displayed in two stages: the crown always changes color before the lower branches (see photo on p. 96, bottom right).

Acer cissifolium may be used as a solitary plant in large parks, or in mixed border plantings. It should be protected from strong sun, especially in sites with dry soil, and it requires enough space to allow for spreading. It is suitable for large gardens but may also be planted in small ones if pruned, preferably in summer.

Acer cissifolium strongly resembles A. henryi, but the latter has entire or very weakly toothed leaves, thinner foliage, and glabrous young shoots and petioles.

in autumn (Westonbirt)

trunk (Lenoir) | in autumn (Mariemont)

Acer cissifolium in autumn (Westonbirt)

Acer ×conspicuum

Van Gelderen & Oterdoom (1994)

Epithet: *Conspicuus,* conspicuous, worthy of notice, referring to the maple's overall appearance.

Origin: Garden. A hybrid of *Acer davidii* × *A. pensylvanicum.*

General appearance: A tree 10 m (33 ft.) tall and similar in appearance to *Acer davidii* but with much less branching.

Trunk: White striped.

Leaves: Three- to five-lobed, large, 5 to 20 cm (2–8 in.) long, 5 to 15 cm (2–6 in.) wide, dark green and glabrous above, lighter below with tiny tufts of reddish down at the base of the veins. Lobes with acuminate tips. Margins serrate. Petiole 2 to 10 cm (0.75–4 in.) long.

Flowers: In terminal racemes, very slightly pubescent, 4 to 15 cm (1.5–6 in.) long.

Fruits: Glabrous, the wings of the samaras forming an obtuse angle.

This maple's epithet is well chosen, for not only is the tree fine looking, but it also is a fast grower. The plant remains a small to medium-sized tree and displays very attractive fall colors, as does *Acer pensylvanicum.* Generally, the tree prefers an acid soil. Hardy in zone 5. Three cultivars have been identified.

CULTIVARS

Acer ×conspicuum 'Elephant's Ear'
Bulk (1990). Netherlands.

A large shrub 8 to 10 m (26–33 ft.) tall, solid and vigorous. The trunk is purple-brown with white stripes. The leaves are three-lobed, ovate at the base, and slightly acuminate at the tip, with serrate margins. The young leaves are yellowish, pendulous, becoming very large when fully grown, between 15 and 30 cm (6–12 in.) long, but not as wide. The size of the leaf is remarkable and assures a vigorous growth rate for this original tree. The fall colors, however, are not special. Hardy to zone 6.

Acer ×conspicuum 'Phoenix'
Esveld (1986). Netherlands.

A large, bushy shrub, with dense growth, reaching 3 to 4 m (10–13 ft.) tall. Sometimes it grows into a tree. The trunk is red-orange with white stripes, and the young shoots are

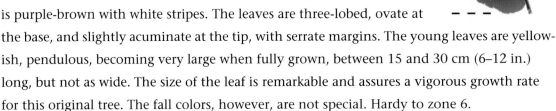

leaves (CECE)	in autumn°
young trunk	

A. ×conspicuum 'Phoenix' in autumn (CECE)

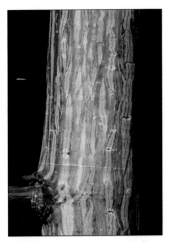

Acer ×conspicuum 'Silver Cardinal'
(Hillier)

Acer ×conspicuum 'Silver Cardinal' (CECE)

Acer ×conspicuum 'Silver Cardinal'
(Hillier)

A. ×conspicuum 'Silver Vein', leaves	*A. ×conspicuum* 'Silver Vein', trunk
A. ×conspicuum 'Silver Vein' (Hillier)	*A. ×conspicuum* 'Silver Vein', flowers
	A. ×conspicuum 'Silver Vein', fruits*

bright red-orange, as are the petiole, buds, and midrib. Undoubtedly one of the finest maples, mainly in winter. It needs a well-drained soil and very sheltered locations. Hardy in zone 6. In autumn, the foliage turns golden yellow starting from the leaf edge. When the leaves have fallen, the tree displays a mass of brilliant orange-red to scarlet twigs with white stripes. This beautiful plant is easy to propagate and grows well, preferably in an acid soil.

Acer ×*conspicuum* 'Silver Cardinal'

Crown Estate Commissioners (1985). England.

A shrub with very fine red bark on young specimens and on the current year's growth. Young leaves are reddish pink, spotted with green, turning dark green when mature with a few remaining yellowish or pink spots. The leaves on immature shoots have small lateral lobes or large teeth. Adult leaves are entire, large, and triangular, with coarse, uneven margins. They often appear to be curved. The petiole is also red. Hardy to zone 6, this maple is however sensitive to spring frosts and suffers from winter sun because of its very thin bark.

Acer ×*conspicuum* 'Silver Vein'

Hillier's Nurseries (1975). England.

A small robust tree or large multistemmed shrub reaching 10 m (33 ft.) tall. Strong branches. Trunk green with strong gray striping. Remarkable bright general aspect in winter sun. The three-lobed leaves have under-developed lateral lobes with forward-facing tips. The leaves are dark green, smooth to the touch, and carried on a red petiole 4 to 10 cm (4 in.) long. The yellow flowers are borne on terminal racemes 10 to 15 cm (4–6 in.) long. Hardy to zone 5, this tough maple is a reliable grower that turns lemon yellow early in the season, but only for a brief period, like one of its parents, *Acer pensylvanicum.*

Acer ×coriaceum

Bosc ex Tausch (1829)

Epithet: *Coriaceus,* leathery, referring to the leaves.

Origin: Southeastern Europe, especially Yugoslavia. A hybrid of *A. pseudoplatanus* × *A. monspessulanum.*

General appearance: A medium-sized, elegant tree, 8 to 15 m (26–50 ft.) tall, densely branched, with a rounded, mushroom-shaped crown. The leathery leaves remain on the tree until early winter.

Trunk: Gray, lightly striped.

Branches: Stiff, thick, gray-brown, and glabrous. The current year's growth is redder and slightly sticky.

Buds: Small, very dark colored, occasionally in groups.

Leaves: Three- to five-lobed, 5 to 8 cm (2–3 in.), broader than long, dark green, glabrous, tough, glossy. Lobes rounded, with green-yellow veins visible to the tips, the two smaller lateral lobes passing for teeth. Base cordate. Petiole greenish red, 3 to 8 cm (1–3 in.) long. Young leaves red.

Flowers: Yellowish, parts arranged in fives, on short, terminal insignificant umbels. Appearing in April.

Fruits: Samaras 2.5 cm (1 in.) long, the wings forming an angle of 60 degrees, the seeds rounded, glabrous, and fairly large.

This maple hybrid has certain features of *Acer monspessulanum:* similar shape, glossy leaves, bluish color on the leaf underside, leaf size, and the three short, broad, forward-facing lobes. From the other parent, sycamore maple, it gets broad leaves with more toothed margins and initial down on the reverse side, large seeds, and more widely diverging samaras. Hardy to zone 5, this very vigorous tree grows fast and reaches 5 to 6 m (16–20 ft.) tall and 7 to 10 m (23–33 ft.) wide in 20 years. Fine specimens prosper in the south of England, including one at Westonbirt Arboretum (Gloucestershire) which stands 15 m (50 ft.) tall. Although this maple has no fall color, it is of interest for its discreet flowers and for its new spring foliage, very light in color. The leaves drop at the end of December or the beginning of January.

Curiously, this splendid hybrid is now rare in cultivation, whereas, according to Leonard Dippel's observations in 1892, it was often planted in 19th-century gardens.

in summer (Hillier)	flowers
young shoot/trunk	fruits in spring (Hillier)
spring flowering (Hillier)	

Acer crataegifolium
Siebold & Zuccarini (1845)

Section: *Macrantha.*

Epithet: *Crataegifolius,* having leaves like *Crataegus,* hawthorn.

Common name: Hawthorn maple.

Origin: Central and southern Japan, in mountainous areas. Introduced in 1879 by Charles Maries for Veitch Nursery.

General appearance: A small deciduous tree, 8 m (26 ft.) tall, or a dense shrub with upright branches that bend outwards and become horizontal.

Trunk: Purple-brown, with green or white-green vertical stripes.

Branches: Young branches are greenish and glabrous.

Buds: Small, greenish, with scales that touch but do not overlap.

Leaves: Variable shape, ovate and acuminate, entire or with two, three, or five insignificant lobes. Base cordate or truncate. Midrib pink. Margins unevenly dentate. Petiole bright red, about 2 cm (0.75 in.) long. Young leaves purplish, becoming glossy green above and lighter green below, glabrous except for a few tufts of hairs on the vein axils.

Flowers: Yellow on a reddish pedicel, in partially upright racemes, 5 to 8 cm (2–3 in.) long. Appearing in spring with the leaves.

Fruits: Small and glabrous. Samaras purple-red, turning red early in the season, the wings almost horizontal.

Propagation: Traditionally, by seed, collected and sown in the fall, germinating in spring; the seedlings show great diversity. By cuttings, which give good results, as does grafting on the other species of section *Macrantha.*

A large bush with striped bark, *Acer crataegifolium* is less spectacular than other similar maples because of its darker leaves and bark. Yet, the large, bright red infructescences light up the dark green summer foliage. Fall color is yellow or orange, or sometimes remains a dark red and green.

This maple can be capricious and a weak grower. It is best planted in part shade among plants of lighter-colored foliage. It is hardy to zones 5 and 6.

flowers	fruits
young shoots (Hemelrijk)	leaves in autumn (Hillier)
trunk (Hillier)	spring (Hillier)

Acer crataegifolium (Hemelrijk)

Acer crataegifolium in autumn (Japan)*

Acer crataegifolium var. *macrophyllum* Hara (1934)

This variety differs from the species by its larger leaves, which are 8 to 10 cm (3–4 in.) long and wide, and by its well-defined lateral lobes at the base of the leaves. It grows into a shrub larger than *A. crataegifolium* 'Veitchii', but the fall colors are far less spectacular.

CULTIVAR

Acer crataegifolium 'Veitchii' Nicholson (1881). England.

A small shrub reaching 2.5 m (8 ft.) tall. Dense growth with branches growing almost horizontally. The young branch is a bright orange-red. The leaves are smaller than those of the species, but are strikingly variegated in summer. Some specimens have white variegation, others pink. In the fall the leaves turn orange-tinted or a crimson-pink color, giving a splendid effect. This old cultivar should be given a choice position to make up for its lack of size. It is quite difficult to propagate. It is however well suited to temperate climates and is hardy to zone 5.

A. crataegifolium var. *macrophyllum* (Esveld)	*A. crataegifolium* 'Veitchii', white variegation°
A. crataegifolium 'Veitchii' in autumn (Hillier)	*A. crataegifolium* 'Veitchii', pink variegation°

Acer davidii

Franchet (1885)

Section: *Macrantha.*

Epithet: *Davidii,* after Father Armand David (1826–1900), French missionary and botanist.

Origin: Central and western China. Introduced from the provinces of Hubei and Sichuan to England in 1879 by Charles Maries for Veitch Nursery. Plants were imported to Europe from Yunnan by George Forrest and Francis Kingdon-Ward and from Hubei by Ernest H. Wilson.

General appearance: An elegant tree or very large shrub, reaching 10 to 12 m (33–39 ft.) tall, sometimes multitrunked. Upright growth, with a spreading crown and with branch tips dropping downwards.

Trunk: Green, gray-green, or reddish, with long white vertical stripes. Varies with place of origin and planting location.

Branches: Young shoots are orange-red or green.

Buds: Long, conical, red, with scales that touch but do not overlap.

Leaves: Shape and size vary. Predominately three-lobed on young trees and on young shoots of older trees. Entire on mature trees, ovate, rounded, tip acuminate and typically reaching 3 to 4 cm (1–1.5 in.). Leaf size reaching 14 to 15 cm (5.5–6 in.) long and half as wide, color deep green with a dark tint on both sides, base rounded to cordate, lobes insignificant, veins prominent and parallel. Margins dentate, crenulate and slightly lobulate on the lower part of the leaf. Petiole 2 to 3 cm (0.75–1 in.) long, yellow to pinkish red. Young leaves purplish, becoming glossy green above and lighter below with coffee-colored tufts of hairs on the axils.

Flowers: Small, yellowish, on long, pendent racemes. Peduncles and racemes of female flowers are larger than those of male flowers. Appearing in May.

Fruits: Samaras yellow-green, 3 cm (ca. 1 in.) long, glabrous, very profuse, the wings forming an obtuse angle or almost parallel.

Propagation: Easy by seed, but this species tends to hybridize with other maples especially *Acer davidii* subsp. *grosseri.* Makes a good rootstock for all the maples of section *Macrantha.*

*A*cer davidii is certainly the most widely grown of the twenty-odd snake bark maples that give good value in the garden. It is also one of the largest. Abundant fruiting covers the pendent branches and fall color is usually noteworthy. The largest specimen grows in the arboretum at Winkworth, in England.

This small tree usually grows to 10 m (33 ft.) tall but can reach 20 m (66 ft.) when competing with other trees for sunlight. It reaches its fullest potential in a solitary location in an open space where its beautiful striated trunk (particularly well marked in winter) is visible at its best advantage. The orange-red leaves in spring are also very ornamental. Abundant fruits cover the hanging branches in early September, and fall coloring is usually noteworthy.

flowers	fruits°
fruits in autumn°	trunk (Kew)
young trunk°	

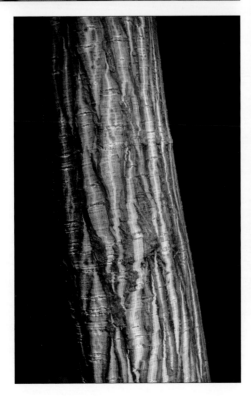

CULTIVARS

Native to distant lands, the forms of *Acer davidii* described hereafter have cultivation requirements that should be considered to obtain the best results when planting these maples outside their habitat. The plants are hardy to zone 5, prefer part shade, and need easy-to-work, light, damp but well-drained, acidic soils. They do not tolerate chalky soils.

Distributed throughout Asia, *Acer davidii* has assumed various forms. For example, the maple discovered by Belgian Joseph Hers, originally named *A. hersii,* is now synonymous with *A. davidii* subsp. *grosseri,* the slight differences between them no longer warranting the distinctive name. The variability of these plants is the result of a good adaptive faculty and a strong tendency to hybridize.

A. davidii in spring | *A. davidii* in winter (Kew)

A. davidii covered in fruits, end of August (Kew)

A. davidii 'Ernest Wilson', leaves | *A. davidii* 'Ernest Wilson', buds opening

A. davidii 'Ernest Wilson', young trunk in winter (BMP) | *A. davidii* 'Ernest Wilson', young tree (Westonbirt)

In 1957 Englishman J. Keenan classified as cultivars two wild forms of *Acer davidii* that had been imported and selected by the Royal Botanic Garden of Edinburgh at the beginning of the century.

Acer davidii 'Ernest Wilson' Keenan (1957). Scotland.

Discovered by Charles Maries in 1907 in central China and introduced by Ernest H. Wilson. A compact, low, spreading tree with a rounded crown. The branches have small bud marks measuring 2 to 3 cm (0.75–1 in.). The leaves are smaller than those of 'George Forrest', the pedicel is short and pinkish green. The tree produces abundant fruit. This cultivar differs from 'George Forrest' by its all-over green color with no other tints in the foliage.

Acer davidii 'George Forrest' Keenan (1957). Scotland.

Introduced by George Forrest and Francis Kingdon-Ward from the province of Yunnan in China. It is characterized by a treelike habit with an open crown, and pendent branching. It is medium size, 8 to 10 m (26–33 ft.) tall. The trunk is purple-green with white stripes, and the young shoots are red. Leaves are green with red tinges and carried on a red or yellow pedicel.

Acer davidii 'George Forrest' (Hillier)

A. *davidii* 'George Forrest', large trunk (Hillier)

A. *davidii* 'George Forrest' in spring (Savill)	A. *davidii* 'George Forrest', young fruits*

113

Acer davidii subsp. *grosseri*

(Pax) de Jong (1994)

Section: *Macrantha.*

Epithet: After German botanist W. C. H. Grosser (1869–1942).

Synonym: *Acer hersii* Rehder (1922).

Origin: Central to northern China. Discovered by Father Giuseppe Giraldi in Shaanxi province and introduced in Europe in 1927. A variable species.

General appearance: A large shrub, 6 to 8 m (20–26 ft.) tall, often multitrunked. Very upright habit.

Trunk: Greenish on young specimens, with age exhibiting white-yellow stripes that give it a veined look.

Branches: Gray-green, few stripes. Young shoots are green to reddish, without stripes.

Leaves: Generally unlobed, broad, ovate, with a cordate base, or three-lobed with two small side lobes, the center lobe an elongated oval-triangular shape, with a very acuminate tip. Thick, 5 to 6 cm (2–24. in.) long, 4 to 5 cm (1.5–2 in.) wide, with a yellow midrib. Margins biserrate, the teeth closely spaced and numerous. Young leaves green, covered for a short time with a brownish down, persisting as only a few reddish tufts. Petiole yellow, 4 to 5 cm (1.5–2 in.) long.

Flowers: Yellowish on pendent racemes, 5 to 8 cm (2–3 in.) long.

Fruits: Samaras 2 cm (0.75 in.) long, glabrous, the wings curved and forming an obtuse angle or almost parallel.

Propagation: Easy, by seed, which is abundant and germinates after only a few weeks of stratification.

This subspecies is so similar to *Acer davidii* 'Ernest Wilson' that the two can be hard to distinguish. The leaves of *A. davidii* subsp. *grosseri* have sharper teeth on their margins, and are smaller and proportionately broader. Furthermore, they change color in autumn from the border of the leaf to the center, displaying a spectrum of shades from red to yellow.

Less demanding than *Acer davidii,* the subspecies is a bit more tolerant of lime but will not put up with waterlogged soils. It is hardy to zone 5 and survives lower temperatures if the wood has hardened-off properly. This maple should not be pruned too heavily. It makes a perfect solitary tree.

branch°	habit (Kew)
leaves in autumn	
trunk°	leaves (Westonbirt)

The maple discovered by Joseph Hers in the Chinese province of Henan in 1919 was initially thought by Alfred Rehder to be a distinct species, but is now included under the name *Acer davidii* subsp. *grosseri* as these two plants are almost identical. The young leaves on the maple discovered by Hers have more acuminate lobes. Furthermore, the Hers maple grows into a larger tree than *A. davidii* subsp. *grosseri.* These differences are considered minor as they are the result of geographical variations and do not deserve giving the plants separate names.

One of the largest specimens of the Hers maple is at the Arboretum des Barres, in France. It was planted in 1925 and was more than 20 m (66 ft.) tall before it was destroyed by a storm in 1999.

Acer davidii subsp. *grosseri*
var. *hersii* (Les Barres)

flowers	flowers (Hemelrijk)
fruits (Les Barres)	leaves in autumn (Westonbirt)
trunk (Les Barres)	autumn (Batsford)

Acer davidii subsp. *grosseri* 'Leiden'

Netherlands.

A fine-looking cultivar with a characteristic brown-red bark, covered with large white vertical stripes of various widths. In summer, the trunk is green and less contrasted. Like subsp. *grosseri,* this cultivar has ovate, very small leaves. Spring leaf color is less spectacular than it is in the other *A. davidii* cultivars. In the fall, 'Leiden' turns red-orange. It is slow growing and sparsely branched.

Other *Acer davidii* cultivars

Acer davidii 'Horizontale'

Villa Taranto (pre-1959). Italy.

As indicated by its name this plant is wider than tall: 5 to 6 m (16–20 ft.) tall and 8 to 10 m (26–33 ft.) wide. The brown and gold young leaves stand out at the start of the season; they are very dark but glossy and contrast well with the lighter colored pink trunk. The leaves then turn to dark green. This cultivar is propagated by grafting onto any rootstock of section *Macrantha.* Fast growing and vigorous, it is a tree for large gardens.

Acer davidii 'Karmen'

Esveld (1985). Netherlands.

A tree or large shrub growing to 10 m (33 ft.) tall with the typical habit of maples in section *Macrantha,* an inverted triangle. Vigorous. The leaves are quite large, 12 to 15 cm (4.75–6 in.) long and 4 to 6 cm (1.5–2.4 in.) wide, and very acuminate; they are brown in spring, becoming dark glossy green in May. The young shoots are glabrous and purple. The petiole and the midrib on the underside are also purple. The trunk is green and smooth, with white stripes and small horizontal purple lenticels.

A. davidii subsp. *grosseri* 'Leiden', flowers	'Leiden', trunk in winter (BMP)
A. davidii 'Karmen', leaves	*A. davidii* 'Karmen' (BMP)
A. davidii 'Karmen', trunk	*A. davidii* 'Karmen', flowers

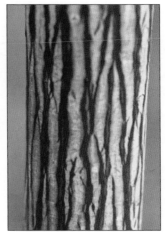

119

Acer davidii 'Madeleine Spitta', leaves in autumn

Acer davidii 'Madeleine Spitta', tree in spring (Hillier)

Acer davidii 'Madeleine Spitta'

W. Fox (1950). England.

A tree growing to more than 12 m (39 ft.) tall, fastigiate, vigorous. The leaves turn orange in autumn and then drop late in the season. This trait does not, however, make this cultivar particularly worthwhile for landscaping.

| *A. davidii* 'Rosalie', leaves | *A. davidii* 'Rosalie', flowers (Herkenrode) |
| *A. davidii* 'Rosalie', young shoots in summer | *A. davidii* 'Rosalie', young trunk in winter |

Acer davidii 'Rosalie'

Esveld (1985). Netherlands.

This tree grows to 12 to 15 m (39–50 ft.) tall, with an open, upright habit. The bark changes color through the seasons: green with white stripes in summer and a reddish-lilac color in winter. The leaves appear early in spring and, like those of *Acer davidii* 'Horizontale', are not damaged by light spring frosts; they are brownish and remain so for quite some time before turning green.

Acer davidii 'Serpentine'

Hooftman (1976). Netherlands.

A low-growing tree reaching 4 to 5 m (13–16 ft.) tall, bushy, and more densely branched than most cultivars of *Acer davidii*. The internodes are shorter and growth is mainly spreading. The branching is irregular, so the tree looks like a mass of untidy branches. The purple-red trunk has white stripes, which give it an all-over light aspect. The branches are quite narrow. The leaves are dark green, glossy, and usually unlobed; they are rather small, 6 to 7 cm (2.4–2.75 in.) long and 3 cm (ca. 1 in.) wide, triangular, and pointed. The petiole is red. The leaves have the peculiar habit of rolling themselves up and shrinking when they are exposed to strong sunshine.

This plant is suitable for small gardens because it does not become too imposing. The abundant display of flowers is followed by the fruits that add to the already very ornamental qualities of this adaptable tree. Hardy to zone 5.

Acer 'Cascade'

An unregistered cultivar with a weeping habit and very pendent branches. Descended from *Acer davidii* 'Serpentine'.

Acer davidii 'Serpentine', young specimen, as the leaves unfurl (Westonbirt)

A. davidii 'Serpentine', leaves unfurling	*A. davidii* 'Serpentine', flowers (BMP)
A. davidii 'Serpentine', leaves (CECE)	*A. davidii* 'Serpentine', fruits°
A. davidii 'Serpentine', young trunk	*A. davidii* 'Serpentine', young trunk in winter

Acer davidii × *A. rufinerve* 'Albo-limbatum'

A handsome hybrid in section *Macrantha* between *Acer rufinerve* 'Albo-limbatum' and *A. davidii*. The latter tends to hybridize easily, but in this case, the *A. rufinerve* heritage seems to be dominant. This may be seen mainly in the upright, narrow habit, whereas the branches of *A. davidii* are generally arching. The bark of the trunk leaves little room for doubt. Leaf variegation is much less pronounced on the hybrid than on the parent tree and even very often absent on certain branches.

The leaf is cordate at the base, entire, and acuminate, looking more like that of *Acer davidii*.

The fruits are borne in profusion and highly ornamental with their colored wings, but they are mostly sterile. This hybrid needs a sheltered site in shade.

This hybrid has not yet been registered.

Acer davidii × *A. rufinerve*
'Albo-limbatum', early fall colors

leaves	abundant fruit
trunk	leaves unfurling (Hillier)

Acer diabolicum

Blume ex Koch (1864)

Section: *Lithocarpa.*

Epithet: *Diabolicus,* of the devil, referring to the hornlike projections on the fruits.

Common names: Horned maple, devil's maple.

Origin: Japan, except Hokkaido Island, in mountainous areas at altitudes of 400 to 1300 m (1320–4290 ft.). Introduced in Europe in 1880 by Charles Maries for Veitch Nursery.

General appearance: A medium-sized, deciduous tree, reaching 15 m (50 ft.) tall, with a rounded crown.

Trunk: Gray-brown, smooth.

Branches: Brown-red, covered with down when young.

Buds: Dark brown, with scales developing freely at the base.

Leaves: Five-lobed, large, 12 to 20 cm (4.75–8 in.) long, sometimes opening red, later turning green. Center lobe large, basal lobes insignificant. White down covers both sides of young leaves, the teeth, and the petiole; later, this down remains only on the petiole and on part of the leaf underside.

Flowers: Dioecious species. Yellow. Female flowers have petals and are in pendent clusters. Male flowers lack petals, are very numerous, have dense, spectacular, red stamens, and are pendent. Appearing before and with the leaves.

Fruits: Samaras up to 4 cm (1.5 in.) large and intertwined. Fruits purple, with two horn-shaped growths (hence the epithet). White hair covers the large nutlets, less densely the wings.

Propagation: The seed has a low rate of germination and is difficult to obtain as the tree is rare.

leaves unfurling*	flowers (Hillier)
fruits°	

A. diabolicum f. *purpurascens* (Hergest Croft)

Too little known, this broad tree displays remarkable flowers, which come out just before the leaves. This characteristic earns the maple a highly visible location in the landscape. It is inconspicuous the rest of the year and devoid of landscaping interest, showing, however, a brownish yellow to reddish brown in the fall. It grows fairly rapidly and is hardy to zone 5.

A form called *Acer diabolicum* f. *purpurascens* has redder young shoots and leaves, but otherwise does not fundamentally differ from the species.

spring flowering (Hillier)	autumn (Lenoir)
leaves in autumn (Lenoir)	trunk (Hillier)

Acer ×dieckii, spring flowering

Acer ×dieckii (Kew)

Acer ×dieckii

(Pax) Pax (1893)

Epithet: *Dieckii,* after Georg Dieck (1847–1925), director of Zoeschen nurseries, near Berlin.

Origin: Garden. A hybrid of *Acer platanoides* × *A. cappadocicum* subsp. *lobelii.*

General appearance: An average-sized, deciduous tree, 15 to 20 m (50–66 ft.) tall. Columnar habit, with dense branching, upright in the center, more horizontal toward the outside.

Trunk: Gray-brown, fissured.

Branches: Brown. Young shoots yellow-green.

Buds: Like *Acer platanoides.*

Leaves: Three- to five-lobed, sometimes seven-lobed, 8 to 12 cm (3–4.75 in.) long, 12 to 15 cm (4.75–6 in.) wide, dark brown, glossy above, with tufts of hair below at the axil of the veins. Lobes large, triangular, tips blunt. Margins entire. Petiole yellow, up to 12 cm (4.75 in.) long.

Flowers: Yellow, numerous, in small corymbs, similar to *Acer platanoides.*

Fruits: Samaras large, 5 to 8 cm (2–3 in.) long, glabrous, the wings forming a wide angle. A group of three samaras is a very rare occurrence (see photograph on opposite page).

Very similar to the maples from which it originated, *Acer ×dieckii* displays an abundant mass of long-lived yellow flowers in the spring. It has inherited the fastigiate tendency of *A. cappadocicum* subsp. *lobelii.* Perfectly hardy, it is suited to large gardens and parks, and is appreciated for its nice proportions. Its coloring comes out progressively in the fall, first yellow, then orange-red. Culture and precautions as for *A. platanoides.*

leaf	leaves
flowers	fruits
fruits	in autumn (Hillier)
trunk	

Acer distylum
Siebold & Zuccarini (1845)

Section: *Parviflora.*

Epithet: *Distylus,* having two styles.

Common names: Linden-leaved maple, lime-leaved maple.

Origin: Japan, although it is rare. Introduced in 1879 by Charles Maries for Veitch Nursery.

General appearance: A small, deciduous tree, up to 10 m (33 ft.) tall in favorable conditions, otherwise a large, broad shrub, with slightly pendulous branches.

Trunk: Brown, lightly furrowed with green and light orange stripes.

Branches: Red-brown. Young shoots are bright light orange.

Leaves: Entire, 15 cm (6 in.) long, 10 cm (4 in.) wide, oval, slightly pointed, asymmetrical, with a cordate base. Midrib orange-red. Leaf color light green above, glossy, and glabrous, lighter colored below. Margins toothed. Petiole bright red, 3 to 4 cm (1–1.5 in.) long. Young leaves orange-red to pinkish.

Flowers: Yellow, small, and persistent. The inflorescence is terminal and an upright spike between two falling petioles.

Fruits: Samaras upright, in groups of two and sometimes three, up to 3 cm (ca. 1 in.) long, the wings forming an angle of 60 degrees.

Propagation: Rather easy, by seed sown in February. Germination is very rapid, but the young plants are very delicate initially, being susceptible to molds and spring frosts, for example.

*A*cer distylum* does not look like a maple at first sight, its leaves resembling more those of the linden tree. This thick shrub for small gardens is appreciated close-up for its remarkable young shoots, its upright and durable flowers, and its agreeable fruit. It retains its yellowish fall color briefly. Hardy to zone 5, it prefers a site in slight shade and a rich, humic soil, corresponding to the soil in its habitat in Japanese forests, at low elevations.

start of flowering	young shoots (Hergest Croft)
flowers*	fruits (Hergest Croft)
a wild specimen in autumn (Japan)*	

Acer elegantulum
Fang & Chiu (1979)

Section: *Palmata.*

Epithet: *Elegantulus,* having an elegant appearance.

Origin: China (Zhejiang and Jiangxi provinces).

General appearance: A small tree, 7 to 8 m (23–26 ft.) tall, with horizontal branches.

Trunk: Green, without stripes, covered with lenticels.

Branches: Green, glabrous.

Leaves: Five-lobed, 8 to 10 cm (3–4 in.) long and wide, glabrous on both sides, except for very small white hairs at the axil of the veins on the underside. Basal lobes small and often opposite the center longer lobe. Margins with forward-pointing, regularly spaced, blunt teeth. Petioles orange-green, 4 to 6 cm (1.5–2.4 in.) long. Young leaves carmine-red.

Flowers: Yellowish with red petals, on a glabrous, terminal, drooping inflorescence.

Fruits: Samaras small, yellowish, 1 to 2 cm (0.4–0.75 in.) long, the wings almost horizontal, the nuts glabrous and flat.

The plant shown in the photographs on the following page grows in the Westonbirt Arboretum, England, as no. 86390720. It came from the Hangzhou botanical garden in eastern China. Planted in 1986, this tree had grown to more than 3 m (10 ft.) in 1998 and is located in semishade in a forest. No further information about this plant is available.

young shoots in spring	glossy leaves
a branch	flowers

135

Acer erianthum

Schwerin (1901)

Section: *Palmata.*

Epithet: *Erianthus,* having wool-covered (downy) flowers.

Origin: China (Sichuan, Guangxi, and Hubei provinces), in mountains. Discovered by Augustine Henry and introduced in Europe in 1901 by Ernest H. Wilson for Veitch Nursery.

General appearance: A large, broad shrub, sometimes a small tree, 6 to 8 m (20–26 ft.) tall.

Trunk: Covered with large white spots. Vertical ridges in relief.

Branches: Young shoots greenish, sometimes covered with bloom.

Leaves: Five-, six-, or seven-lobed, 7 to 15 cm (2.75–6 in.), dark green above, lighter colored below, covered with white down at the axil of the veins. Lobes ovate, terminating with an inclined tip, base truncate or cordate. Margins strongly and irregularly toothed. Petiole 3 to 10 cm (1–4 in.) long, very red.

Flowers: Yellowish, with long stamens, and with ovaries covered with silky hair (hence the epithet). Inflorescence an upright spike, 4 to 8 cm (1.5–3 in.) long.

Fruits: Samaras small, 2 to 3 cm (0.75–1 in.) long, closely grouped on the peduncle, the wings horizontal, the nuts downy, becoming glabrous when ripe.

Propagation: Easy, by seed, or by grafting on *Acer palmatum.*

The interesting flowering of *Acer erianthum* closely resembles those of *A. caudatum* subsp. *ukuruduense* and *A. spicatum.* The bright red fruits of *A. erianthum* are very ornamental almost all summer and only lose their color in the fall. This feature earns this maple a place in the garden as a specimen tree where it can be seen in full sight. Fall color is yellow and unassuming. Winter branch structure is attractive.

flowers (Batsford)	fruits (BMP)
pruinose branches	fruits
habit (Hillier)	

A. erianthum, spring flowering (Kew)

| fruits (BMP) | trunk |

Acer fabri
Hance (1884)

Section: *Palmata.*

Epithet: *Fabri,* after the Rev. Father Ernest Faber, who collected this plant in China in 1887.

Origin: Eastern Himalayas and southeastern China. Introduced in England by Ernest H. Wilson in 1901.

General appearance: A tree, 20 m (66 ft.) tall in habitat, much smaller in cultivation, usually evergreen.

Trunk: Dark brown, smooth.

Branches: Dark green, slender, glabrous. Young shoots red.

Leaves: Entire, oblong, 5 to 15 cm (2–6 in.) long, 3 to 5 cm (1–2 in.) broad, tough, glossy dark green on both sides, tips acuminate. Margins entire or slightly incised, never toothed. Young leaves reddish.

Flowers and fruits: Not observed.

❧

This tree is very closely related to *Acer laevigatum* but much more appealing. Unfortunately, it is not very hardy, and because of its evergreen foliage must be restricted to protected regions of southern England, France, Ireland, the United States, and Portugal.

Acer ×freemanii
Murray (1969)

Epithet: *Freemanii,* after Oliver M. Freeman (b. 1891), a plant breeder at Arnold Arboretum.

Origin: A natural and artificial hybrid of *Acer rubrum* × *A. saccharinum.*

General appearance: A tree, 20 to 25 m (66–82 ft.) tall, with upright branches and an oval or rounded crown. Tree height intermediate between that of the two parent species.

Trunk: Grooves vertical and superficial.

Branches: Dark brown. Young shoots reddish brown.

Leaves: Very variable in size and shape, intermediate between the two parents. Five-lobed, green and smooth above with a red midrib, glaucous below. Lobes less deeply cut than those of *Acer saccharinum* and more toothed than those of *A. rubrum,* basal lobes small. Petiole red.

Flowers: Similar to those of *Acer rubrum.*

Fruits: Samaras 3 to 6 cm (1–2.4 in.), reddish brown, striped like those of *Acer saccharinum.* Many seeds are sterile.

Artificially hybridized by Freeman, this maple exists also occasionally in nature, where the two parent trees grow in close proximity. The parents flower early in the season and simultaneously. Both belong to section *Rubra* and are hardy to zone 4. The hybrid is a better tree than *Acer saccharinum,* mainly for urban settings. It is a deeper red color than *A. rubrum.*

CULTIVARS

The American selections 'Armstrong', 'Autumn Fantasy', 'Celebration', and 'Marmo' have upright habit and attractive fall colors. They have been sold in the United States since about 1970. All the cultivars are hardy to zone 5. Some cultivars are also available in Europe; two examples are described below.

Acer ×freemanii 'Autumn Blaze'
Jeffers (1980). United States.

Rather widespread in Europe, this cultivar grows to a respectable 20 m (66 ft.) tall. The habit is fairly straight and narrow, but broadens with age. The bark is similar to that of *Acer rubrum,* and the branches are reddish brown in winter, with small red buds. The shape of the terminal leaves (see photograph on opposite page) is rather different from that of the mature leaves. This cultivar has been selected for its remarkable fall color.

Acer ×freemanii 'Elegant'
Grootendorst (1969). Netherlands.

Synonym, *Acer saccharinum* 'Elegant'. This cultivar is more compact than *A. saccharinum,* with upright branches. The leaves are smaller and have more lobes.

A. *×freemanii*, leaves (Hemelrijk)   A. *×freemanii* 'Autumn Blaze' (BMP)

A. *×freemanii* in autumn   A. *×freemanii* in autumn (Hemelrijk)

A. *×freemanii*, trunk

Acer glabrum
(Hooker) Wesmael (1890)

Originating in western North America, this small tree can be found in patches in the Rocky Mountains as well as in the Black Hills of South Dakota. Sometimes shrublike, it carries dark red branches, very upright, ending in characteristic purple young shoots. The leaves have five (sometimes three) lobes, with a fine structure and a variable size. The lobes are acuminate, strongly and doubly serrate. The leaf is green and glossy above, glaucous below. Hardy to zone 4, this species is found along rivers or at the lower level of forests. It has four subspecies, three of which were identified by Murray, and a fourth one, more important, described hereunder.

Acer glabrum subsp. *douglasii*
(Hooker) Wesmael (1890)

Section: *Glabra.*

English: Rocky Mountains maple

Origin: North America's Pacific Coast (southern Alaska to southern British Columbia, and on Vancouver Island), on cliffs and rocky outcrops.

General appearance: Usually a large shrub, becoming a small tree in the southern part of its habitat, where it can reach 8 to 10 m (26–33 ft.) tall, with a trunk diameter of 25 cm (10 in.). Very upright branches, almost fastigiate.

Trunk: Dark red-brown, rough like the thick branches.

Branches: Red-brown. Young shoots are smoother and redder than mature ones.

Buds: Diameter of 0.6 to 1.2 cm (0.2–0.5 in.), smooth, with a pair of highly visible scales. On opening, they release a glossy red, sometimes yellow, leaf.

Leaves: Three- or five-lobed, 8 to 12 cm (3–4.75 in.) long, dark green above, gray-green below, glabrous on both sides. Lobes separated by little space, and on young leaves with five lobes, the two smaller lobes are toothlike. Margins doubly and roughly toothed. Petiole reddish, 2 to 6 cm (0.75–2.4 in.) long, drooping.

Flowers: Yellowish green, 0.5 cm (0.2 in.) long, on short peduncles, in pendent clusters, at the end of and along the branchlets. Male and female organs on separate flowers and usually on separate trees. Appearing with the leaves.

Fruits: Samaras 2 to 3 cm (0.75–1 in.) long, the wings curved, forming a very small angle, often parallel, green or pink initially, turning light brown in the fall. Seed envelope deeply cleft and veined.

This tree has ornamental value in North America, where it takes nice fall colors. The wood is moderately tough and heavy, very light brown in color, and has no economic value. The plant has trouble adapting to climates in Europe and is very inconspicuous and lacks ornamental value.

A. glabrum (CECE)	*A. glabrum*, fruits*
A. glabrum subsp. *douglasii*	*A. glabrum*, fruits (BMP)
A. glabrum subsp. *douglasii*, fruits	*A. glabrum* subsp. *douglasii*,
A. glabrum subsp. *douglasii*, branch	buds in winter

Acer griseum

(Franchet) Pax (1902)

Section: *Trifoliata.*

Epithet: *Griseus,* gray, referring to the color of the down on new leaves.

Common name: Chinese paperbark maple.

Origin: Central China. Introduced in Europe in 1901 by Veitch Nursery.

General appearance: A tree, to 10 m (33 ft.) tall, with main branches upright and with a rounded crown.

Trunk: Orange brown to cinnamon brown, more or less glossy depending upon the individual. The bark peels off in long flakes that roll up on themselves, a phenomenon that occurs on the entire tree and increases with age.

Branches: Dark red-brown, glabrous.

Buds: Small, very dark.

Leaves: Consist of three leaflets, each 4 to 8 cm (1.5–3 in.) long, half as wide, bright green above, glaucous below. Center leaflet largest, oval-lanceolate, and roughly toothed from the middle to the point; side leaflets smaller, slanted, without a petiole, toothed, with a wavy margin. Petiole downy. Young leaves are red-brown and downy when opening.

Flowers: Yellow, in groups of three or five, on a downy, drooping peduncle, 2.5 to 3 cm (ca. 1 in.) long. Appearing with the unfolding leaves.

Fruits: Samaras 3 to 4 cm (1–1.5 in.) long, the wings almost parallel at an angle between 60 and 90 degrees, the nuts and wings very downy.

Propagation: Relatively difficult by seed due to a strong parthenocarpic tendency, which results in most seed (90 percent) being sterile. The seed is very hard and requires 2 to 3 years of stratification. Seedlings are very similar to each other. By cuttings, a method requiring much skill.

Discovered by Ernest H. Wilson in 1901, this magnificent tree, interesting from many points of view, is probably the most prized maple of the Western world. Its unique bark and its orange-red to scarlet autumn foliage earn it a choice location in any landscape. It is slow growing, hardy, and easily cultivated, prospering in rich, neutral or acid soil. It is not recommended for soils with insufficient drainage or for sites dominated by large trees. It will be more appreciated in a solitary position in an open space.

Acer griseum is immediately distinguished from the other trifoliolate maples of the group by the appearance of its bark, but also by the teeth that border the leaflets. The leaflets of *A. maximowiczianum* are larger and slightly more toothed, while those of *A. triflorum* are less pointed and more deeply cleft.

leaves unfurling	leaves (CECE)
flowers (Herkenrode)*	fruits (Herkenrode)*
in autumn (CECE)	start of fall coloring (Westonbirt)

A. *griseum* (Hillier) | A. *griseum*, trunk°

A. *griseum* lining a driveway (Hergest Croft)

Acer griseum (Winterthur)*

Acer griseum (Kew)

Acer heldreichii

Orphanides ex Boissier (1856)

Section: *Acer.*

Epithet: *Heldreichii,* after Theodor H. H. von Heldreich (1822–1902), director of the botanical gardens in Athens, Greece.

Common names: Balkan maple, Greek maple.

Origin: Balkan states and Greece.

General appearance: A large deciduous tree, more than 25 m (82 ft.) tall, with a straight trunk and with broadly spreading, domelike branching.

Trunk: Gray, smooth like the branches, sometimes vertically striped on older trees.

Branches: Brownish. The current year's growth is a lighter brown.

Buds: Red to dark brown, very pointed.

Leaves: Five-lobed, sometimes three-lobed, 10 to 15 cm (4–6 in.) long, broader than long, glossy dark green above, grayer below, very thin, glabrous on both sides except for a tuft of small hairs on the upper side at the base and brownish down along the main vein on the underside. Lobes oblong, the three terminal lobes well separated, almost down to the base. Margins roughly toothed. Petiole yellow, up to 20 cm (8 in.) long.

Flowers: Yellow, in short and broad upright umbels. Appearing relatively late in May.

Fruits: Smooth, samaras 3–5 cm long, the wings at an angle of 60 degrees.

Propagation: Preferably by seed, but garden seed is often of hybrid origin. By grafting on *Acer pseudoplatanus.*

Characterized by a tall, straight crown and a smooth, lightly colored trunk, this tree is often mistaken for *Acer pseudoplatanus,* sycamore maple. It may however be distinguished from large-leaved maples by its deeply cleft leaves with very close lobes. Although it does not display spectacular coloring, this hardy tree is often planted in a solitary location for its elegant habit.

flowers (Hemelrijk)	fruits in summer (Hergest Croft)
trunk (Hergest Croft)	the largest tree of its kind in England, more than 25 m (82 ft.) tall (Hergest Croft)

Acer heldreichii subsp. *trautvetteri*

(Medvedev) Murray (1982)

Section: *Acer.*

Epithet: *Trautvetteri,* after Ernst R. von Trautvetter (1809–1889), director of the Saint Petersburg (Russia) botanical garden.

Common name: Redbud maple.

Origin: Caucasus, eastern Turkey, and Iran, in mountains at altitudes above 1500 m (4950 ft.). Introduced by G. van Volxem in 1866.

General appearance: A large deciduous tree, up to 20 or 25 m (66–82 ft.) tall, with a trunk circumference of 2 m (6.5 ft.). The main branches are often upright in the center, more horizontal at the outside. The crown is rounded.

Trunk: Gray-brown, vertical fissures with large scales.

Branches: Reddish brown, glabrous, and glossy. Dark red in winter.

Buds: Dark brown in winter, very thick and scarlet red before opening.

Leaves: Five-lobed, large, 15 to 18 cm (6–7 in.) long, dark green and glabrous above, lighter, matt green and slightly glaucous below, with some tufts of down at the axils of the main veins where they join the petiole. Base slightly cordate. Lobes deeply cleft three-quarters of their length. Margins roughly and irregularly toothed. Petiole red, to 20 cm (8 in.) long. Young leaves often scarlet red.

Flowers: Yellow, in terminal panicles, upright then drooping.

Fruits: Samaras large, 7 cm (2.75 in.) long, deep red, the wings parallel or overlapping, the nutlets initially downy, becoming glabrous.

Propagation: Easy, by seed, as long as the seeds are not from hybrids. By grafting on *Acer pseudoplatanus.*

flowers (Batsford)*	early autumn (Hillier)
dried fruits	
fruits (Wakehurst)	fruit detail (Hillier)

This tree has a definitely more ornamental character than does *Acer heldreichii,* thanks to its colorful, scaly buds, which are very large before opening, its very red fruit clusters, its young red leaves, and its yellow to red fall colors. A keen eye will recognize the imposing candelabra-shaped silhouette of this specie. It can be distinguished from sycamore maple by its more deeply cleft leaf and from *A. velutinum* by the less rounded lobes. A rapid grower, it is easily cultivated in sites with damp soil and moderate temperatures. This tree is particularly suitable for large gardens and parks.

Acer heldreichii subsp. *trautvetteri,* large trunk (Wakehurst)

A. heldreichii subsp. *trautvetteri* (Wakehurst)

A. heldreichii (Kew)

Acer henryi

Pax (1889)

start of
flowering*

Section: *Negundo.*

Epithet: *Henryi,* after Irish plant hunter Augustine Henry, who discovered this maple.

Origin: Central China (Hubei and Sichuan provinces). Introduced in 1903 by Ernest H. Wilson for Veitch Nursery.

General appearance: A small tree or usually a large shrub, 10 to 12 m (33–39 ft.) tall and wide.

Trunk: Gray-brown.

Branches: Olive green, glabrous.

Leaves: Consists of three leaflets, each 6 to 10 cm (2.4–4 in.) long and 2 to 3 cm (0.75–1 in.) broad, oval, toothed from the middle on and ending with a long point, but less toothed than *Acer cissifolium.* Leaves are entire, mostly on the older branches. Petiole 5–10 cm (2–4 in.) long, red-brown with a green vein. Young leaves remarkable for their pinkish red color, turning glossy dark green on both sides. Down is present, mostly on the leaf underside, on the veins.

Flowers: Dioecious species, but becoming monoecious with age. With whitish petals that fall before or while the flower opens and is fertile. Borne in drooping spikes, at the axil of the new shoot. Sessile, without a peduncle. Appearing in May, before the leaves.

Fruits: On numerous racemes 10 to 15 cm (4–6 in.) long, almost sessile. Samaras about 2 cm (0.75 in.) long, the wings nearly horizontal.

Propagation: If not pollinated, the seeds develop by parthenogenesis (they are all sterile).

Acer henryi, which is closely related to *A. cissifolium,* is distinguished from the latter by its red young shoots. Leaf margin varies considerably in this species: trees originating from China and introduced by Wilson have glossy, entire leaflets that turn to yellow and glossy red in the fall, while the leaflets of other trees have a more toothed margin and are broader and duller looking.

This maple is a nice example of a specimen tree for the garden, grown as a solitary plant so that its very elegant habit may be appreciated.

leaves (Lenoir)	in autumn (Arnold Arboretum)
flowers	fruits (Hillier)
trunk (Caerhays Castle)	in autumn (Hillier)
	leaves in autumn

A. henryi, in spring (Hillier)

A. henryi, an old tree (Caerhays Castle) | *A. henryi,* trunk (Morris Arboretum)*

A. henryi, start of fall coloring (Hillier)

Acer ×hillieri

Lancaster (1979)

Epithet: *Hillieri,* after British nurseryman Sir Harold Hillier (1906–1984).

Origin: Hillier nursery. A hybrid of *Acer miyabei* × *A. cappadocicum*. Cultivated since 1935 by Harold Hillier, this hybrid had only one known relative, *Acer miyabei*. Later, around 1979, in the Hergest Croft arboretum, Roy Lancaster, the caretaker of the Hillier nursery, noticed the existence of a similar but more yellow hybrid. Close to it grew an *A. miyabei* and an *A. cappadocicum* 'Aureum', which he guessed to be the "parents" of this hybrid. He later decided that the parents of the Hillier hybrid must be the already known *A. miyabei* and *A. cappadocicum*. These two hybrids (described hereunder) with almost the same ancestors have received the following cultivar names:

> *Acer ×hillieri* **'Summergold'** Banks (1979), *A. miyabei* × *A. cappadocicum* 'Aureum'.
>
> *Acer ×hillieri* **'West Hill'** Hillier & Sons (1970), *A. miyabei* × *A. cappadocicum*.

General appearance: The original tree, dating back to 1935, is 12 m (39 ft.) tall, almost the adult height of *Acer miyabei*. The crown is rounded.

Trunk: Vertical striation.

Branches: Dark brown. Young shoots are reddish brown.

Leaves: Five-lobed, sometimes seven-lobed, 10 to 13 cm (4–5 in.) long, 8 to 10 cm (3–4 in.) wide. The upper surface is green, glabrous, and glossy, with prominent yellow veins, the backside glabrous except for a tuft of brown hair at the base of the veins. Lobes long, acuminate. Margins entire, wavy, sometimes crumpled. Petiole glabrous, at most 14 cm (5.5 in.) long, on young leaves.

Flowers: Yellowish. The inflorescences in upright corymbs carry as many flowers as those of *Acer cappadocicum* and more than those of *A. miyabei*.

Fruits: Nutlets round, flattened, covered with a white down.

When the leaf with its larger central lobe is considered, *Acer ×hillieri* more closely resembles *A. miyabei* than *A. cappadocicum;* lobes of the latter are broader and more triangular. The vertically ridged trunk of the hybrid is also closer to that of *A. miyabei*.

 Acer ×hillieri 'West Hill' is a beautiful tree, showing a nice yellowish color when the buds open as well as in the fall.

trunk	*A. ×hillieri* 'West Hill' (Hillier)
flowers	fruits

Acer ×hillieri 'Summergold'

Banks (1979). England.

Acer ×hillieri
'Summergold'
(Hergest Croft)

Origin: Hergest Croft arboretum; raised by Mr. Banks, owner of the arboretum. A hybrid of *Acer miyabei* × *A. cappadocicum* 'Aureum'.

General appearance: An average-sized tree, with dense, upright branching.

Branches: Brown, glabrous. Young shoots are green.

Leaves: Five-lobed, the basal lobes less developed than the others, the center lobes elongated and acuminate. Leaf surface glabrous and glossy, color golden yellow in summer. Margins entire.

Among the beautiful hybrids of section *Platanoidea* (for example, *Acer ×dieckii, A. platanoides* × *A. truncatum, A. ×zoeschense*), *A. ×hillieri* 'Summergold' fills out well the range of yellow-leaved medium to tall trees. Indeed, only *A. cappadocicum* 'Aureum', *A. negundo* subsp. *californicum,* and *A. pseudoplatanus* 'Corstorphinense' display almost uniformly yellow leaves in summer. 'Summergold' grows well and is hardy to zone 5.

Acer ×hillieri 'Summergold' (Hergest Croft)*

Acer ×hillieri 'Summergold', flowers (Great Park)

Acer ×hillieri 'Summergold' in spring (Great Park)

Acer ×hillieri 'Summergold' (Hergest Croft)

Acer ×hybridum
Bosc (1821)

Epithet: *Hybridus,* of hybrid origin.

Origin: Garden. Parentage uncertain, perhaps *Acer opalus* × *A. monspessulanum.*

General appearance: A tree, 15 m (50 ft.) tall, with a dense, rounded crown and relatively upright branches.

Trunk: Gray-brown, fissured, and very superficially corky.

Branches: Green, glabrous.

Leaves: Three-lobed, 5 to 12 cm (2–4.75 in.), tough, glossy, dark green above, gray-green below, with down only along the main veins. Base slightly cordate. Lobes rounded, slightly acuminate, and forward-pointing. Petiole yellowish, glabrous, rather thin, shorter than the leaf; it does not contain any milky sap.

Flowers: Yellowish, in panicles 8 to 15 cm (3–6 in.) long. Appearing in May.

Fruits: Samaras parallel.

❧

Several renowned botanists have tried to identify the parentage of *Acer ×hybridum.* Some determined the parents to be *A. pseudoplatanus* and *A. opalus.* The ideal way to resolve the question would be to cross the supposed parent species and then name the new hybrid. Indeed, hybrid plants of each species result from normal tests in most nurseries and arboreta. After the two parents are identified, the new plant could be described and named, the name then registered and published.

    Acer ×hybridum is perfectly hardy and of moderate growth. Fall color is a very short-lived yellow.

leaves (Hillier)	flowers and fruits
trunk	in spring (Hillier)

Acer hyrcanum

Fisher & Meyer (1837)

Section: *Acer.*

Epithet: From Hyrcania, a Persian province, close to the Caspian Sea.

Common name: Balkan maple.

Origin: Southeastern Europe, the Balkans, and western Asia. Plants differ more or less from region to region.

General appearance: A deciduous tree, 6 to 15 m (20–50 ft.) tall, sometimes a large multitrunked shrub, with dense branching and a rounded, open, spreading habit.

Trunk: Light orange-brown bark, with thin scales.

Branches: Light brown, redder than the trunk.

Buds: With red-brown, gray-bordered scales.

Leaves: Five-lobed, rarely three-lobed, 8 to 12 cm (3–4.75 in.) long, green, glossy above, glaucous below except for some tufts of down along the main vein, the three central lobes with broad, angular, blunt points. Margins entire, not toothed. Petiole rosy brown, 5 to 10 cm (2–4 in.) long.

Flowers: Yellow-green, on short peduncles, inflorescence in upright corymbs. Appearing with the leaves.

Fruits: Upright, glabrous. Samaras 3 cm (ca. 1 in.) long, the wings almost parallel, the nutlets well rounded.

Propagation: By seed, but few fruits are available due to the plant's strong parthenocarpic tendency. By grafting on *Acer pseudoplatanus,* which produces unsatisfactory results.

Broadly distributed from Europe to western Asia, *Acer hyrcanum* has given rise to many subspecies. It is similar to *A. opalus* but distinguished by its deeper and angular lobes. It also is similar to *A. campestre,* although its petiole does not contain any milky sap; both maples are about the same height and have yellow foliage in the fall. *Acer hyrcanum* is well suited to large gardens or parks, isolated or in groups. It grows well in calcareous soils and survives hot, dry summers. It is not recommended for northern Europe, except in temperate regions with a maritime climate.

leaf (Westonbirt)	leaves in autumn
flowers (Westonbirt)	fruits
in autumn (Westonbirt)	

165

Acer hyrcanum in spring (Kew)

Acer hyrcanum var. *granatense*

Synonym: *Acer granatense* Boissier (1838).

General appearance: A small shrub, 2 to 3 m (6.5–10 ft.) tall, with dark brown, glabrous branches.

Leaves: Five-lobed, small, 3 to 4 cm (1–1.5 in.) long, 4 to 5 cm (1.5–2 in.) wide, green, smooth above, rough below. Distinguished by flat, very thin leaves.

Acer hyrcanum subsp. *keckianum*

Epithet: *Keckianus,* after Karl Keck (1825–1894), an Austrian botanist.

Origin: Lebanese mountains and western Turkey.

General appearance: A small bushy tree, 4 to 5 m (13–16 ft.) tall and wide, with relatively horizontal branching.

Trunk: Gray-brown.

Leaves: Five-lobed, small, 2 to 3 cm (0.75–1 in.) long, 3 to 4 cm (1–1.5 in.) wide, slightly tomentose below. Lobes very symmetrical, the two front lobes wavy. Margins roughly toothed. Petiole short, 2 to 5 cm (0.75–2 in.) long.

Flowers and fruits: Similar to the species.

This large, slow-growing shrub is distinguished from the species by a smaller leaf and petiole, as well as by down on the leaf underside. Like the species, it turns an attractive yellow color in the fall. Hardy to zone 5.

A. hyrcanum var. *granatense*	*A. hyrcanum* var. *granatense* (Hillier)
A. hyrcanum subsp. *keckianum* (Hillier)	*A. hyrcanum* subsp. *stevenii* (Hemelrijk)
A. hyrcanum subsp. *tauricolum* (Hillier)	

167

Acer japonicum

Thunberg ex Murray (1784)

Section: *Palmata.*

Epithet: *Japonicus,* from Japan.

Common names: Full-moon maple, Japanese maple.

Origin: Japan (Hokkaido and Honshu islands), in mountain forests, in understory.

General appearance: In habitat, where it grows in the understory of mixed forests, it is a small multi-trunked tree. Elsewhere it reaches 10 to 15 m (33–50 ft.) tall. Deciduous, with a dense, rounded crown.

Trunk: Gray-brown, smooth, without ridges.

Branches: Glabrous, like the young shoots.

Buds: Dark red, ovoid, pointed.

Leaves: Seven- to eleven-lobed, rather large, 8 to 15 cm (3–6 in.) , and dark green on both sides. Lobes large, separated at two-thirds of their length, pointed. Margins doubly and very finely toothed. A thin down remains on the petiole, at the junction with the leaf, and in the axils of the veins.

Flowers: Purple-red, with yellowish stamens, in pendent clusters, with relatively long peduncles. Appearing in April, before the leaves.

Fruits: Samaras 2 to 3 cm (0.75–1 in.) long, hairy initially, becoming glabrous, always hanging under the leaves, opposite, the wings usually horizontal. Seeds rather large.

Propagation: By grafting on *A. palmatum.* By seed, which ripens in October but must be stratified for at least a full year.

Known and described two hundred years ago, the Japanese maple is remarkable and, rather curiously, mainly represented by its cultivars rather than by the type species. It is a large tree, with fairly rapid growth in good conditions and magnificent carmine-red and orange fall colors. An understory tree, it fits very well in an open area or in the shade of larger trees. It prefers light clay or sandy soil and moderate humidity. It is not suitable for heavy calcareous soil. Although hardy to zone 5, this maple is sensitive to spring frosts.

flowers	autumn (Westonbirt)
dried fruits	fruits
leaves unfurling (Westonbirt)	

Acer japonicum in spring (Westonbirt)

Acer japonicum in early autumn (Winkworth)

Acer japonicum in autumn (Kohan, Lake Shikotsu, Hokkaido)*

Acer japonicum in summer (Westonbirt)

Acer japonicum
'Aconitifolium'°

CULTIVARS

Acer japonicum 'Aconitifolium'

Meehan (1888). England.

A small tree, 5 m (16 ft.) tall, easily recognized by its dense, rounded crown. It is certainly the most beautiful and most typical cultivar of the species. It is ornamental from early spring, with large inflorescences appearing simultaneously with the light green foliage. The leaves are large, 10 to 15 cm (4–6 in.), and resemble those of *Aconitum,* the monkshood genus. The 9 to 11 lobes are deeply cleft at their extremities, broadly open, and narrowing down to the point of intersection of the ribs; the length of the lobes may vary between 7 and 17 cm (2.75–6.75 in.), the width between 6 and 14 cm (2.4–5.5 in.). The leaves are slightly pubescent and in summer are a deep green. The thick, curved petiole tends to carry the leaf horizontally. The foliage persists on the branch in fall, allowing plenty of time to appreciate its superb carmine-red to purple color. The fruits are also purple-red and ornamental.

Acer japonicum 'Aconitifolium U.S.A.'

United States.

Acer japonicum 'Aconitifolium U.S.A.'
(Herkenrode)

A cultivar with a provisional name, since its taxonomy is uncertain. The leaves are very similar to those of the species but larger. This plant grows well and has attractive fall coloring.

A. japonicum 'Aconitifolium', flowers	*A. japonicum* 'Aconitifolium', fruits
A. japonicum 'Aconitifolium' in autumn	*A. japonicum* 'Aconitifolium' in autumn
A. japonicum 'Aconitifolium' in autumn (Herkenrode)	

A. japonicum 'Attaryi' (CECE)	*A. japonicum* 'Attaryi' in autumn
A. japonicum 'Dissectum' (CECE)	*A. japonicum* 'Fairy Light'

Acer japonicum 'Attaryi'

Vertrees. United States.

A small tree or large upright shrub, 12 m (39 ft.) tall. The trunk is gray and smooth. The leaves are very wide, 15 to 25 cm (6–10 in.) long, and have seven to nine lobes deeply cleft to two-thirds of their length. The petiole is long, 5 to 10 cm (2–4 in.). This cultivar strongly resembles the type *Acer japonicum* and *A. japonicum* 'Ō isami', with more lobes. It is hardy to zone 5. Fall color is scarlet red or a lighter orange color. The taxonomy of this cultivar is confused; it appears this maple should now be known as *A. japonicum*.

Acer japonicum 'Dissectum'

Kolding Botanical Garden, Denmark.

The leaf is similar to that of 'Green Cascade', but slightly less cleft. The fall color is just as remarkable. The name 'Dissectum' is already in use for a cultivar of *Acer palmatum* and should thus not be used for this maple.

A. japonicum 'Green Cascade' (CECE)	*A. japonicum* 'Green Cascade', leaves in autumn
A. japonicum 'Green Cascade' in autumn (Lenoir)	*A. japonicum* 'Green Cascade' in summer (Hillier)

Acer japonicum 'Fairy Light'

Teese (1979). Australia.

This small, elegant tree has an upright, bushy habit. It is slow growing, reaching about 3 m (10 ft.) tall when mature. Its leaves, like those of 'Green Cascade', are deeply divided. The lobes are threadlike at the base and separated from the point at which they are attached to the petiole. The light green leaves turn brilliant yellow, then scarlet red in fall. This cultivar was selected by A. J. Teese of Monbulk, Victoria (Australia).

Acer japonicum 'Green Cascade'

Wright (1955). United States.

As its name indicates, this small tree of 1 to 2 m (3–6.5 ft.) tall has a weeping habit. It must be staked, however, if a spreading plant is not wanted. It may occasionally cover an embankment. Its leaves are similar to those of *Acer japonicum* 'Aconitifolium' but smaller; they have 9 to 11 lobes, each 8 to 10 cm (3–4 in.) long, and very narrow on the first third of the length and attached to the leaf's base. Fall color is orange-red.

A. japonicum 'Ō isami' (CECE)

A. japonicum 'Ō isami', end of summer (Herkenrode)

A. japonicum 'Ō isami' in autumn

Acer japonicum 'Ō isami'

Koidzumi (1911). Japan.

A large shrub reaching 5 to 8 m (16–26 ft.) tall and wide, with a rounded crown, and gray-brown smooth trunk. The plant is hardy and of average growth. The leaves are large, to 15 to 25 cm (6–10 in.) long, with 9 to 13 lobes cleft on one-half their length, pointed, strongly toothed, and showing even rather deep slits. A light pubescence is visible on the face of the young leaf and gives it a silvery aspect. The leaves are soft green to pink on unfurling, becoming dark green in the summer, with some silvery pink reflections. In the fall, the green combines with the reds, yellows, and oranges to produce spectacular effects. The colors then turn from bright to deep red. This cultivar is well suited to average-sized gardens.

Acer japonicum 'Ōtaki'

Japan.

A large, vigorous-growing shrub, averaging 4 to 5 m (13–16 ft.) tall and 2 to 3 m (6.5–10 ft.) wide when mature. The leaves have 9 to 11 lobes, divided on one-half their length and very closely packed, deeply cleft and toothed. The leaves have a diameter of 6 to 8 cm (2.4–3 in.) and are often larger when young. The short petiole is 2 to 3 cm (0.75–1 in.) long and rather stiff. The branches are thick, short, and rather stiff. In summer, the leaves are deep green, sometimes slightly bluish in a shady site. Fall color varies from red to orange-yellow.

A. japonicum 'Ōtaki', leaves (CECE)	*A. japonicum* 'Ōtaki', spring flowers
	A. japonicum 'Ōtaki', fruits

A. japonicum 'Ōtaki' in autumn (Herkenrode)

Acer japonicum 'Taki no gawa'

Japan.

The name of this cultivar is not yet finalized, since the leaves of American trees differ from those of their European counterparts. The latter have larger leaves with deeper lobes, grow to 6 or 8 m (20–26 ft.) tall, and have a broad mushroom-shaped crown. The buds of 'Taki no gawa' open early, and red fall color appears early in October.

Acer japonicum 'Vitifolium'

N. E. Brown (1876). United Kingdom.

It is the largest and oldest cultivar of this species, bearing large leaves ensuring a rapid growth. The leaves are very similar to those of *Acer japonicum,* slightly more cleft and larger, fanning out. The crown is round and the adult tree height verges on 12 m (39 ft.). This plant provides a real show in the fall, as may be seen from the picture on p. 180, taken in Weston-birt in early autumn.

A. japonicum 'Taki no gawa' in spring (BMP)
A. japonicum 'Taki no gawa', flowers*

A. japonicum 'Taki no gawa' in autumn (Herkenrode)*

A. japonicum 'Vitifolium' in spring (Savill) | *A. japonicum* 'Vitifolium', flowers*

A. japonicum 'Vitifolium', flowers

A. japonicum 'Vitifolium' in spring (Westonbirt)

A. japonicum 'Vitifolium' in autumn (Westonbirt)

A. japonicum 'Vitifolium', frosted leaves in autumn | *A. japonicum* 'Vitifolium' in autumn (Lenoir)

Acer laevigatum
Wallich (1830)

Section: *Palmata.*

Epithet: *Laevigatus,* smooth, polished, referring to the leaves.

Origin: Central and eastern China (Hubei and Sichuan provinces) and southeastern Asia. Introduced in Europe by Ernest H. Wilson in 1902.

General appearance: A tree, reaching 10 to 15 m (33–50 ft.) tall, with upright habit and sparse branching. The Westonbirt tree (see p. 180) is 7 m (23 ft.) tall, with a trunk diameter of 26 cm (10.5 in.) at a height of 1.5 m (5 ft.).

Trunk: Smooth, olive green with brown veins.

Branches: Green, sometimes reddish.

Leaves: Entire, evergreen, 8 to 15 cm (3–6 in.) long, 3 to 3.5 cm (1–1.4 in.) wide, smooth and glossy. Margins very slightly toothed, red. Petiole short, only 1 cm (0.4 in.) long. Young shoots glabrous, hanging, rosy red.

Flowers: Yellow, in corymbs on a red panicle.

Fruits: Samaras reddish, with a rounded end, 4 to 7 cm (1.5–2.75 in.) long, the wings forming a right or obtuse angle.

❧

This tender tree is hardy only to zones 7 and 8 (down to –5°C or 23°F). It is very seldom encountered In Europe, since it can only survive in favorable microclimates. It is semi-evergreen and interesting for its young pink-reddish shoots. *Acer laevigatum* looks like *A. fabri* and *A. oblongum,* which are also tender, but leaves of the latter species have three veins at the base.

Acer longipes

Franchet ex Rehder (1905)

Section: *Platanoides.*

Epithet: *Longipes,* having an elongated point.

Origin: China (Sichuan province). Introduced in Europe by Ernest H. Wilson in 1908.

General appearance: A tree, 15 to 20 m (50–66 ft.) tall, with a rounded, mushroom-shaped crown.

Trunk: Brown-green.

Branches: Reddish brown. Young shoots dark brown, glabrous.

Leaves: Invariably three-lobed, 7 to 15 cm (2.75–6 in.) long, green covered below with a brownish down turning to rusty brown at the end of summer. Lobes elongated, triangular, ending in a very acuminate point. Margins entire.

Flowers: On a short, glabrous peduncle, in panicles 10 cm (4 in.) long.

Fruits: Samaras 3 cm (ca. 1 in.) long, the wings rather short and forming a right angle.

*A*cer longipes is common in Sichuan province, China, but rather rare in Europe. Its upright silhouette is very similar to that of maples in section *Macrantha,* but it can be identified easily in early spring when the characteristic three-lobed leaf develops long points. The red stipules are present at this stage and are very ornamental. The leaves are red in summer, turning yellow in the fall. This tree should be planted more often. Hardy to zone 5.

flowers (Great Park)	branches in spring
leaves (Hillier)	spring (Hillier)
fruits (Hillier)	

Acer longipes subsp. *amplum*

(Rehder) de Jong (1994)

Section: *Platanoides.*

Epithet: *Amplus,* numerous.

Origin: China (Sichuan, Hubei, Guangxi, and Zhejiang provinces). Discovered by Ernest H. Wilson in Zhejiang in 1901 and immediately imported to the West.

General appearance: A medium-sized tree, 15 to 20 m (50–66 ft.) tall in habitat, but much shorter in cultivation.

Trunk: Dark gray, lightly striated or smooth.

Branches: Brown-green. Young shoots are more yellow.

Buds: Green.

Leaves: Five-lobed, 8 to 12 cm (3–4.75 in.) long and wide, often wavy. Center lobe broader than the others. Margins entire. Petiole long at 5 to 15 cm (2–6 in.), very thin, and hanging. Young leaves open coppery red, turning green in summer.

Flowers: Yellowish white, relatively few, in a large panicle, 10 to 15 cm (4–6 in.) long.

Propagation: Very easy by seed. Equally easy by grafting on *Acer platanoides* or *A. cappadocicum.*

*A*cer longipes subsp. *amplum* was discovered in the Tien Tai mountain range, and originally named var. *tientaiense* (Schneider) Rehder (1911).

This maple strongly resembles *Acer cappadocicum,* but has broader and larger lobes. Hardy to zone 5, it is fast growing and suitable for all soils except excessively alkaline ones. Its main ornamental advantages lie in its flowering and in its orange to pale yellow fall color.

CULTIVAR

Acer longipes subsp. *amplum* 'Gold Coin'
Esveld (1985). Netherlands.

A small, multitrunked tree, showing good vigor. The bark is brown, the young shoots green. The leaves have five lobes and are broadly cordate at the base. The basal lobes are small, the center one is very broad, ovoid, and acuminate. The young leaves are red, turning to a golden yellow then to green on the older branches. Fall color is whitish yellow. Hardy to zone 6.

young shoots	leaves
flowers*	fruits
trunk	habit (Hillier)
	leaves in autumn (Batsford)

Acer macrophyllum
Pursh (1814)

opening buds

Section: *Lithocarpa.*

Epithet: *Macrophyllus,* having large leaves.

Common names: Big-leaf maple, Oregon maple.

Origin: Western North America (British Columbia to California). Introduced in England by David Douglas in 1826. It is the only arborescent maple in western North America.

General appearance: A large tree, more than 25 m (82 ft.) tall, with a short trunk and a broad crown. All plant parts are large, including leaves, petioles, flowers, and fruits.

Trunk: Dark brown and smooth on young trees, with many low branches. Becoming fissured, striated, and grayer, with time.

Branches: The current year's branches are greenish and smooth.

Buds: Covered by the petiole in summer. Thicker, with brown scales, in winter.

Leaves: Five-lobed and the largest leaf in genus *Acer* (see photograph on opposite page) at 15 to 30 cm (6–12 in.). Center three lobes larger than the others and themselves lobed. Petiole long at about 20 cm (8 in.), yellowish, containing a milky sap. Young leaves often downy, becoming smooth and glossy, lighter above and darker below.

Flowers: Large, yellow, and fragrant, forming large drooping inflorescences (see photograph on opposite page). Appearing with the first leaves.

Fruits: Samaras large, 7 cm (2.75 in.) long, covered with brownish very stinging hairs, the wings glabrous.

Propagation: Very easy, by seed. Seedlings grow well. Seed collectors will want to wear gloves when harvesting the seed.

flowers°	leaves (BMP)
fruits	as a street tree°
trunk (Hergest Croft)	

Originating in Oregon, in the western United States, *Acer macrophyllum* is found at lower elevations in large conifer forests, where it appreciates shade and a relatively humid environment. The tree's root system has adapted to these conditions and is very broad and superficial. The bark holds the humidity, thus favoring the proliferation of mosses on the trunk and the thick branches. The tree does not harden-off well in Europe, due to the lack of summer and fall warm periods, and thus is prone to frost damage. Even the larger English specimens do not rival trees in their native environment.

The landscaping value of this tree resides in the unusual size of its flowers, fruits, and leaves, the largest in the genus *Acer*. Hardy to zone 5, it has no particular fall coloring.

CULTIVARS

Acer macrophyllum 'Kimballiae'
Harrar (1940). United States.

Very different from the species, it often assumes a shrublike habit less than 10 m (33 ft.) tall. The leaves are divided into three to five well-separated leaflets, each 8 to 10 cm (3–4 in.) long. This cultivar is seldom cultivated.

Acer macrophyllum 'Seattle Sentinel'
Mulligan (1954). United States.

This is the fastigiate cultivar of *Acer macrophyllum*, growing up to 15 m (50 ft.) tall. The leaves are smaller than those of the species, with a similar shape. The leaf is glossy green above, light green below. The length of the leaf varies between 15 and 25 cm (6–10 in.), and the width between 18 and 24 cm (7–9.5 in.). This tree does not change color in the fall. Hardy to zone 6. It is very rarely cultivated.

Acer macrophyllum 'Variegatum'
Schwerin (1893). Germany.

A very old cultivar. The reddish-green leaves have whitish spots and are thus tri-colored. The red color often disappears, yielding a more classical green and white mix. The leaf is 10 to 12 cm (4–4.75 in.) long and broad. The petiole is reddish. Old specimens of this cultivar progressively lose their coloring.

A. macrophyllum in spring (Westonbirt)*	*A. macrophyllum* 'Variegatum'
A. macrophyllum 'Seattle Sentinel', trunk	*A. macrophyllum* 'Seattle Sentinel' (Hillier)

Acer mandshuricum

Maximowicz (1867)

- - -

Section: *Trifoliata.*

Epithet: *Mandshuricus,* from Manchuria.

Common name: Manchurian maple.

Origin: Eastern Siberia, Manchuria, and central China. Plants sent from Saint Petersburg to the Royal Botanic Gardens, Kew, in 1904.

General appearance: A small tree, sometimes a broad shrub, reaching 5 to 6 m (16–20 ft.) tall.

Trunk: Dark brown, rough.

Branches: Brown, slender, and slightly drooping.

Buds: Small, dark.

Leaves: Consist of three leaflets, each 5 to 7 cm (2–2.75 in.) long, 2 to 3 cm (0.75–1 in.) wide, dark green above, blue-green below. Terminal leaflet oblong, lanceolate, and acuminate, lateral leaflets smaller with shorter peduncles. Petiole 4 to 6 cm (1.5–2.4 in.) long, with a reddish tint.

Flowers: Yellowish green, same as the stamens.

Fruits: Glabrous, purple-red.

Propagation: Very difficult, since viable seed is very rare. Furthermore, the embryo resides in a thick shell. By grafting on *Acer griseum.*

Coming from northeastern Asia, *Acer mandshuricum* needs lots of warmth in late summer to mature and yield fertile seeds. This small tree has no particular soil requirements. It is slow-growing. Hardy to zone 4.

   With its gracious bearing and horizontal branches, it makes an excellent specimen tree. It bears colorful fruit in the summer and has attractive red-orange leaves in the fall. This maple strongly resembles *Acer triflorum* and *A. griseum.*

leaves unfurling*	flowers
leaves in autumn	fruits*
in autumn (CECE)	habit (Hergest Croft)

Acer maximowiczianum

Miquel (1867)

Section: *Trifoliata.*

Epithet: *Maximowiczianum,* after Russian botanist Carl Maximowicz (1827–1891).

Common name: Nikko maple.

Synonym: *Acer nikoense* Maximowicz (1867).

Origin: Japan (southern Honshu, Kyushu, and Shikoku islands) and China (Hubei and Anhui provinces).

General appearance: A small, compact tree, 5 to 6 m (16–20 ft.) tall in continental Europe and 10 m (33 ft.) tall in England. In habitat, it reaches 12 to 16 m (39–53 ft.) tall with a trunk diameter of 30 to 40 cm (12–16 in.).

Trunk: Young trees gray-brown and striated. Older trees gray and rough, but not as much so as *Acer triflorum* or *A. griseum.*

Branches: Brownish and pubescent.

Buds: Long, triangular, surrounded by scales.

Leaves: Consist of three leaflets, each 5 to 15 cm (2–6 in.) long, 2 to 5 cm (0.75–2 in.) wide, the center leaflet largest, the other two more oval. Midrib prominent, mostly on the leaf underside, and very pubescent. Margins entire to superficially toothed, with very fine hairs. Petiole strong, 3 to 5 cm (1–2 in.) long, brownish, covered with hairs. On opening, the leaves are brown and covered with a thick down, turning dark green above and grayer below due to the down.

Flowers: Yellow, a little more than 1 cm (0.4 in.) in diameter, generally grouped in threes, on a pubescent, drooping peduncle. The trees often bear either all-male or all-female flowers. When male and female flowers appear on the same tree, they grow on separate branches.

Fruits: Seed brown, thick, and ligneous. Wings 4 cm (1.5 in.) long, 2 cm (0.75 in.) wide, rounded, lying parallel or forming an angle of up to 60 degrees, very pubescent (see photograph on opposite page).

Propagation: More than half the seeds are sterile. Only 10 percent of fertile seeds germinate after 3 to 4 years of stratification.

leaves unfurling	habit (Sheffield Park)*
flowers	fruits
trunk (Von Gimborn)°	leaves in autumn

Acer maximowiczianum in spring (Kew)

Acer maximowiczianum (Westonbirt)

This very hardy tree (to zone 4) is slow growing. Although it prefers light humic soils, neither too heavy nor too humid, it nevertheless adapts to limestone. It is suitable in full sun and open sites. This beautiful plant has a nicely a proportioned silhouette. *Acer maximowiczianum* is best appreciated in a solitary setting, in small or medium-sized gardens, if correctly pruned. Its color sequence is interesting throughout the vegetative cycles, beginning with very spectacular red-brown young shoots, followed by bronze-green leaves that turn vivid green, and finally reddish in the fall. Branch coloring is very irregular in fall. Rarely do trees exhibit uniform fall color; instead, several leaf colors are present at any time.

  Acer maximowiczianum looks very much like *A. griseum* and *A. triflorum,* but is larger and has larger leaves. It is not as beautiful, however, as either of them.

Acer maximowiczianum in autumn (CECE)

A curiosity, *Acer maximowiczianum* × *A. griseum*°

Acer micranthum

Siebold & Zuccarini (1845)

Section: *Macrantha.*

Epithet: *Micranthus,* having small flowers.

Common name: Small-flowered maple.

Origin: Japan. Introduced in Europe around 1880.

General appearance: A small deciduous tree, sometimes a large shrub, rarely more than 6 m (20 ft.) tall. Young plants are delicate looking but fill out with age.

Trunk: Many branched, smooth and red-brown.

Branches: Compared to the trunk, young branches are redder and thinner; they are often curved.

Buds: With scales that touch but do not overlap.

Leaves: Five-lobed, sometimes seven-lobed, elongated. Lobes well separated, tips acuminate. Margins irregularly serrate. Veins sometimes with very small hairs.

Flowers: Yellowish, in pendent clusters, 6 to 8 cm (2.4–3 in.) long. Appearing in May.

Fruits: Numerous and very small (the smallest in the genus *Acer*). Samaras 1 to 2 cm (0.4–0.75 in.) long, glabrous, the wings horizontal, forming an obtuse angle, the nutlet glabrous.

Propagation: Very difficult, by seed, due to the very low rate of germination. Easy by cuttings, or by grafting on any other maple of section *Macrantha*.

*A*cer micranthum is hardy and slow growing. This small plant is well suited to small gardens. It has ornamental flowers and young leaves, the latter staying red-orange till July. Fall color is a remarkable fiery red. The tree's structure and shape give it a discreet, refined aspect, and it remains elegant even in winter due to its reddish branches.

Acer micranthum is closely related to *A. tschonoskii,* which is larger and broader. The latter also has larger samaras, a characteristic that distinguishes it from *A. micranthum*.

CULTIVAR

Acer micranthum 'Candelabrum'

This unique plant grows in the Sir Harold Hillier Gardens and Arboretum, where it is much taller than the species (see photograph on p. 199). The leaves are also larger than those of the species, and the upright branches are similar to those of other maples in section *Macrantha*. The origin of this cultivar is unknown, but it might be the product of a hybrid seed, since many other maples belonging to the same section grow in proximity.

A. micranthum (Hergest Croft)	*A. micranthum,* flowers*
	A. micranthum, fruits*
A. micranthum in autumn (Herkenrode)	

Acer micranthum in autumn (Westonbirt)

Acer micranthum 'Candelabrum' in spring (Hillier)

Acer miyabei

Maximowicz (1888)

Section: *Platanoidea.*

Epithet: *Miyabei,* after Japanese botanist Kingo Miyabe (1860–1951).

Common name: Miyabe's maple.

Origin: Northern Japan. Introduced in England in 1895.

General appearance: An elegant tree, reaching 20 to 25 m (66–82 ft.) tall, with upright habit.

Trunk: Orange-brown, strongly striated, lightly and irregularly peeling, and corky.

Branches: Dark brown.

Buds: With six to eight scales.

Leaves: Five-lobed, 10 to 15 cm (4–6 in.) long, olive green, slightly rough-textured above and below. Lobes elongated, lobulate (mainly the central one), ending in a rounded point. Young leaves pink-red (see photograph on opposite page), covered with down which persists on the underside and on the petiole. Yellow vein visible later in the season on both sides of the leaf. Petiole yellow, about 15 cm (6 in.) long.

Flowers: In upright corymbs, 10 to 12 cm (4–4.75 in.) long.

Fruits: Covered with down. Samaras 2 cm (0.75 in.) long, the wings horizontal.

Propagation: Difficult, by seed, since the seeds ripen slowly and are not readily available in the trade. By grafting on *Acer campestre,* but grafts do not take well.

Because it is difficult to propagate, *Acer miyabei* is very rarely cultivated in Europe or in Japan, where it is native. It is similar to *A. campestre* in its bark and horizontal branching, but more elegant. In spring, its dark bark contrasts attractively with the yellowish young shoots and flowers. Leaves are dark green in summer, returning to yellow in the fall.

CULTIVARS

Crossing *Acer miyabei* with *A. cappadocicum* 'Aureum' has yielded the hybrid *A.* ×*hillieri,* described elsewhere in this work.

SUBSPECIES

A Chinese form, recognized by Edward Murray as *Acer miyabei* subsp. *miaotaiense,* is endemic in the provinces of Gansu, Shaanxi, and Zhejiang. It does not readily propagate itself and is threatened by the clearing of forests.

new leaves (Hemelrijk)   flowers (Lenoir)

autumn (Hemelrijk)   fruits (Hillier)

trunk (Hillier)

Acer miyabei (Hergest Croft)

Acer mono in autumn (Hillier)*

Acer mono in autumn (Japan)*

Acer mono

Maximowicz (1867)

Section: *Platanoidea.*

Origin: Central and northeastern China, eastern Siberia, Korea, and Japan. Introduced by Charles Maries in 1881.

General appearance: An elegant, medium-sized tree, reaching 20 to 25 m (66–82 ft.) tall, with a rounded, spreading, pyramidal crown.

Trunk: Very light gray-yellow, smooth, without ridges.

Branches: Brown-yellow, glabrous. Young shoots are yellow in summer, red in winter (only on young trees).

Buds: Dark red in winter.

Leaves: Five- to seven-lobed, broader than long, 9 to 16 cm (3.5–6.4 in.) wide and 8 to 13 cm (3–5 in.) long, green, glabrous, covered below with tufts of hair at the axil of the veins. Lobes very variable, triangular, with elongated tips depending on the variety, base cordate, never truncate, side lobes tapering downward (see photograph on opposite page). Margins entire, sometimes red-purple at leaf opening (see photograph on opposite page). Petiole long, containing a juicy sap.

Flowers: Greenish yellow, in umbels 5 to 8 cm (2–3 in.). Appearing before or with the leaves.

Fruits: Very close together (see photograph on opposite page), with very short wings.

Propagation: By grafting on *Acer platanoides.*

*A*cer mono is a tree showing good growth quality, healthy and resistant. It is very hardy and matures well and adapts to all growing sites, even mountains. The English champion in Hergest Croft (see photograph on p. 207) is 20 m (66 ft.) tall with multiple trunks from the base, as in nature, where straight, upright trees are seldom encountered. This maple is often planted in large parks where it is admired for its fall color.

Acer mono is the Asiatic equivalent of *A. cappadocicum,* which it resembles in many respects. The trunk of *A. mono,* however, is smooth and light-colored and its samaras have short wings. *Acer cappadocicum* has longer, more pointed leaf lobes and it suckers. In spite of these differences, *A. mono* is difficult to identify with certainty, due to the highly polymorphic leaves. Much literature exists on this variable tree, taking into account its wide geographical dispersion.

leaves (Hillier)	in autumn°
flowers	leaves in autumn (Hemelrijk)
fruits (Les Barres)	branches in winter in the
branch with fruit	wild (Hokkaido)*

Acer mono in spring (Arnold Arboretum)*

Acer mono in autumn (Lake Hibara, Honshu, Japan)*

Acer mono (Hergest Croft), the largest in England

Acer mono in autumn (Hokkaido, Japan)*

Acer mono subsp. *okamotoanum*

(Nakai) de Jong (1996)

Acer mono subsp.
okamotoanum in spring
(Savill)

Section: *Platanoidea.*

Origin: Ullung-do, an island off eastern South Korea. Endemic on that island. Introduced in England by James G. S. Harris in 1982.

General appearance: A tree 10 to 12 m (33–39 ft.) tall, with a flat crown.

Trunk: Dark brown, smooth.

Leaves: Five- to seven-lobed, broad, to 12 to 15 cm (4.75–6 in.) wide, light green above, lighter green below. Lobes short, abruptly acuminate, broadly ovoid. Margins entire, very wavy, especially on the acuminate point of the lobe.

Fruits: Samaras 3 to 4 cm (1–1.5 in.) long, closely spaced, the nutlets flat.

Approximately 300 km (186 mi) from Korea, Ullung Island harbors this unique subspecies of *Acer mono*. It would be interesting to find out how and when the subspecies established itself on the island. It is relatively new to Europe, though some specimens are flourishing there, notably in England and Belgium, where they appear to be hardy. The observed specimens show good growth and yellow fall color, similar to that of the species.

Acer mono f. *ambiguum* (Hillier)

Acer mono var. *mayrii* in autumn (Sapporo, Japan)*

Acer mono f. *ambiguum*

(Dippel) Rehder (1939)

Origin: Japan. Widespread in mountainous regions.

General appearance: Similar to the species, but distinguished by its rough bark and by pubescence on the leaf underside. Hardy to zone 5.

Leaves: Fall color is yellow.

Acer mono var. *mayrii*

(Schwerin) Nakai (1930)

Epithet: *Mayrii,* after German professor H. Mayr (1865–1911).

Origin: Northern Japan (only on Hokkaido Island) and the Sakhalin Islands. Discovered by Mayr in 1886.

General appearance: A tree to 20 to 25 m (66–82 ft.) tall in habitat, but much smaller in cultivation, where it may also become shrublike.

Branches: Dark red-brown. Young shoots are greenish, glabrous.

Leaves: Five-lobed, typically almost rectangular (see photograph above), green above and below. Lobes very broad, ovoid, rounded, ending in a very thin point. Petiole long and glabrous.

CULTIVARS

Acer mono 'Hoshi yadori'

Kingsville Nursery (1968). United States.

A small tree or large shrub, 6 to 7 m (20–23 ft.) tall. Leaves are decorated with creamy white spots and dots and are very similar to those of the species. The leaves are tender and very sensitive to sun; they do best in a somewhat shady site. A very beautiful cultivar. Hardy to zone 5.

Acer mono 'Marmorata'

Nicholson (1881). England.

A large shrub, to 8 m (26 ft.) tall. Spring color is superb: the large green leaves have a rosy red border. The leaves slowly turn to green, leaving some light-colored slightly patterned spots. Hardy to zone 5.

Acer mono 'Tokiwa nishiki'

A very large shrub, 6 to 7 m (20–23 ft.) tall. The leaves have five or seven lobes, the central lobe often being triangular. Generally, the leaf shape is similar to that of the species but sprinkled all over with white in a very irregular pattern. The petiole is thin and drooping. This interesting plant is fit for garden compositions calling for contrasts. Hardy to zone 6. Requires the usual care given cultivars.

Acer mono 'Usugumo'

A small, slow-growing shrub, only reaching up to 2 m (6.5 ft.) tall. The leaves have seven to nine triangular lobes, each ending in a long point. Leaf size is uniform and ranges from 8 to 11 cm (3–4.4 in.). This attractive, unique plant is characterized by its spotted foliage. Each leaf is irregularly spotted with white dots and rosy reflections. In the spring, the young leaf is truly magnificent, with its pink color and its upright position on the reddish petiole. The pink turns progressively to green and only persists in some locations, giving the whole this patterned aspect. This small maple will find its place in small, protected gardens. Hardy to zone 6.

A. *mono* 'Marmorata' in spring

A. *mono* 'Usugumo' in spring*   A. *mono* 'Usugumo'°

A. *mono* 'Hoshi yadori'°   A. *mono* 'Tokiwa nishiki'°

Acer monspessulanum

Linnaeus (1753)

Section: *Acer.*

Epithet: *Monspessulanus,* from Montpellier, France.

Common name: Montpelier maple.

Origin: Southern and central Europe and the Mediterranean basin.

General appearance: An elegant, compact tree reaching 7 to 10 m (23–33 ft.) tall, rarely 15 m (50 ft.), with dense, impenetrable branching and a rounded crown.

Trunk: Dark, with crevices.

Branches: Lighter colored than the trunk.

Buds: Ovoid, pointed, covered with numerous dark brown scales.

Leaves: Three-lobed, tough, glossy, thick, dark green above, lighter green below. Lobes 3 to 6 cm (1–2.4 in.) long. Base cordate. Margins entire. Petiole 3 to 5 cm (1–2 in.) long, with down at the junction of the ribs and the petiole.

Flowers: Yellow-green, on 4-cm (1.5-in.) long peduncles, growing on young shoots, forming inflorescences of drooping umbels, abundant.

Fruits: Numerous. Samaras 1.5 cm (ca. 0.5 in.) long, sometimes reddish, the wings parallel or intertwined.

Propagation: Easy by seed, but the species hybridizes easily with *Acer campestre.*

This tree is suitable for a warm climate and is adapted to calcareous and stony soils. Shade and cold, damp, acid soils must be avoided. *Acer monspessulanum* is disease resistant and hardy to zone 5. Fall color is red-orange, although cultivated trees do not display the full coloring that trees in habitat do. Because it tolerates heat, this maple is suitable for urban surroundings, terraces, and container cultivation. It resembles *A. campestre,* except that its petiole is free of milky sap, its leaves always have three lobes, and its samaras lie parallel. The flowers appear before the leaves and are remarkable and ornamental.

trunk°	flowers (Hillier)
fruits°	fruits

in full bloom (left) with *Betula* 'Jermyns' (right) in spring (Hillier)

212

Acer ×*martinii*

Jordan (1852)

Synonyms: *Acer ×peronai* Schwerin (1901), *A. perrieri* Chabert (1909).

Origin: Naturally occurring hybrid of *Acer monspessulanum* × *A. opalus* in southern France, Switzerland, Yugoslavia, and Italy (Apennines).

General appearance: A small tree, 8 to 10 m (26–33 ft.) tall, with a dense crown. The crown is rounded initially, becoming oblong with time.

Trunk: Differs from *Acer monspessulanum*. Scaly bark resembles that of *A. pseudoplatanus*.

Branches: Brown and glabrous.

Buds: Woolly hairs on the bud scars, later becoming glabrous.

Leaves: Variable as the tree ages. Three-lobed, occasionally with two additional but smaller basal lobes. Size varies from 7 to 12 cm (2.75–4.75 in.). Texture thick; upper side lustrous, glabrous, and rugged; underside bluish green.

Flowers: Yellow, on a raceme 5 cm (2 in.) long, in groups of 7 to 11. Appearing simultaneously with the leaves.

Fruits: Similar to those of the parent species. Wings of the samaras parallel.

*A*cer ×*martinii* is a naturally occurring hybrid. Fall color varies from yellow to orange and is similar to that of *A. opalus*. The leaves of trees growing in the Vachères forest of southern France resemble those of *A. monspessulanum*. *Acer ×martinii* should not be confused with *A. ×peronai*, a hybrid of *A. monspessulanum* and a variety of *A. opalus* endemic to Italy. *Acer monspessulanum* hybridizes equally easily with *A. campestre* (see *A. ×bornmuelleri*). Note that the hybrids of *A. monspessulanum* have different local names, leading to much confusion.

A. ×martinii (La Vachère, France)

A. ×martinii, fruits (La Vachère, France)

A. monspessulanum in autumn (Turkey)°	*A. monspessulanum* (Bokrijk)
A. monspessulanum subsp. *ibericum*	*A. monspessulanum* subsp. *turcomanicum*
A. monspessulanum subsp. *ibericum* in spring	*A. monspessulanum* subsp. *ibericum* (Kew)

Acer morifolium

Koidzumi (1914)

Section: *Macrantha.*

Epithet: *Morifolius,* having leaves like *Morus,* mulberry-tree.

Common name: Yaku maple.

Origin: Japan (Yaku and Tanego islands). Very recently imported.

General appearance: A large shrub, 8 to 10 m (26–33 ft.) tall.

Trunk: Green, with thin white striation.

Branches: Greenish, little striation. Young shoots reddish.

Leaves: Usually three-lobed, about 10 cm (4 in.) long, dark green above, slightly lighter green below. Lateral lobes insignificant. Petiole 5 to 8 cm (2–3 in.) long, red. Young leaf red, very acuminate, with prominent red veins.

Flowers: Yellowish on a short raceme.

Fruits: Numerous. Samaras small, 2 cm (0.75 in.) long, the wings forming an obtuse angle.

This tree is very rare in Europe where the first specimens were planted only recently. The species is often compared with *Acer capillipes,* since the two maples have similar leaf shape and a large number of fruits. The difference lies in their color: *A. morifolium* has less contrast, mostly in the fall when it takes its yellow tint.

Originating in Japan, this species has the same ornamental qualities and cultivation requirements as other maples in section *Macrantha,* except that it is slightly less hardy, to zones 6 and 7.

in spring (Westonbirt) | leaves
| young shoot
| trunk

Acer negundo

Linnaeus (1753)

Section: *Negundo.*

Epithet: *Negundo,* an old generic name given to some maples.

Common names: Ash-leaved maple, box elder.

Origin: North America, from New York state to the Rocky Mountains. Widely distributed in the Mississippi basin. Also occurs in Florida.

General appearance: A medium-sized tree, 12 to 20 m (39–66 ft.) tall, with a trunk diameter no more than 80 to 90 cm (32–36 in.). The rounded, broadly spreading crown is 5 to 10 m (16–33 ft.) wide, and the tips of the branches are pendulous. The sparse branching gives the tree a light, airy look.

Trunk: Light gray becoming brown and fissured with age.

Branches: Olive green, covered with a whitish bloom, glabrous, and very strong. Twigs are identical.

Leaves: Consist of three or five leaflets, rarely seven or nine, glossy light green and glabrous above, lighter green and slightly downy or sometimes glabrous below. Leaflets oval, 5 to 10 cm (2–4 in.) long, pointed, and roughly toothed at the end. The terminal leaflet has three lobes, the two lateral lobes with forward-pointing tips, and the terminal lobe sometimes assuming a wholly different shape. Rib greenish yellow. Petiole long, with a brown-red top.

Flowers: Dioecious species. Sometimes greenish yellow, without petals. Male flowers in dense red panicles at the end of the new shoot, each flower carried by a hairy peduncle, 2.5 to 3.5 cm (ca. 1 in.) long. Female flowers in drooping clusters. Wind-pollinated.

Fruits: Grouped in long drooping clusters, highly visible. Wings of samaras 3 to 5 cm (1–2 in.) long, at a maximum angle of 60 degrees, very thin, almost translucent.

Propagation: Easy by seed. Often used as rootstock for many cultivars and subspecies (more than 30); grafting is done in February on seasoned wood, or in July on green wood, with the rootstock in a container. Cuttings give good results but are little used.

pubescent petiole	trunk (New Mexico)
pubescent leaf underside	
male flowers	fruits

Acer negundo (Arenberg Park)*

*A*cer negundo likes humid areas, similar to its natural habitat. Seeds and young plants grow very rapidly, and the tree resists cold and hot spells. It is short-lived, between 50 and 60 years, and resembles *A. cissifolium*. The autumn foliage is clear and fresh, with a soft yellow color.

Widely cultivated in the 19th century, this species gave rise to numerous cultivars that are more ornamental than the species, due to their light and patterned colors. Some cultivars, however, have a tendency to revert to the shape and characteristics of the type.

At one time, this species was a source of maple sugar and syrup. Today is it used primarily for its ornamental value, although its mediocre and fragile wood is still used for pallets.

Native to North America, *Acer negundo* and its three recognized subspecies have been cultivated in Europe, where, in the 19th century, many selections were made. A large number of them were selected by German botanist Fritz von Schwerin, but many are no longer cultivated. The cultivars presented here below represent the best examples of the older cultivars as well as some new Dutch selections. All cultivars are hardy to zone 5.

Acer negundo (Glenwood, New Mexico)

PRINCIPAL CULTIVARS

Acer negundo 'Auratum'
Späth (1901). Germany.

A small tree or large shrub, up to 6 m (20 ft.) tall. The leaves are yellow when exposed to the sun, greener in the shade and at the end of summer. In the spring, when unfurling, a majority of the young leaves are a brilliant red, giving beautiful contrasts (see photograph on opposite page). The branches are green and glabrous. The flowers of this female cultivar are white.

Acer negundo 'Aureo-marginatum'
Dieck (1885). Germany.

Synonym, *Acer negundo* 'Aureo-limbatum'. A very widely distributed cultivar, reaching 8 to 10 m (26–33 ft.) tall, strong and fast-growing. The leaves are identical to those of the species, but have a creamy yellow margin, while the young shoots are green and lack bloom. The young leaf often has a pink-red margin.

Acer negundo 'Baron'
MacBeath (1982). Canada.

A new cultivar that may reach 20 m (66 ft.) tall and is very resistant to cold. Fruits are sterile, so propagation is by grafting.

Acer negundo 'Crispum'
Loddiges (1826). England.

A small tree or shrub having crumpled leaflets and, often, irregular leaf borders.

Acer negundo 'Elegans'
Schwerin (1901). Germany.

A slow-growing, small tree reaching 7 to 8 m (23–26 ft.) tall, with a relatively dense crown. The branches are green, smooth, and pruinose. The leaves have a yellow margin with some pink in the spring; they are slightly crumpled and smaller than those of the type. The petiole is purple-red and is very visible.

A. negundo 'Auratum', young plant (Bokrijk)

A. negundo 'Auratum' in spring

A. negundo 'Auratum', leaves

A. negundo 'Auratum', fruits (Lenoir)

Acer negundo 'Flamingo',
young shoot in summer

Acer negundo 'Flamingo'

Bastiaanse (1976). Netherlands.

A small tree or very large shrub, 8 to 9 m (26–30 ft.) tall. The branches are rather upright and the green twigs are glabrous and pruinose. The leaves, smaller than those of the type, generally have five or seven leaflets. They are green with a white margin, and on older branches provide a very ornamental contrast with the younger pink-red shoots; this combination of colors gives the tree a remarkable aspect in spring and early summer. The younger leaves later become more whitish and are generally browned by sun. The fruits are intertwined.

Acer negundo 'Heterophyllum'

Späth & Otto (1883). Germany.

Synonym, *Acer negundo* 'Laciniatum'. A small tree to about 8 m (26 ft.) tall. The branches are glabrous. The leaflets are very narrow, elongated, and crumpled, with entire margins; they are a very soft green.

Acer negundo 'Kelly's Gold'

Duncan & Davies (1989). New Zealand.

A small tree to 5 or 6 m (16–20 ft.) tall, looking very much like *Acer negundo* 'Auratum'. The fruits are scarlet red in early autumn.

Acer negundo 'Odessanum'

H. Rothe (1890). Ukraine.

A strong bushlike maple, to 7 or 8 m (23–26 ft.) tall. It has a magnificent yellow color when growing in a site with full sun, and like *Acer negundo* 'Auratum' is greener in shade. Unlike the latter, 'Odessanum' has very downy branches and seems more hardy.

A. negundo 'Heterophyllum' in spring (Hillier)

A. negundo 'Elegans' (Hillier) | *A. negundo* 'Heterophyllum' (Hillier)

Acer negundo 'Variegatum'

Wiegers (1809). Germany.

Synonym, *Acer negundo* 'Albo-variegatum'. An old cultivar. This small tree is 10 m (33 ft.) tall and has very good growth and hardiness. The leaflets are the same size as those of the type, and their border is irregularly tinted in pink and white when unfurling; only the creamy white pattern persists through the summer. The fruits (see photographs on p. 228) are also patterned, but are sterile. In fall, the foliage takes on a whitish, rather dull coloring.

Acer negundo 'Versicolor'

Dieck (1885). Germany.

A large cultivar, growing to 10 to 15 m (33–50 ft.) tall. The young shoots are green. The older leaves are dark green with light green margins, or just yellow if they develop in the shade. This male clone bears white flowers.

Acer negundo 'Violaceum'

Miller (1826). United Kingdom.

A tree, to 20 m (66 ft.) tall. The purplish-red young branches have a thick bloom. The young leaves are also purplish brown, later greener and darker. The stamens are bright red. Leaflets vary from 3 to 11 in number. This maple makes very rapid growth in a favorable soil (see photograph on p. 229).

A. *negundo* 'Kelly's Gold' in spring (Savill)	A. *negundo* 'Kelly's Gold' in spring
	A. *negundo* 'Kelly's Gold', leaves
	A. *negundo* 'Odessanum'
A. *negundo* 'Odessanum'°	A. *negundo* 'Odessanum' (CECE)

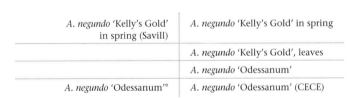

A. negundo 'Variegatum' (Bokrijk)

A. negundo 'Variegatum'°

A. negundo 'Variegatum', leaves (CECE)

A. negundo 'Variegatum', fruits (BMP)

A. negundo 'Violaceum' in flower (Hillier)

| *A. negundo* 'Violaceum', flower detail | *A. negundo* 'Violaceum', leaves and young shoots |

Acer negundo subsp. *californicum*

(Torrey & Gray) Wesmael (1890)

Section: *Negundo.*

Epithet: *Californicus,* from California.

Origin: United States (California and humid regions of Arizona).

General appearance: A tree, up to 25 m (82 ft.) tall, very dense, with branching starting at the base of the trunk.

Trunk: Light brown

Branches: Very thick, covered with a thick, stringy down persisting through summer.

Buds: Covered with down like the branches.

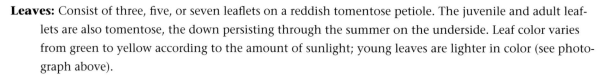

Leaves: Consist of three, five, or seven leaflets on a reddish tomentose petiole. The juvenile and adult leaflets are also tomentose, the down persisting through the summer on the underside. Leaf color varies from green to yellow according to the amount of sunlight; young leaves are lighter in color (see photograph above).

Flowers: Very similar to those of the type, except the stamens of male trees are more colorful and more spectacular than those of the species.

Fruits: Abundant, pubescent, and greenish. Samaras 5 cm (2 in.) long, the wings at a right angle.

*A*cer negundo subsp. *californicum* is among the hardiest maples and can be used as a windbreaker. It is a very strong grower, possibly the strongest of the maples. It grows to 10 m (33 ft.) tall and 8 m (26 ft.) wide in 10 years. It is hardy to zones 5 and 6. The subspecies has value as an ornamental plant, thanks to its interesting flowers and leaves. The leaves range in color from green to yellow, a function of the amount of sunlight they receive.

male flowers

female flowers

Acer negundo subsp. *californicum* in spring flowering (Hillier)

Acer nipponicum

Hara (1938)

Section: *Parviflora.*

Epithet: *Nipponicus,* from Nippon, an old name for Japan.

Common name: Nippon maple.

Origin: Japan (Honshu, Shikoku, and Kyushu islands), in mountain forests. A rare tree.

General appearance: A medium-sized, deciduous tree, 15 to 20 m (50–66 ft.) tall. Well framed.

Trunk: Gray-brown, smooth, like the branches.

Branches: Young shoots are strong, vigorous growing, and a glossy light green.

Buds: The terminal bud is often destroyed or aborted. Growth occurs through a succession of forked branches.

Leaves: Five-lobed, large, tough, 8 × 8 to 16 × 16 cm (3 × 6.4 in.), evenly divided, with an embossed and uneven texture. Leaf underside is pubescent in spring, later glabrous. Lobes oval, terminating in a short point. Margins doubly toothed. Petiole green, with an uneven texture, and up to 15 cm (6 in.) long. All parts of the leaf are a uniform light green.

Flowers: Yellow-green, small, numerous, in drooping panicles. Appearing after the leaves, often late in the season. Very long inflorescences of maple flowers appear first, the female flowers appear later and are shorter.

Fruits: Samara wings 3 to 5 cm (1–2 in.) long, thick, pubescent, with a slightly wavy border, forming an obtuse angle, the seeds large, round but flattened, often sterile.

Propagation: Only by seed, since this plant is isolated in its group and has no other maple on which it can be grafted. Cuttings give no results. Seed must be sown soon after it is collected, as it quickly loses its viability. Young seedlings show little diversity. *Acer nipponicum* generally begins producing flowers in its 20th year.

*A*cer nipponicum* is endemic in the mountain forests of Japan, at altitudes of 900 to 1800 m (2970–5940 ft.). It is hardy to zone 5. In cultivation, the tree is only found in a few botanical gardens. The most beautiful example grows in the botanical garden at Zuider Park, The Hague, Netherlands, and is 15 m (50 ft.) tall.

The leaves of this species could be compared with those of *Acer tegmentosum,* but *A. nipponicum* has unique and spectacular inflorescences that differ from those of any other maple. This feature is its main landscaping interest. The leaves are uniformly green, turning a fleeting golden yellow to brown-yellow in the fall.

habit (Hillier)	flowers
	fruits
leaves	autumn*

Acer oblongum

Wallich ex de Candolle (1824)

Section: *Pentaphylla.*

Epithet: *Oblongus,* oblong, referring to the leaf shape that is longer than broad.

Common name: Flying-moth tree.

Origin: Himalayas and western and southern China. Introduced to Europe from the Himalayas in 1824, and from China by Ernest H. Wilson in 1901.

General appearance: A deciduous or semi-evergreen tree. In China, it reaches 5 to 10 m (16–33 ft.) tall, twice that height in the Himalayas, but such trees are not hardy throughout Europe. The crown is broad and dense.

Trunk: Gray to red-brown, peeling in irregular plates.

Branches: Green, glabrous.

Leaves: Neither lobed nor toothed, oblong or oblong-ovate, 5 to 10 cm (2–4 in.) long, hard, tough, very smooth above, glaucous below. The Himalayan form reaches 12 to 15 cm (4.75–6 in.) long. Young leaves a soft green, others dark green. Three-lobed leaves may be observed on some old trees.

Flowers: Yellowish green, parts arranged in fives, in terminal panicles. Appearing with the leaves.

Fruits: Samaras 2 to 3 cm (0.75–1 in.), the nutlets 3 to 4 mm (ca. 0.1 in.).

Propagation: By cuttings.

Long known to botanists, this exceptional tree is rare in cultivation because of its susceptibility to frost. It prospers in the mild southwestern climate of England, although it remains scarce there. This plant is interesting for its persistent foliage and its widespread, falling branches. It is used as a street tree in southeastern China and Southern California (United States). Very beautiful specimens grow in southern France in mediterranean climate.

habit (Serre de la Madone)	young shoots
	fruits

a young tree in spring (Hillier)

Acer obtusifolium
Sibthorp & Smith (1809)

Section: *Acer.*

Epithet: *Obtusifolius,* having leaves with obtuse (rounded) lobes.

Synonym: *Acer syriacum* Boissier & Gaillardot (1856).

Origin: Eastern Turkey, Syria, Lebanon, Palestine, and Cyprus (on the northern flank of Mount Trodos).

General appearance: A large evergreen or semi-evergreen shrub, 5 to 6 m (16–20 ft.) tall, with an ovoid rounded shape and dense branching. Sometimes it forms a small tree. No part of the plant is pubescent.

Trunk: Olive green, smooth.

Branches: Reddish brown. Young shoots also reddish brown.

Leaves: Tough, polymorphic, three-lobed or entire, ovate-elongate. Young leaves toothed, their central lobe more elongated than the other lobes, the bronze-red color outstanding. Mature leaves broad, 4 to 10 cm (1.5–4 in.) long, 3 to 6 cm (1–2.4 in.) wide, dark glossy green, with three lobes. Most leaves on old specimens are entire. Petiole 5 cm (2 in.) long.

Flowers: Yellowish green, in clusters, on short lateral shoots.

Fruits: Globose. Samaras 2 cm (0.75 in.) long, the wings forming an angle of 60 degrees.

Propagation: By seed, or by grafting on *Acer monspessulanum* or *A. pseudoplatanus.*

The leaves are evergreen but may fall in colder climates. The species is hardy to zone 7 and suited only to a mild climate similar to that of southern England, unless it is cultivated in pots and protected during the winter. It is very drought resistant and adapts to poor soils. *Acer obtusifolium* is sometimes used as a cut hedge in Cyprus and could be perfectly suitable for planting in the regions bordering the Mediterranean.

Acer obtusifolium, flowers (Hemelrijk)

Acer obtusifolium, leaves

Acer oliverianum

Pax (1889)

Section: *Palmata.*

Epithet: *Oliverianus,* after English botanist Daniel Oliver (1830–1916).

Origin: Central China (Yunnan and Hubei provinces). Discovered by Augustine Henry and introduced in 1901 by Ernest H. Wilson for Veitch Nursery.

General appearance: A small, upright tree, 8 to 12 m (26–39 ft.) tall, typically multitrunked.

Trunk: Greenish on young subjects, then brown.

Branches: Green, smooth. Young shoots are purplish brown.

Leaves: Five-lobed, palmate, 5 to 10 cm (2–4 in.) long, dark green. Lobes ovoid to triangular, and rather pointed, the center lobe being the largest. Base truncate or slightly cordate. Margins very strongly but regularly toothed. Petiole 3 to 6 cm (1–2.4 in.) long, orange-red, with juvenile down visible along the ribs. Young leaves are soft green, contrasting well with the older leaves.

Flowers: Small, whitish, with purple sepals and white petals, on a drooping peduncle, 4 to 8 cm (1.5–3 in.) long, issuing from a terminal bud. Inflorescence in corymbs. Appearing rather late, in May, well after the leaves.

Fruits: Small and glabrous. Samaras with thin red peduncles, the wings 3 to 4 cm (1–1.5 in.) long, 1 cm (0.4 in.) wide, and almost horizontal.

Propagation: Difficult, since the seeds must be sown immediately after they are collected. By grafting on *Acer palmatum.*

This delicate shrub has remarkable fall color ranging from orange-yellow to brown-red. In winter, its greenish bark is a beautiful sight. The bicolored summer leaves, light green and dark green, are also characteristic of the species.

This very beautiful but rare maple strongly resembles *Acer palmatum* but has a stiffer, more upright habit and glossier leaves. It makes a good accent plant. The species is hardy only in zones 6 and 7. It is not disease resistant. Young shoots that fail to ripen properly in summer do not withstand rigorous winters, leading to the plant's decay. It is thus important to plant *A. oliverianum* in warm, protected spots.

A. oliverianum (Bamboo Farm)

A. oliverianum, leaves | *A. oliverianum,* young shoots in summer

A. *oliverianum*, leaves unfurling
(Herkenrode)

A. *oliverianum*, start of flowering

A. *oliverianum*, trunk

A. *oliverianum*, in flower

A. *oliverianum*, fruits (Hillier)

Acer oliverianum subsp. *formosanum*

(Koidzumi) Murray (1969)

Section: *Palmata.*

Epithet: *Formosanus,* from Formosa, an old name for Taiwan.

Synonym: *Acer serrulatum* Hayata (1918).

Origin: Taiwan, in mountain forests, at an altitude from 1000 to 2500 m (3300–8250 ft.).

General appearance: A deciduous tree, 20 to 25 m (66–82 ft.) tall, vigorous growing.

Trunk: Olive green, bark rather thin, smooth, sometimes slightly striated.

Branches: Green with reddish highlights. Young shoots green.

Leaves: Five-lobed, palmate, 10 to 12 cm (4–4.75 in.) long, broader than long, dark glossy green with purple reflections, glabrous below. Base truncate to cordate, the two basal lobes either horizontal or backward-pointing. Margins roughly toothed, teeth purplish red and forward-pointing. Petiole long, thin. Young leaves are purplish red, and the central lobe is larger than the lateral lobes.

Flowers: Yellow, with five petals. Inflorescences terminal umbels. Appearing with the leaves.

Fruits: Samaras almost horizontal.

Subsp. *formosanum* is very abundant on the island of Taiwan where it is endemic. It differs from the Chinese species by its great size.

Strong and fast-growing in the wild where it reaches 20 m (66 ft.) tall, this maple is slower growing in cultivation. Hardiness does not seem to be a problem in The Netherlands, northwestern Belgium, or England.

The purplish color of the leaves is very characteristic at the end of summer, turning rapidly in fall to carmine-red and then yellow.

leaves	young shoots in summer
start of fall coloring*	habit (Batsford)
young trunk	

Acer opalus
Miller (1768)

Section: *Acer.*

Epithet: *Opalus,* a misspelling of *Opulus,* an old name for maples.

Common name: Italian maple.

Origin: Central Europe and the Mediterranean basin.

General appearance: A medium-sized, deciduous tree, 10 to 12 m (33–39 ft.) tall, with a short trunk. Can also be shrublike. The domelike crown is broad and rounded.

Trunk: Orange-gray, bark formed by square or rectangular scales, varying in size up to 15 to 20 cm (6–8 in.).

Branches: Reddish green, glabrous, covered with lenticels.

Buds: Thick, ovoid, pointed, covered with 10 to 12 light or dark brown overlapping scales.

Leaves: Three- or five-lobed, broad, rounded, 10 to 12 cm (4–4.75 in.), dark green, glossy, and glabrous above, light gray and always downy below. Base cordate. Lobes short, broad, with small sinuses. Petiole 6 to 8 cm (2.4–3 in.) long. Young leaves are red-bronze.

Flowers: Pale yellow, with large petals, on 3- to 4-cm (1- to 1.5-in.) long peduncles, in drooping corymbs, which distinguishes it from *Acer pseudoplatanus*. Abundant. Appearing in March, before the leaves.

Fruits: In clusters of 8 to 15, very variable in shape. Samaras 3 to 5 cm (1–2 in.) long, the nutlets large, glabrous, and green, the wings brownish.

Propagation: Easy, by seed, collected in autumn and sown the next spring. The difficulty resides in finding viable seed, since the species has a strong parthenocarpic tendency.

This beautiful tree should be planted more often. Solitary or in a group, it produces attractive glossy yellow spring flowers which are admired for their precocity and abundance. In April, it displays coppery orange-red unfolding leaves, while in summer its rounded, harmonious silhouette will soften the all-green monotony of the landscape. If grown in a site with sun and with well-drained soil, this maple will in fall adorn itself with colors ranging from yellow to orange. Originating from southern Europe, it tolerates heat very well, but is also hardy to zone 5. It grows equally well in sandy or rocky soils, or even calcareous or clayey.

leaves unfurling	flowers*
leaves in spring	fruits (Les Barres)
leaves°	trunk°
fruits in spring (Les Barres)	

Acer opalus in spring (Les Barres)

Acer opalus (Kew)

Acer opalus subsp. *obtusatum*

(Willdenow) Gams (1925)

Section: *Acer.*

Epithet: *Obtusus,* rounded, referring to the lobes.

Common name: Bosnian maple.

Origin: Central and southeastern Europe, southern Italy.

General appearance: A medium-sized tree, 20 m (66 ft.) tall, with a broad, rounded crown. Sometimes shrublike with multiple stems.

Trunk: Brown-green, similar to *Acer opalus.*

Branches: Brown. Young shoots are light brown.

Buds: Brown, pointed, with 10 pairs of scales.

Leaves: Five-lobed, larger than in the type species, 10 to 12 cm (4–4.75 in.), dark green and smooth above, lighter green and densely tomentose below. Lobes short, very rounded, blunt. Petiole yellow.

Flowers: Yellow, numerous, in hanging umbels.

Fruits: In numerous short clusters, on a brown, hairy peduncle. Samaras 2.5 to 3 cm (ca. 1 in.) long, the nutlets round, green, and glabrous, the wings brown.

Propagation: Difficult by seed due to strong parthenocarpic tendency.

A. opalus subsp. *obtusatum* (Hemelrijk)	*A. opalus* subsp. *obtusatum,* large trunk (Kew)
A. opalus subsp. *obtusatum,* flowers	

A. opalus subsp. *obtusatum* (Kew)

This tree of nice proportions and beautiful habit is suitable for large parks. Many-flowered, like the species, *Acer opalus* subsp. *obtusatum* acquires a yellow coloring just before the leaves unfurl. In summer it is dark green and in fall the opal color fades quickly. The subspecies is hardy to zone 5 and well adapted to Europe where it is sadly too rarely encountered in gardens.

The Kew specimen shown above is one of the most beautiful; it is 17 m (56 ft.) tall and has a circumference of 2.45 m (just under 8 ft.).

❧

Acer opalus "subsp. *tomentosum*"

The tomentose variety of *Acer opalus* has strong, tough, arched leaves that are similiar in size to those of the species. The epithet refers to the thick down on the backside of the ribs. Very seldom encountered in cultivation, this maple generally grows in a copse, where it forms a large clump.

Acer palmatum

Introduction

Long cultivated in Japan where it is venerated, *Acer palmatum* is but one example of the Japanese people's historic interest in the plant kingdom. This species is present in every garden in that country, private or public, sometimes in places of worship. It is often found as bonsai on terraces or inside houses.

Swedish botanist Carl Thunberg visited Japan and described *Acer palmatum* in his *Flora Japonica*, published in 1784, but, due to the nation's strong century-old isolationist and protectionist tendencies, the species was not exported until around 1830. It created extraordinary interest when it arrived in the West.

Acer palmatum is an important species, with as many cultivars (about 350) as all the other maple species and subspecies put together. Known as Japanese maple, it should not confused with *A. japonicum,* also called Japanese maple. The mix-up occurs often in the West where people forget that several species of maples originate from Japan.

Acer palmatum and the author, in spring (Hergest Croft)

Acer palmatum
Thunberg ex Murray (1784)

Section: *Palmata.*

Epithet: *Palmatus,* palmate, shaped like a hand.

Common name: Japanese maple.

Origin: Japan (Honshu and Shikoku Islands, rarer on Hokkaido), eastern China, Taiwan, and Korea. Introduced from Japan in 1820.

General appearance: A hardy, rounded tree, as wide as it is tall, reaching 12 to 15 m (39–50 ft.) in habitat, but only half that height in cultivation.

Trunk: Smooth, reddish brown on young trees, turning gray-brown with age.

Branches: Reddish to brown-red, glabrous, slender.

Buds: Very small, reddish, always in pairs.

Leaves: Five- or seven-lobed, palmate, 5 to 10 cm (2–4 in.) long, always colorful, glabrous on both sides. Lobes ovate and lanceolate, deeply divided to two-thirds the length. Margins doubly toothed. The color varies with the season: opening red-orange, turning green in summer; young shoots are lighter and have orange-red margins. In the fall, all hues from purple-red to yellow may appear.

Flowers: Small, with creamy white petals and purple-red sepals. Appearing rather late, in small hanging clusters.

Fruits: Very small, even smaller than those of the cultivars. Samaras 1 cm (0.4 in.) long, red, glabrous, often curved, the wings forming an obtuse angle.

Propagation: Easy, by seed, which ripens in September. Cultivars, however, are generally propagated by grafting, sometimes by cuttings. Propagating cultivars by seed involves recombining chromosomes, a process that leads to great diversity in the seedlings, which always differ from the parent plant. This potential for variability has given Japanese growers the opportunity to select and create the largest variety of cultivars. Seed produced by trees in nature is much more stable than that produced by cultivated trees.

leaves unfurling with flowers	young summer shoot
flowers	fruits
old trunk (Westonbirt)	fall colors (Great Park)
	fall colors (Westonbirt)

Acer palmatum, an old tree (Wakehurst)

Acer palmatum, a large tree in autumn (Westonbirt)

Acer palmatum group, in autumn (Great Park, near Savill)

Acer palmatum backlit in autumn (Westonbirt)

In nature, *Acer palmatum* grows in mountain forests at elevations from 100 to 1200 m (330–3960 ft.). The soil is naturally well draining, which is why this species favors light acid, humic soils and dislikes compact soils and excess water. It is well suited for shady sites, where it grows faster than in sun, but becomes less compact; in shade the leaves are a uniform green color. *Acer palmatum* is certainly the most popular tree for small gardens. Besides offering a wide range of colors that vary with the seasons, it also comes in all shapes and sizes that fit perfectly with other plants in a landscape.

The weakness of this species is its great vulnerability to spring frost, which kills the young shoots and thus damages the tree's silhouette. The tree must be planted in a protected spot. It is also very sensitive to verticillium wilt, a disease spread by spores. Care must be taken not to contaminate young grafted plants.

The Japanese have been cultivating this tree for more than three centuries and have created several hundred varieties, offering thus a wide diversity of shapes, sizes, and colors.

CULTIVARS

Maples are mentioned in a Japanese poem dating from the 7th century, while the first botanical descriptions date from 1695. When the cultivars were introduced in the United States and Europe, they were given names in Latin, English, or French. These names were in addition to the original names, which had been translated from Japanese. Thus, many homonyms were created. The confusion led nurseryman J. D. Vertrees to study maple names and in 1978 he proposed a new classification and taxonomy in his book *Japanese Maples*. Among other things, Vertrees distinguished between two subspecies of *A. palmatum*: subsp. *amoenum* and subsp. *matsumurae*. The photographs on the opposite page illustrate the incredible diversity of this species, a subject that demands its own copiously illustrated book in the future.

A. palmatum 'Beni tsukasa' in spring (Savill)	*A. palmatum* 'Red Pygmy' in spring
A. palmatum 'Asahi zuru'	*A. palmatum* 'Higasa yama'
A. palmatum 'Katsura' in spring	*A. palmatum* 'Chishio Improved' in spring
A. palmatum 'Shigitatsu sawa' in spring	*A. palmatum* 'Seiryū' in autumn

Acer paxii
Franchet (1886)

Section: *Pentaphylla.*

Epithet: *Paxii,* after German botanist and taxonomist Ferdinand A. Pax (1858–1942).

Origin: Widespread in southern China. Discovered by Father Delavay in Yunnan province.

General appearance: A small evergreen tree, 8 to 10 m (26–33 ft.) tall, generally shrublike.

Trunk: Dark gray, smooth.

Leaves: Evergreen, tough, polymorphic. Three-lobed, sometimes unlobed and ovate. Varying leaves appear on the same shoot. The three-lobed leaf is large, with an ovate base, the lobes often being simple teeth growing halfway down the leaf. Margins entire. Dark green and glossy above, glaucous below, 5 to 8 cm (2–3 in.) long, 3 to 6 cm (1–2.4 in.) wide.

Flowers: Small, white, in panicles as in *Acer oblongum.* Appearing with the new leaves.

Fruits: Samaras 2 to 3 cm (0.75–1 in.) long, the wings forming an angle of 60 degrees, the nutlets and ends of the wings rounded.

Propagation: By grafting on *Acer buergerianum,* which is very closely related.

Originating in a humid and warm setting, *Acer paxii* nevertheless withstands the rigor of winter in southern and western England. It survives, but produces little or no fruit, unless it is raised in a greenhouse or under special conditions. It could certainly grow in the U.S. Southeast. The light green leaves contrast nicely with the red-orange fruits, particularly at the end of summer. The permanence of the leaves is an advantage in winter. It is hardy to zone 8.

leaves | fruits

tree

Acer pectinatum

Wallich ex Nicholson (1881)

Section: *Macrantha.*

Epithet: *Pectinatus,* like a comb, referring to the fringe of hair bordering the margin.

Origin: Southern Himalayas, eastern Nepal, Bhutan, northern Myanmar, and eastern China (Yunnan province).

General appearance: A shrubby tree, 15 to 18 m (50–59 ft.) tall, often multitrunked, upright, with broadly spreading branches.

Trunk: Light brown or green, sprinkled with whitish striations.

Branches: Red-brown, glabrous, sometimes covered lightly with a whitish bloom.

Buds: Red, large, 1.5 cm (ca. 0.5 in.) in diameter.

Leaves: Three-lobed, sometimes with two additional small basal lobes, 8 to 14 cm (3–5.5 in.) long, 5 to 10 cm (2–4 in.) broad, terminal leaves sometimes larger (20 × 16 cm or 8 × 6.4 in.) when grown in shade. Color dark green, glabrous above, grayish below, slightly pubescent, adorned with small tufts of very small red hairs at the axil of the ribs. Base cordate. Lobes triangular, ovate, acuminate; lateral lobes with forward-pointing ends. Margins very fine and deeply toothed, teeth ending in very small reddish hairs. Petiole 5 to 8 cm (2–3 in.) long, glabrous, very red.

Flowers: Yellow, on recumbent narrow spikes, 7 to 12 cm (2.75–4.75 in.) long.

Fruits: Borne on racemes by small peduncles. Samaras 2 to 2.5 cm (0.75–1 in.) long, the wings almost horizontal.

*A*cer pectinatum grows naturally in a large region on the southern flank of the Himalayas, much farther west than its Chinese subspecies. Despite this distance, the two taxa share certain characteristics: striated trunk; funnel-shaped, upright branching; recumbent twigs; and three-lobed, broad, acuminate leaves. The species differs from the subspecies by having broader, more pointed lobes.

This species and its subspecies grow into respectably sized trees with striped bark. Like other maples of section *Macrantha,* they can be used as beautiful accent trees in highly visible locations, close to large protecting trees. The esthetic qualities of these maples are enhanced when they are underplanted with smaller shrubs, perennials, or ground covers.

In 1977, Murray regrouped four species––*Acer forrestii, A. laxiflorum, A. maximowiczii,* and *A. taronense*––under *A. pectinatum,* which is the oldest valid name among them.

leaves unfurling	habit (Hillier)
leaves	
flowers	trunk (Hillier)
young fruits*	

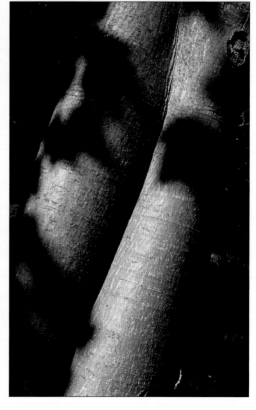

Acer pectinatum subsp. *forrestii*

(Diels) Murray (1977)

Section: *Macrantha.*

Epithet: *Forrestii,* after Scottish botanist George Forrest.

Origin: Western China (Yunnan province), in the Yulong Mountains.

General appearance: A large shrub, 15 m (50 ft.) tall, often multitrunked, upright, forming a large, spreading crown with long branches curving downward and sometimes hanging vertically at their tips. Gracious habit.

Trunk: Variable color, from red-brown to green, slightly striated with white.

Branches: Green, with white striation. Young shoots are very thin, very long, and reddish brown.

Leaves: Three-lobed, sometimes five-lobed, 10 to 12 cm (4–4.75 in.) long, 7 to 10 cm (2.75–4 in.) wide, dark green, adorned below with tufts of red hair at the axils of the veins. Central lobe longer than the others, very acuminate, and ending in a very thin point. Margins doubly and rather roughly toothed. Petiole 4 to 8 cm (1.5–3 in.), rhubarb red, rather characteristic. Young leaves on young trees are more variable in size and generally larger; their teeth are more irregular, with two extra lobes at the base and a longer central lobe.

Flowers: Brownish green, on short terminal hanging racemes. Appearing with the young leaves.

Fruits: Glabrous, 2 cm (0.75 in.). Samaras in pendent racemes, the wings almost horizontal.

flowers

fruits

A beautiful specimen growing at Caerhays Castle Gardens in Cornwall, England (zone 7), has reached 18 m (59 ft.) tall. The region's favorable climate has allowed the tree to attain this large size. Elsewhere in England, this maple is smaller.

Acer pectinatum subsp. *forrestii* is difficult to distinguish from *A. pectinatum* subsp. *laxiflorum.* It may be recognized by its hanging twigs, sometimes vertical, its variably sized young leaves, and its bright red petioles. Subsp. *forrestii* is otherwise similar to *A. pectinatum* and its flowering is similar to that of *A. davidii,* which is typical for section *Macrantha.*

In addition to attractive fall color, the leaves of this maple remain a long time on the tree.

habit (Westonbirt)	leaves*
	trunk*
in autumn (Herkenrode)	

CULTIVARS:

Acer pectinatum subsp. *forrestii* 'Alice'

Esveld (1981). Netherlands.

A large shrub, 5 to 6 m (16–20 ft.) tall, rather broad. The leaves are 8 to 15 cm (3–6 in.) long and 4 to 7 cm (1.5–2.75 in.) wide; they have three lobes with acuminate tips. Young leaves are reddish pink in the summer, contrasting well with the glossy dark green foliage. The petiole is carmine-red, as is the young shoot, and even glossier in winter. The shrub has real landscaping interest. Unfortunately, this cultivar is not hardy and must be protected from cold winds.

Acer pectinatum subsp. *forrestii* 'Sirène'

Esveld (1988). Netherlands.

A spreading shrub with widely recumbent shoots. The trunk is a very attractive purple-red, partly striated with white. The leaves have three lobes, the central one elongated. When unfolding, young leaves are a glossy dark purple color, progressively turning to their dark green summer coloring. Fall color is attractive on some trees, but not regularly on all.

Acer pectinatum subsp. *forrestii* 'Sparkling'

Esveld (1989). Netherlands.

A large shrub with an upright, rather bare silhouette, or a small fastigiate tree not more than 7 to 8 m (23–26 ft.) tall. The trunk is greenish. The leaves have three lobes, the central lobe longer and broader than the others. The leaves are dark green in the summer, and the contrast with the red petiole is even more marked than in 'Alice'. The tree has good growth and the plant looks strong, but it needs a warm autumn, since the shoots do not tolerate frost in an early winter.

A. pectinatum 'Alice' (CECE)	*A. pectinatum* 'Alice'°
A. pectinatum 'Alice' (BMP)	
A. pectinatum 'Sirène' (CECE)	*A. pectinatum* 'Sirène'°
	A. pectinatum 'Sparkling' (BMP)

Acer pectinatum subsp. *laxiflorum*
(Pax) Murray (1977)

Section: *Macrantha.*

Epithet: *Laxiflorus,* broad flowered.

Synonym: *Acer laxiflorum* Pax 1902.

Origin: Western China. Collected by E. Pratt in Tatsien-lu and by the Rev. Father Ernest Faber at Mount Emei.

General appearance: A small tree, 6 to 12 m (20–39 ft.) tall, developing large horizontal branching, often curved.

Trunk: Brown-green, with white striation.

Branches: Light green to gray-green. Knots closely space between numerous small lateral shoots, yielding dense foliage. Young shoots are red, glabrous.

Buds: With scales that touch but do not overlap.

Leaves: Entire, sometimes three-lobed with two small basal lobes, 5 to 10 cm (2–4 in.) long, 3 to 5 cm (1–2 in.) broad, medium green and smooth above, covered with russet down below, then almost glabrous, slightly tough. Lobes oblong, ovate, with a cordate or rounded base, tip acuminate. Margins finely toothed. Rib yellow. Petiole yellow, 2 to 4 cm (0.75–1.5 in.) long.

Flowers: Yellowish, large.

Fruits: Samaras on long racemes, the wings at a right angle. Most fruits have an atrophied samara.

This maple's place of origin has been the occasion of much controversy. Very rare in cultivation, this medium-sized tree has dense cascading foliage, almost covering the branch. In the fall, it cedes nothing to the other subspecies, retaining its orange to red-yellow spotted leaves for a long time. Its broader leaves distinguish it from the other members of the group.

habit (Hillier)	
flowers*	fruits
trunk	leaves in autumn

Acer pectinatum subsp. *maximowiczii*

(Pax) Murray (1977)

Section: *Macrantha.*

Epithet: *Maximowiczii,* after Russian botanist Carl Maximowicz (1827–1891).

Origin: Western China (Hubei, Gansu, and Sichuan provinces). Introduced in Europe in 1912 by Ernest H. Wilson.

General appearance: A small tree or large shrub, 12 to 15 m (39–50 ft.) tall, with upright, funnel-shaped branching.

Trunk: Green with white stripes.

Branches: Glabrous, reddish to brown in summer, red in winter. The stripes appear on the oldest branches.

Leaves: Three- or five-lobed, ovate or oblong, shape varies on the same tree, dark glossy green, paler along the midrib, whitish green below with tufts of hair on the axils of the ribs. Central lobe elongated, lateral lobes short, tips forward-pointing. Base insignificant. Margins doubly toothed.

Flowers: Reddish, sometimes yellowish, on short, glabrous, upright racemes.

Fruits: Samaras 3 cm (ca. 1 in.) long, the wings at a right angle.

Propagation: Difficult, but grafting is possible on all the members of this section.

The bark of young individuals of *Acer pectinatum* subsp. *maximowiczii* is more striated and lighter than that of any other member of the *A. pectinatum* group. Moreover, the long branches turn bright red in winter. Mature trees, however, have green bark, occasionally with white stripes, and the branches do not turn red in winter. The dominating leaf color in fall is yellow with orange hues. The tree is hardy but relatively sensitive to spring frosts.

flowers	fruits
in autumn (Hillier)	in spring (Hillier)
young shoots on a young trunk	

Acer pectinatum subsp. *taronense*

(Handel-Mazzetti) Murray (1977)

Section: *Macrantha.*

Epithet: *Taronense,* from the river Taron (Irrawaddy), in Yunnan province, China.

Origin: Northeastern Myanmar and China (Sichuan and Yunnan provinces).

General appearance: A medium-sized tree, to 15 m (50 ft.) tall. Branches upright, then pendulous.

Trunk: Gray-brown, lightly striated with white.

Branches: Reddish brown, slender, light striation. Young shoots are reddish brown.

Leaves: Five-lobed, dark green above, lighter below, with tufts of brown hair at the axils of the ribs. Lobes triangular and ovate, basal lobes shorter than the others. Margins doubly toothed.

Flowers: Yellow-green, on a terminal hanging raceme.

Fruits: Samaras crimson, 3 cm (ca. 1 in.) long, glabrous, the wings forming a right or obtuse angle.

*A*cer pectinatum subsp. *taronense* bears long, upright branches, which become strongly recumbent, like those of subsp. *forrestii.* The leaves of the two subspecies are similar in size and are borne on a deep red petiole. The difference between the two is evident in spring, when the young leaves of subsp. *taronense* are glossy purple-green and the flowers reddish. This reddish tint disappears progressively. Small tufts of hair are located at the axils of the ribs.

Like other members of the *Acer pectinatum* group, subsp. *taronense* is a beautiful solitary tree, best placed where its deep yellow coloring can be observed in spring and fall. The leaves drop early.

young leaves*	leaves (CECE)
flowers	habit (CECE)
fruits*	

267

Acer pensylvanicum
Linnaeus (1753)

Section: *Macrantha.*

Epithet: *Pensylvanicum,* from Pennsylvania.

Common names: Moosewood, striped maple, snake bark maple, goosefoot.

Origin: Eastern North America, along the Saint Lawrence and Ohio rivers. Described by Carl Linnaeus in 1753 and introduced to Europe in 1755. It is the sole American species in section *Macrantha* with striated bark.

General appearance: A tree 12 m (39 ft.) tall with a tendency to branch early, thus looking shrubby, multitrunked.

Trunk: Reddish brown, with white striation.

Branches: The ends of the branches are very ornamental, turning a bright orange-red in winter.

Buds: With two shiny red scales.

Leaves: Five-lobed, large, 12 to 20 cm (4.75–8 in.). Basal lobes two, insignificant. Tips of lobes forward-pointing. Margins very finely and doubly toothed. Young leaves covered with brown-red woolly down, which disappears later, remaining only on the ribs and part of the petiole.

Flowers: Yellow-green, with parts arranged in fives, about 5 mm (ca. 0.2 in.) wide, forming drooping clusters about 10 cm (4 in.) long (see photograph on opposite page). Appearing with and after the leaves.

Fruits: Samaras small, 1 cm (0.4 in.) long, the wings forming an obtuse angle, the nutlets flat.

Propagation: Easy, by seed, the traditional method of propagating this species. Seed is collected in autumn, stratified in winter, and sown in spring. By grafting on all species of section *Macrantha*. By layering of low branches, the typical method of propagation in habitat.

bud in winter (BMP)

*A*cer pensylvanicum prefers the shade, a temperate climate, and moderately moist soil. An understory tree in Canadian and American forests, it adapts well to the area's low temperatures (−35°C or −31°F), thanks to a very warm autumn, which allows the wood to harden-off. The leaves turn pale yellow in early fall, but also drop rather early.

This maple can be used as a medium-sized specimen tree or planted underneath the canopy of large park trees. It is the American counterpart of *Acer tegmentosum,* which also likes the understory of mixed pine, beech, and oak forests.

The greenish bark, striated with white in the summer, becomes redder in winter and more ornamental.

leaves (CECE)	flowers*
autumn°	fruits (CECE)
trunk (Les Barres)	branches in winter (BMP)

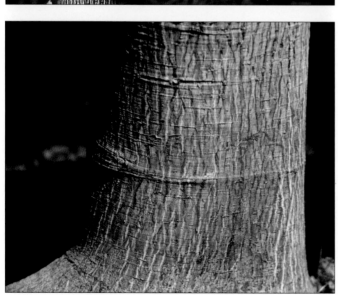

A. pensylvanicum 'Erythrocladum' (CECE)	*A. pensylvanicum* 'Erythrocladum' in autumn (Hillier)
A. pensylvanicum 'Erythrocladum', branches°	*A. pensylvanicum* 'Erythrocladum', young shoots (Savill)

CULTIVAR

Acer pensylvanicum 'Erythrocladum'

Späth (1904). Germany.

This old cultivar is a slow-growing small tree but generally assumes the shape of a large shrub, with many almost-fastigiate branches. The bark color changes through the seasons more markedly than does that of *Acer pensylvanicum*: the branches in summer are dull green, unstriated, and glabrous, turning salmon pink to red in winter. The base of the trunk is yellowish, slightly veined with white. The leaves are large, 12 to 18 cm (4.75–7 in.) in size. The terminal leaf has three lobes and is smaller than the other leaves and acuminate. The margin is roughly toothed. This tree is easily propagated. It needs light soil and light shade.

A. pensylvanicum (Herkenrode)*

A. pensylvanicum, large trunk (Hemelrijk)	*A. pensylvanicum*, start of autumn (Hillier)

Acer pentaphyllum
Diels (1931)

Section: *Pentaphylla.*

Epithet: *Pentaphyllus,* having five leaflets.

Origin: China (Sichuan province). Discovered in 1929 by Joseph Rock in the Yulong Valley and immediately introduced in the United States.

General appearance: A small tree 10 m (33 ft.) tall, sometimes shrublike, with spreading branches.

Trunk: Light gray. Branches brownish, rather thin.

Leaves: Consist of four to seven leaflets, generally five, each lanceolate, pointed at the base, blunt at the tip, glabrous and glaucous below, 3 cm (ca. 1 in.) long and 1 cm (0.4 in.) broad, dark green. The lower leaflets are sessile, those at the top have a short petiole.

Flowers: Yellowish, in terminal corymbs.

Fruits: Numerous, in large panicles, but with a strong parthenocarpic tendency.

❧

Very rare in the wild, *Acer pentaphyllum* is seldom encountered in cultivation. A few highly specialized nurseries are propagating it. The species is tender, hardy only in protected areas of zones 7 and 8.

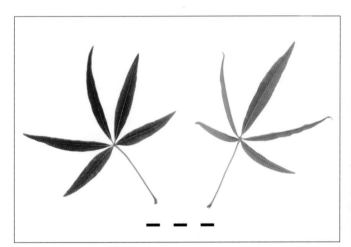

Acer platanoides in spring (Kew)

Acer platanoides
Linnaeus (1753)

Section: *Platanoidea.*

Epithet: *Platanoides*, like *Platanus*, sycamore, plane tree.

Common name: Norway maple.

Origin: Northern and continental Europe, Asia Minor, and China. Introduced rather late in England.

General appearance: A very large deciduous tree, reaching 30 m (100 ft.) or more tall, with a broad, rounded crown.

Trunk: Dark gray-brown, smooth on young and middle-aged trees, fissured vertically with age.

Branches: Green, glabrous, covered with many lenticels.

Buds: Red-brown, lateral, close to the branch, with overlapping scales.

Leaves: Five- to seven-lobed, large, 12 to 20 cm (4.75–8 in.), larger on young trees, glossy green above, smooth below, a light down persisting at the axils of the veins. Lobes acuminate. Margins with spaced, pointed teeth. Petiole 8 to 15 cm (3–6 in.) long, thin, often reddish, exuding a milky sap when broken.

Flowers: Yellow, 0.8 cm (ca. 0.25 in.) in diameter, between 30 and 40 in terminal upright umbels. The distribution of the sexes on the inflorescences varies from year to year. Lasting two weeks, appearing before the leaves.

Fruits: Glabrous, in drooping clusters, on peduncles 5 to 8 cm (2–3 in.) long. Samaras large, 3 to 4 cm (1–1.5 in.) long, the wings forming an obtuse angle.

Propagation: Self-seeds. Seed germinates after several weeks of stratification in humid, cool conditions. Cultivars are propagated by grafting buds in summer.

The Norway maple, along with *Acer pseudoplatanus* (sycamore maple), is the largest maple in Europe and probably the dominant species. It is found throughout the continent, from the Ural Mountains to the Pyrenees and from the Balkans to central Scandinavia, where it is particularly frequent. Because it is widely distributed in nature, the Norway maple is very adaptable. It resists very low temperatures and droughts, and it tolerates almost all soils, with the exception of those that are too acidic or very sandy, which might explain its absence in coastal zones. In the wild, it is usually found in forests or woods. Alas, it is seldom planted in large parks.

flowers opening°	in spring (Savill)
flowers (Savill)	
fruits+	trunk (Westonbirt)

in autumn

fall color (Mariemont) | leaves in autumn

Often going unnoticed, so familiar is its silhouette to our eyes, Norway maple displays magnificent and abundant lemon-yellow flowers in spring, and sometimes in fall takes on a more golden color. *Acer platanoides* is the type species for section *Platanoides* and ranges from Europe to Japan. With *A. cappadocicum,* it is the largest representative of the section.

Acer platanoides has long been exploited for its hard white wood. It was introduced and planted in large quantities in North America, where its great adaptability and resistance have made it a choice pioneer plant.

The ornamental value of *Acer platanoides* extends to its numerous cultivars (at least 90), which are more colorful than the species. The cultivars come in shapes and sizes more adapted to all landscape situations, including use in smaller gardens and urban settings. Some of these cultivars are illustrated and described hereafter.

CULTIVARS

Many cultivars of the plane maple decorated parks and gardens in the 19th century, but most of them are no longer cultivated. Only the best are still commercially available, and most of these have purple foliage.

Among the cultivars are those with classical habits, such as 'Columnare', 'Globosum', or 'Erectum', or unique leaves, such as 'Palmatifidum' or 'Cucullatum', which continue to be propagated although they are rare. Most of the new cultivars have been created to fit into restricted spaces. Those of American origin, such as the selections of E. H. Scanlon—'Almira', 'Cavalier', 'Cleveland', and 'Olmsted'—are very small compared with the species. This characteristic allows them to adapt to urban use while retaining the strength and hardiness of *Acer platanoides.* All the cultivars are hardy in zones 4 and 5 and withstand pollution well. They are easy to propagate and cultivate, developing well in all non-acidic soils.

Acer platanoides 'Almira' (Hemelrijk)

Acer platanoides 'Ascendens' on unfurling (Hemelrijk)

Acer platanoides 'Almira'

Scanlon (1955). United States.

A small tree, 8 to 10 m (26–33 ft.) tall, very slow growing and similar in shape to 'Globosum'. The leaves are a glossy green. This tree is suitable for container culture.

Acer platanoides 'Charles F. Irish'

Scanlon (1955). United States.

A tree 15 to 20 m (50–66 ft.) tall, with a rounded crown. It is very similar to the species and the largest cultivar of *Acer platanoides*.

Acer platanoides 'Cleveland'

Scanlon (1948). United States.

A medium-sized tree, 10 to 12 m (33–39 ft.) tall, with a rounded crown. Leaves are glossy green in the summer, turning progressively to orange-red in the fall.

A. platanoides 'Cleveland' (CECE)	*A. platanoides* 'Cleveland', flowers (CECE)
A. platanoides 'Cleveland' in autumn (CECE)	*A. platanoides* 'Charles F. Irish' (Hemelrijk)
A. platanoides 'Charles F. Irish', early spring (Hemelrijk)	

Acer platanoides 'Columnare'

Carrière (1878). France.

An old, fastigiate cultivar, 15 to 20 m (50–66 ft.) tall. Fall color an attractive golden yellow.

Acer platanoides 'Crimson King'

Barbier & Company (1937). France.

A medium-sized tree, about 20 m (66 ft.) tall, with a rounded crown like that of the species. The leaves also resemble those of the species. They are crimson-red in the spring, turning darker until they drop. Fall color is not special.

Acer platanoides 'Crimson Sentry'

McGill & Son (1974). United States.

Smaller than 'Crimson King', only 8 to 10 m (26–33 ft.) tall, with a fastigiate and very dense habit. The leaves are also slightly smaller than those of 'Crimson King' but glossier.

Acer platanoides
'Columnare' in autumn°

A. *platanoides* 'Crimson King' (Bokrijk)   A. *platanoides* 'Crimson Sentry'°

A. *platanoides* 'Crimson King' (CECE)   A. *platanoides* 'Crimson Sentry'°

281

Acer platanoides 'Cucullatum'

Carrière (1866). France.

An erect tree, 20 m (66 ft.) tall. The leaves are green and overlapping. The points of the lobes are crimped.

Acer platanoides 'Deborah'

Cannor Nurseries (1975). Canada.

A medium-sized tree, 12 to 15 m (39–50 ft.) tall, with an erect habit. The young leaves are purple-red (see photograph on opposite page), later turning to green, then orange-red in autumn.

Acer platanoides 'Dilaceratum'

Dieck (1885). Germany.

A small tree, 5 to 6 m (16–20 ft.) tall. The small crimped leaves are dark glossy green with yellow-green spots.

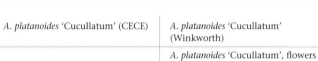

A. platanoides 'Cucullatum' (CECE)

A. platanoides 'Cucullatum' (Winkworth)

A. platanoides 'Cucullatum', flowers (Hemelrijk)

A. platanoides 'Deborah', young shoot	A. platanoides 'Dilaceratum'°
	A. platanoides 'Dissectum', flowers (Hillier)
A. platanoides 'Drummondii' (Hillier)	A. platanoides 'Drummondii'°
A. platanoides 'Drummondii'°	

Acer platanoides 'Dissectum'

Späth (1834). Germany.

A rare tree in cultivation. The green leaves are deeply cleft. On unfurling, the young leaves are red-brown and glossy. Rare in cultivation.

Acer platanoides 'Drummondii'

Schwerin (1910). Germany.

A large beautiful tree, 15 to 20 m (50–66 ft.) tall, with habit similar to that of the species. The leaves are strongly and remarkably spotted in cream white on their margins, the center remaining green.

Acer platanoides 'Erectum'

Slavin (1932). United States.

A small tree with erect branches, almost fastigiate. Leaves yellow-green in spring, greener in summer.

Acer platanoides 'Faassen's Black'

Faassen-Hekkens (1946). Netherlands.

A tree 15 to 20 m (50–66 ft.) tall. The leaves are similar in size to those of the species. Attractive flowers contrast with the purple-red young leaves. The orange-red fruits are very ornamental. This cultivar is similar to 'Crimson King' but has slightly paler leaves. It was selected by the former Tips Nurseries in Belgium, under the name of 'Globosum Purpureum'.

Acer platanoides 'Globosum'

Van Houtte (1873). Belgium.

A very beautiful cultivar, 8 to 12 m (26–39 ft.) tall, with a flat crown, and globular, very dense branching. This shape is retained without cutting or pruning but develops slowly. The green leaves are similar in shape but smaller than those of the species. In early spring, the wholly folded young leaves present a remarkable appearance: olive green, with red bracts and beautiful yellow flowers—truly magnificent. This old cultivar is still very much in use. Its globular habit and its proportions make it suitable for urban sites, tree rows, lane borders, and so forth.

A. platanoides 'Erectum' (Hillier)	*A. platanoides* 'Erectum', leaves (Hillier)
	A. platanoides 'Faassen's Black'*

A. platanoides 'Globosum' (Bokrijk)

Acer platanoides 'Goldsworth Purple'

Slocock (1947). England.

A medium-sized tree, 12 to 15 m (39–50 ft.) tall, with a broad, rather irregular crown. The leaves are similar in size and shape to those of the species. They are purple-red in spring, darker and dull at the end of summer; they may be a brighter shade of red in the fall, if the summer has been very warm and dry. In the spring, the yellow flowers contrast well with the purple-red leaves, as do the red samaras in autumn.

Acer platanoides 'Heterophyllum Variegatum'

Baudrillier (1880). France.

A small tree, 6 to 8 m (20–26 ft.) tall, with a columnar habit. The leaves are small, generally irregular, sometimes with only three lobes; the margins are yellow with orange spots. This cultivar is very rare in cultivation, although some old specimens may be encountered. Some British nurseries still offer it to the public.

Acer platanoides 'Maculatum'

Nicholson (1881). England.

A small to medium-sized tree, up to 10 to 12 m (33–39 ft.) tall. The leaves have five lobes; of a rather special shape, the two basal lobes are very small or even absent. Some leaves have only three lobes. The leaves have irregular yellow spots. Young leaves are orange with pink spots; later turning to yellow with a dark green center. In fall, the spring coloring returns with hues of yellow and orange.

Acer platanoides 'Meyering'

Grootendorst (1969). Netherlands.

A medium-sized tree, 12 to 15 m (39–50 ft.) tall, with very classical leaves. The uniqueness of this cultivar is the leaf coloring: bronze-red in the spring, green in summer, and very ornamental in autumn, with all the hues between red and orange.

A. platanoides 'Globosum', flowers (Hillier)	*A. platanoides* 'Goldsworth Purple'*
A. platanoides 'Heterophyllum Variegatum'	*A. platanoides* 'Heterophyllum Variegatum'°
A. platanoides 'Maculatum' in spring	*A. platanoides* 'Maculatum'
A. platanoides 'Maculatum' (CECE)	*A. platanoides* 'Meyering' (Hillier)

Acer platanoides 'Maculatum' in spring (Kew)

Acer platanoides 'Olmsted'

Scanlon (1955). United States.

Another Scanlon creation, with a pyramidal habit and leaves slightly smaller than those of the species. Good growth and good branch structure make this tree very suitable for rocky sites.

Acer platanoides 'Oregon Pride'

Pacific Coast Nursery (1979). United States.

This newish cultivar is not yet available in Europe. It has very deeply cleft leaves, similar to those of 'Palmatifidum' and 'Dissectum'.

Acer platanoides 'Palmatifidum'

Taush (1829). Germany.

Synonym, *Acer platanoides* 'Lorbergii'. An average-sized tree, 12 to 15 m (39–50 ft.) tall, with unique, elegant foliage. The lobes of the leaves are dissected to the base and partly overlapping each other. Fall color is a fleeting yellow-orange.

A. platanoides 'Palmatifidum' (CECE)	*A. platanoides* 'Palmatifidum', flowers and fruits (CECE)
A. platanoides 'Palmatifidum'	*A. platanoides* 'Palmatifidum' (CECE)
A. platanoides 'Palmatifidum' (Taviet, Belgium)	

Acer platanoides 'Pyramidale Nanum'°

Acer platanoides 'Reichenbachii' (Ravenstein)°

Acer platanoides 'Pyramidale Nanum'

Van Houtte (1877). Belgium.

Synonyms, 'Nanum', 'Nanum Pyramidale', 'Pyramidale'. A small tree of very slow growth but with very dense branching. The leaves are small but similar in shape to the species. The size of this cultivar and its dense branching make it perfect for small gardens.

Acer platanoides 'Reichenbachii'

Caspary (1874). Germany.

A large tree, 15 to 20 m (50–66 ft.) tall, slightly smaller than the species. Although the young spring shoots and petioles are red, the overall appearance of this cultivar is very dark, particularly at the end of summer. Leaf color ranges from very dark green to deep purple.

Acer platanoides 'Royal Crimson'

Scanlon (1967). United States.

Similar to 'Crimson King', the only difference being a superior red summer coloring. This cultivar differs little in size and shape from the other, already numerous cultivars, all in the purple range. It is not available in Europe.

A. platanoides 'Reichenbachii' (Westonbirt)	*A. platanoides* 'Schwedleri', flowers°
A. platanoides 'Schwedleri', leaves, upper side	
A. platanoides 'Schwedleri', leaf backside	*A. platanoides* 'Schwedleri' in spring (Savill)

291

Acer platanoides 'Royal Red'

Pacific Coast Nursery (1963). United States.

The size of this cultivar is large for a tree with purple leaves. 'Royal Red' is almost indistinguishable from 'Crimson King': tree height and leaf shape are similar. This cultivar has the advantage of rapid growth.

Acer platanoides 'Schwedleri'

Koch (1869). Germany.

A magnificent, medium-sized tree, easily exceeding 20 m (66 ft.) tall. Its attractive yellow flowers appear simultaneously with the purple-red young leaves. The leaves later turn to green, retaining however a purple hue. Fall coloring is more reddish. Pruning this tree after the leaves drop yields shoots with more color the following spring.

Acer platanoides 'Stollii'

Späth (1888). Germany.

A small tree, 6 to 8 m (20–26 ft.) tall. The leaves are five- to sometimes three-lobed, with a truncate base, dark green above, lighter green below. They have no particular fall coloring. This cultivar is rarely found under its true name, *Acer platanoides* 'Oekonomierat Stoll'.

Acer platanoides 'Walderseei'

Späth (1904). Germany.

A small tree, 8 to 10 m (26–33 ft.) tall. The leaves are light colored, spotted, with grayish tints. Young leaves are yellowish in spring, becoming unevenly green with yellow spots and silvery reflections. This rather unique tree is a slow grower. It is difficult to propagate.

A. platanoides 'Schwedleri' (Bokrijk)	*A. platanoides* 'Stollii' (CECE)
	A. platanoides 'Walderseei' (CECE)
A. platanoides 'Walderseei'°	*A. platanoides* 'Walderseei' in spring (Hemelrijk)
	A. platanoides 'Walderseei' (CECE)*

Acer platanoides subsp. *turkestanicum*

(Pax) de Jong (1994)

Section: *Platanoides.*

Epithet: *Turkestanicus,* from Turkestan.

Origin: Turkmenistan and northeastern Afghanistan

General appearance: A medium-sized tree, 12 to 15 m (39–50 ft.) tall, with broad, dense branching. Similar to the species but smaller.

Trunk: Dark brown.

Branches: Reddish brown. Young shoots are greenish red.

Leaves: Usually five-lobed, sometimes three-lobed, thick and slightly tough, 8 to 10 cm (3–4 in.) long, 10 to 12 cm (4–4.75 in.) broad, glossy, dark green above, lighter below, with down at the axils of the ribs. Central lobe with two large teeth. Tip acuminate. Base cordate. Margins entire. Petiole brown, slightly pubescent.

Flowers: Greenish yellow, in terminal erect panicles.

Fruits: Samaras 3 to 6 cm (1–2.4 in.) long, the wings almost horizontal, the nutlets flat.

Although de Jong classified this maple in 1994 as a subspecies of *Acer platanoides* on the basis of its characteristics, it is nevertheless a variation of *A. platanoides* subsp. *platanoides,* resulting from an adaptation to climactic conditions harsher than those in its original surroundings. Hardy to zone 5.

This maple is already growing in some arboreta, including Hillier.

in spring (Savill)

| flowers | fruits |

Acer platanoides × *A. truncatum*

Origin: Hillier nursery. A hybrid of *Acer platanoides* × *A. truncatum,* both in section *Platanoides.*

Name: This hybrid is still unnamed and is tagged as *"A. platanoides* × *A. truncatum."*

General appearance: A tree reaching 12 m (39 ft.) tall in 25 years. Upright with a rounded crown.

Leaves: Five-lobed, 10 cm (4 in.) long, 10 to 12 cm (4–4.75 in.) wide, glossy, green, some leaves showing brown hues like those of *Acer truncatum.* Basal lobes opposite and almost horizontal, central lobe either broad, triangular, and acuminate, or with two parallel sides bearing acuminate teeth, as in *A. platanoides.* Base truncate. Margins entire. Petiole yellow, 8 to 15 cm (3–6 in.) long.

Flowers: Few and yellow on large inflorescences.

Fruits: Wings of the samaras forming an obtuse angle.

It is interesting to note that this attractive hybrid exhibits a perfect mixture of the characteristics of its two parents. The photograph of the inflorescence (p. 297, right column, center) shows a leaf with some lobes resembling those of *Acer truncatum* and others resembling *A. platanoides.* In general, this hybrid is more like *A. truncatum*; the texture of the trunk is similar. The size of the flower, however, is closer to that of *A. platanoides.* Finally, its beautiful orange fall color seems to be a mixture of both parents.

Two other hybrids of the same parentage are available commercially in the United States. In both of them, the characteristics of *Acer platanoides* seem to predominate. The first, 'Norwegian Sunset', shows good growth, has a strong frame, and displays red to orange leaves in the fall. The second, 'Pacific Sunset', is smaller but displays glossy green foliage turning to carmine-red in the fall.

leaves	in spring (Hillier)
leaves in autumn	
trunk	flowers
	fruit

Acer pseudoplatanus

Linnaeus (1753)

Section: *Acer.*

Epithet: *Pseudoplatanus,* false *Platanus,* sycamore, plane tree.

Common names: Sycamore maple, great maple, Scottish maple.

Origin: Central and southern Europe, Caucasus, and north of Asia Minor. Introduced thereafter in England and western Europe, in areas with a maritime climate.

General appearance: A large deciduous tree, 25 to 35 m (82–116 ft.) tall.

Trunk: Size impressive. The gray bark peels off in elongated scales, variable in size, revealing the reddish brown layer below.

Branches: Brown or greenish, glabrous.

Buds: Large, ovoid, 8 to 10 mm (ca. 0.4 in.) in diameter, with overlapping yellow-green, dark brown-bordered scales.

Leaves: Five-lobed, large, 20 to 30 cm (8–12 in.), dark green above, gray-green to light purple below with more down. Lobes deeply divided. Margins with simple, thick, and irregular teeth. Petiole 8 to 20 cm (3–8 in.) long, greenish yellow or reddish, covered with brownish hair.

Flowers: Greenish yellow, in large cylindrical inflorescences, drooping, 15 to 20 cm (6–8 in.) long. Appearing after the leaves.

Fruits: Samaras 5 cm (2 in.) long, seeds thick and round.

Propagation: Easy, by seed. Equally easy by grafting.

The sycamore maple, along with *Acer platanoides* (Norway maple), is the largest European maple and comparable in size to its American relative, *A. saccharum* (sugar maple). In spring, the scent of the large flowers will be appreciated but, alas and unlike its cousin, it has no fall coloring. Indeed, it is a commonplace dark green, with no ornamental value, except for the leaf underside which is an attractive reddish brown.

The imposing silhouette of the sycamore maple will be more noticeable in winter, mainly on gigantic older specimens. It is long-lived, some trees having been known for more than five centuries.

leaves with young shoots	leaves unfurling
A. pseudoplatanus (left) and 'Atropurpureum' (right), leaf undersides	flowers
trunk°	fruits

One advantage of the sycamore maple is that it can be used as rootstock for propagating most maples, even those belonging to a different section. It is also "the" reference plant from which many cultivars were derived (more than a hundred), a stable and large maple, the largest in existence. It self-seeds and is invasive in gardens.

The quality of sycamore maple wood has been known for centuries. The wood has been widely used in construction and in the manufacture of common implements requiring resistance and strength, such as pulleys, screws, flails, and axles. Cabinet and violinmakers use the wood for its good shaping qualities. It makes an almost white fine-grained, satinlike, glossy wood suitable today for the production of veneer.

Originating in central Europe, *Acer pseudoplatanus* has colonized northern Europe from the Atlantic Ocean to the Baltic Sea in modern times, while remaining absent from the coastal regions. It grows well in mountains, up to altitudes of 1800 m (5940 ft.), where it turns attractive fall colors. It is very hardy and prefers forest clearings, in full sun or part shade, and deep, mineral-rich, well-drained soils with little acidity. Its roots are deep and strong. The leaves are often disfigured by characteristic black spots, a disease caused by the fungus *Rhytisma acerinum,* tar spot.

Acer pseudoplatanus f. purpureum
(Loudon) Rehder (1949)

While the leaves of most trees of *Acer pseudoplatanus* are various shades of green on the underside, in some regions of Europe trees in nature have leaves with a reddish-purple underside. This reddish-purple form, known botanically as *A. pseudoplatanus* f. *purpureum,* caught the attention of botanists and horticulturists, who propagated it by seed and eventually produced a hybrid with the green form. Thus, there exists a whole range of trees with intermediate colors. It seems that there is no dominant form in the case of hybrid.

Other methods of propagating, namely, grafting (with some reservations), layering, or cutting, produce clones that retain the selected characteristics (in this case, the purple-red leaf underside). These plants, the results of artificial propagation, are called cultivars. Seeds of the cultivars always grow into plants that are different than the original plant and may in turn hybridize with other members of the *Acer pseudoplatanus* group. In conclusion, it is

Acer pseudoplatanus (Grez-Doiceau, Belgium)*

Acer pseudoplatanus (Yorkshire, England)* | *Acer pseudoplatanus,* large trunk°

today very difficult to affirm with certainty that the species known as *A. pseudoplatanus* has a green leaf with a green or purplish backside. Too many hybridizations have occurred. Genetic analysis of an old specimen would be the only way to determine if the color is fixed or not.

The two photographs below show a form of *Acer pseudoplatanus* that may be encountered in nature, as well as a cultivar widely commercialized in the 19th century.

Acer pseudoplatanus f. *purpureum**

Acer pseudoplatanus 'Atropurpureum', leaf underside°

CULTIVARS

Acer pseudoplatanus is a variable species with more than 100 registered cultivars. These may be classified by number of lobes (from three to five) and by leaf color (upper surface with or without spots, underside red or green). Some cultivars have very curiously shaped leaves. As is true for cultivars of other maple species, many cultivars of *A. pseudoplatanus* have disappeared. Described here are a few older cultivars still available commercially and some new ones. All the cultivars mentioned below are hardy to zone 5, as is the species.

Acer pseudoplatanus 'Atropurpureum'

Groinland (1862). Germany.

A large tree, 25 m (82 ft.) tall. Leaves dark green above, deep purple-red below; this coloring persists through summer and autumn. The young shoots are reddish brown and the fruits dark purple-red. Even if it has the same shape as the type, this cultivar may be immediately recognized by its darker aspect, similar to *Acer platanoides* 'Reichenbachii', and its smaller size. Moreover, its leaf underside is much redder than all other shades of red-brown present in the species.

A. pseudoplatanus f. *purpureum*, growing in a copse (Mariemont)

A. pseudoplatanus 'Atropurpureum', group (Westonbirt)

Acer pseudoplatanus 'Brillantissimum'

Clark (1905). England.

A small tree, 10 to 15 m (33–50 ft.) tall, globose habit and dense branching. Slow growing but often grafted on a 180- to 200-cm (6- to 6.75-ft.) rootstock to compensate for this handicap. Spring leaves a splendid salmon pink, turning orange-yellow then green in the summer. Leaf underside is green, which differentiates this cultivar from 'Prinz Handjéry'. The soft yellow-green leaves of summer turn brown in sun. No particular fall coloring. A great classic of English gardens. Available throughout Europe.

	A. pseudoplatanus 'Brillantissimum' on unfurling
A. pseudoplatanus 'Brillantissimum' in spring	*A. pseudoplatanus* 'Brillantissimum', flowers
A. pseudoplatanus 'Prinz Handjéry' (left), 'Brillantissimum' (right), leaf upper sides	*A. pseudoplatanus* 'Prinz Handjéry' (left), 'Brillantissimum' (right), leaf undersides

Acer pseudoplatanus 'Brillantissimum' on unfurling (Savill)

Acer pseudoplatanus 'Brillantissimum' in spring (Trompenburg)

Acer pseudoplatanus 'Bob', leaves, upper side (CECE)

Acer pseudoplatanus 'Bob', leaves, underside (CECE)

Acer pseudoplatanus 'Bob'

Vaillant (1727). France.

An unregistered cultivar. Originated in Belgium and available commercially since 1985. A tree of good proportions, reaching 20 m (66 ft.) tall. The attractive pink color of unfolding leaves is close to that of 'Simon Louis Frère', but the leaf underside is redder.

Acer pseudoplatanus 'Corstorphinense'

Sutherland (1883). Scotland.

A majestic tree 15 to 20 m (50–66 ft.) tall, with a round, broad crown. The leaves are yellow in spring, turning to yellow-green in summer; they are not prone to sunburn. The leaf has three lobes, or is often triangular with a very large central lobe. The leaves drop early in the fall compared with other cultivars or the species, and fall color is not special. The cultivar name refers to the plant's origin in Corstorphine, a suburb of Edinburgh, Scotland.

Acer pseudoplatanus 'Erythrocarpum'

Vaillant (1727). France.

Found in the wild in the Swiss and Bavarian Alps, this form has been cultivated by a French nursery, yielding this very ancient cultivar. It becomes a large, elegant tree, comparable in size to the species, but with slightly smaller and glossier leaves. The petiole and fruits are deep red. The cultivar name means red fruit.

A. *pseudoplatanus* 'Corstorphinense' in spring (Westonbirt)

A. *pseudoplatanus* 'Corstorphinense', leaves | A. *pseudoplatanus* 'Erythrocarpum'°

307

Acer pseudoplatanus 'Kaki'

Selected in 1957 by Mr. Charlier of Esneux Arboretum, Belgium. Grows to 20 m (66 ft.) tall. Leaves are similar to those of the species, unfolding light green, changing colors several times in spring, then stabilizing in early summer. Beige-white dots remain until fall on the leaf upper surface; the leaf undersurface is pink-red. The leaves are slightly affected by sun.

Acer pseudoplatanus 'Leopoldii'

Vervaene Nursery (1864). Belgium.

A beautiful tree, 20 to 25 m (66–82 ft.) tall. A champion specimen attains 30 m (100 ft.) with a trunk circumference of 4.5 m (14.5 ft.). The leaves are the same size as those of the species and very ornamental. In spring, they are coppery red, later turning to green, while retaining large yellow and white spots. The cultivar was named for Belgian King Leopold I (1790–1865).

A. *pseudoplatanus* 'Leopoldii' (La Bouverie, Belgium)

A. *pseudoplatanus* 'Leopoldii' (Hillier)

A. *pseudoplatanus* 'Nizetii'

A. *pseudoplatanus* 'Kaki', leaves, upper side

A. *pseudoplatanus* 'Kaki', leaf, underside

A. *pseudoplatanus* 'Nizetii' in spring (Rond-Chêne)

Acer pseudoplatanus 'Negenia'

NAKB (1948). Netherlands.

An attractive, conical cultivar, suitable for urban sites. Very widely used. Bears green leaves on a red petiole. The fruits are very large and yellow, but few in number. No special fall coloring. NAKB is the Dutch Selection Service for Horticulture.

Acer pseudoplatanus 'Nizetii'

Makoy (1887). France.

Very similar to 'Leopoldii', but not as colorful. The leaf underside is purple, adding to the overall drab and dark aspect. A good grower.

A. pseudoplatanus 'Prinz Handjéry'°

| *A. pseudoplatanus* 'Prinz Handjéry' on unfurling | *A. pseudoplatanus* 'Prinz Handjéry', flowers° |

Acer pseudoplatanus 'Prinz Handjéry'

Späth (1883). Germany.

A small, slow-growing tree, very similar to 'Brillantissimum', from which it may be distinguished by deeper sinuses between the lobes, which are cut more deeply, while the leaf underside is browner. The latter characteristic makes this cultivar more resistant to sunburn in summer. Spring coloring is very remarkable.

Acer pseudoplatanus 'Simon Louis Frères'

Acer pseudoplatanus 'Variegatum' (Wakehurst)

Acer pseudoplatanus 'Rotterdam'

Vink (1944). Netherlands.

A beautiful, slow-growing cultivar, reaching 20 to 25 m (66–82 ft.) tall. The habit is conical and the tree has good wind resistance. The leaf is similar to that of the species.

Acer pseudoplatanus 'Simon Louis Frères'

Deegen (1881). France.

An attractive tree, about 10 m (33 ft.) tall, slow growing, sometimes shrublike. The leaves are similar to those of 'Leopoldii'—light pink when unfolding—but the underside is glaucous, sometimes stippled in yellow.

Acer pseudoplatanus 'Variegatum'

This name is given to some cultivars with characteristics identical to those of 'Leopoldii'. The leaves, however, are more drab, since only the white spots remain, and they are not as glossy. This dulling of features is often the case with old cultivars, where the traits for which the plant was selected disappear progressively.

Acer pseudoplatanus 'Worley'

Willkomm (1879). Germany.

Common name, yellow sycamore. A tree to 20 m (66 ft.) tall with beautiful golden yellow leaves in spring, a deeper color than those of 'Corstorphinense'. Leaves are greener in summer (see photograph on p. 312). A good growth for a yellowish maple. Incorrect synonyms include 'Woorley', 'Woorlaii', 'Worlei', and 'Worlem'.

Acer pseudoplatanus 'Zenith'

NAKB (1952). Netherlands.

This cultivar, selected by the Dutch Selection Service for Horticulture (NAKB), has not been sold commercially because its early growth is too slow.

A. pseudoplatanus 'Variegatum' (Hergest Croft)

A. pseudoplatanus 'Worley'° | A. pseudoplatanus 'Zenith' (Hillier)

Acer pseudosieboldianum in autumn (Westonbirt)

Acer pseudosieboldianum

(Pax) Komarov (1904)

Section: *Palmata.*

Epithet: *Pseudosieboldianus,* false *sieboldianus,* referring to this maple's similarity to *A. sieboldianum.*

Common name: Korean maple.

Origin: Korea, China, and Manchuria. It is the equivalent of the Japanese *Acer sieboldianum.* Introduced in Europe in 1904.

General appearance: A small tree or large shrub, about 8 m (26 ft.) tall, deciduous, with open branching.

Trunk: Gray-green, smooth.

Branches: Brown-green, glabrous, and sometimes sticky.

Buds: Small, red.

Leaves: Nine- to eleven-lobed, circular, but larger than those of *Acer sieboldianum,* 10 to 12 cm (4–4.75 in.), green above. Lobes elongated, straight; tip narrows to a sharp point, slightly recumbent, and sometimes with a red border. Base cordate. Margins doubly toothed except where the lobes meet. Young leaves slightly silky below.

Flowers: Creamy yellow, with purple-red sepals. Inflorescences in umbels, terminal, borne by a recumbent glabrous peduncle, 3 to 4 cm (1–1.5 in.) long. Appearing simultaneously with the leaves.

Fruits: In groups of three or four pairs, on a pedicel 1 cm (0.4 in.) long. Samaras 1.5 to 2 cm (ca. 0.75 in) long, the wings forming an obtuse angle, the nutlets round and glabrous.

Propagation: Easy, by seed.

In its natural habitat, *Acer pseudosieboldianum* grows at low levels, preferring humid but well-drained sites where it is protected from cold winds. It nevertheless can be grown in sunnier locations.

Although it is well adapted to Europe and hardy to zone 4, like its parent *Acer sieboldianum* it unfortunately is not fully appreciated for all that it has to offer: remarkable flowering and fall colors similar to those of *A. japonicum, A. shirasawanum,* and *A. circinatum.* The distinctions between *A. pseudosieboldianum* and each of these species are as follows:

mass of flowers	flowers (Herkenrode)
flowers (Lenoir)	fruits
in autumn (CECE)	leaves in autumn
	trunk

- *Acer pseudosieboldianum* differs from *A. sieboldianum* by its larger leaves (which often present two additional lobes), its glabrous and slightly sticky branches, and a less developed root system.

- *Acer pseudosieboldianum* and *A. circinatum* have in common a large seed with horizontal samaras and a glabrous, slightly sticky branch. They differ by the shape of the branches, those of *A. pseudosieboldianum* always being forked and orange-red at their extremities during the winter.

- *Acer pseudosieboldianum* differs from *A. shirasawanum* which has upright inflorescences and infructescences.

- The difference between *Acer pseudosieboldianum* and *A. japonicum* is subtler, the latter having stiffer and stronger branches with shorter young shoots. Moreover, the flowers have glossier sepals. It may also be noted that in spring the envelope of the flower buds of *A. pseudosieboldianum* is highly visible and very ornamental (see photograph on p. 315). After the fall coloring, the leaf becomes brown and remains on the tree.

  Some specialized nurseries are beginning to propagate this very attractive maple via seed and are growing large quantities of it.

Acer pseudosieboldianum in early summer (Herkenrode)

Acer pseudosieboldianum subsp. *takesimense*

(Nakai) de Jong (1994)

Section: *Palmata.*

Epithet: *Takesimensis,* from Takeshima, in South Korea.

Origin: Korea.

General appearance: A small deciduous tree, vigorous growing, with an upright, narrow habit.

Trunk: Green, slightly striated with white, with some brownish parts.

Branches: Green, sticky, rather thick, 0.8 to 1 cm (0.25–0.4 in.) in diameter. Young shoots are soft green.

Leaves: Eleven-lobed, 10 to 12 cm (4–4.75 in.) long, 12 to 15 cm (4.75–6 in.) wide, glossy, dark green, with some hairs at the axil of the veins. Base cordate. Margins roughly and strongly toothed. Young leaves tender green to bronze-orange. Petiole green or reddish green, 5 to 8 cm (2–3 in.) long, very erect, carrying an almost horizontal leaf.

❦

*A*cer pseudosieboldianum subsp. *takesimense* displays a very strong character, with a growth of about 1 m (3 ft.) per year on the top branches. It is hardy to zone 5, accepts a relatively poor soil, and may withstand temperatures as low as –20°C (–4°F). Fall color is purple-red.

As is true for the species, the subspecies bears young shoots that are sometimes sticky. This characteristic is also found in *Acer circinatum* and *A. circinatum* 'Monroe'.

Acer pseudosieboldianum subsp. *takesimense* in summer

Acer pseudosieboldianum subsp. *takesimense* in autumn

Acer pubipalmatum

Fang (1932)

Section: *Palmata.*

Epithet: *Pubipalmatus,* having a pubescent (hairy) palm (hand), referring to the leaves.

Origin: China (Zhejiang province).

General appearance: A small deciduous tree, 8 to 10 m (26–33 ft.) tall, with a narrow, upright habit.

Trunk: Gray-green, lightly striated.

Branches: Green, pubescent. Young shoots are red-brown.

Leaves: Seven-lobed, sometimes five-lobed, 6 to 10 cm (2.4–4 in.), dull medium green above and below, with a red border. Lobes deeply divided and well separated, the two small basal lobes opposite, the central lobe slightly larger and longer than the others. Base truncate. Margins doubly and cleanly toothed, the teeth very small and forward-pointing. Petiole 4 to 6 cm (1.5–2.4 in.) long, pubescent.

Flowers: Small, with white petals and purple-red sepals, in panicles on a very long peduncle.

Fruits: Samaras small, 2 to 2.5 cm (0.75–1 in.) long, pubescent, the wings forming an obtuse angle.

Propagation: As for *Acer palmatum.*

This tree is more erect, taller in the adult stage, and less dense than *Acer palmatum*. It also is less demanding, healthier, and stronger growing than its Japanese counterpart. The leaves of the two species are very similar except the leaf of *A. pubipalmatum* has seven lobes, a truncate base, and pubescence. The solid green leaves of *A. pubipalmatum* turn scarlet red in the fall.

This rare tree should be planted under optimal conditions, namely, a light, humic soil, slightly moist, and well protected, but allowing for maximum warmth at the end of summer.

leaves	branches*
flowers*	fruits
	leaves in autumn*

Acer pycnanthum

K. Koch (1864)

Section: *Rubra.*

Epithet: *Pycnanthus,* having flowers in dense clusters.

Common name: Japanese red maple.

Origin: Japan, a very restricted zone in the Nagano (Honshu) region.

General appearance: A medium-sized tree, often growing to 20 m (66 ft.) tall, broad, and well framed.

Trunk: Brownish, rough.

Branches: Red to brown-red.

Buds: Terminal buds larger than those of *Acer rubrum.*

Leaves: Three-lobed, 4 to 7 cm (1.5–2.75 in.) long, 3 to 6 cm (1–2.4 in.) wide, deep green, glabrous, smooth, glossy above, typically glaucous gray below. Lobes generally well marked. Base cordate. Petiole reddish, often rather long. Young leaves brown-red on opening, later brown-green (see photograph on opposite page).

Flowers: Red, on lateral inflorescences. Appearing very early in spring before the leaves, as with *Acer rubrum.*

Fruits: Appearing early in the year, ripening in June.

Propagation: By grafting on *Acer rubrum.*

*A*cer pycnanthum is the Japanese equivalent of the American species *A. rubrum,* with much smaller tree and leaf size. It is relatively hardy (zone 5). The tree is remarkable during two months in spring for its flowering, close to that of *A. rubrum,* and its beautiful foliage, with its very surprising red and brown hues. Rather classical and commonplace in the summer, it stands out again in the fall with its red and yellow colors.

This species is rather sparsely distributed in Japan and grows in humid mountainous areas, at altitudes between 400 and 500 m (1320–1650 ft.). It is slow growing and recommended for use in our gardens and parks for the nice contrast it presents in springs with trees and shrubs displaying lighter leaves and flowers.

unfurling leaves	young leaves
leaves*	leaves in autumn (Lenoir)
trunk	flowers
	fruits

unfurling in spring (Hillier) | in autumn (Herkenrode)*
in spring (Hillier) |

Acer ×rotundilobum

Schwerin (1894)

Epithet: *Rotundilobus,* with rounded lobes.

Origin: Garden. A hybrid of *Acer monspessulanum* × *A. opalus* subsp. *obtusatum.*

General appearance: A large shrub or medium-sized tree, 15 m (50 ft.) tall.

Trunk: Grayish, fissured, peeling off in small irregular plates.

Branches: Dark gray. Young shoots reddish.

Leaves: Three-lobed, uniform in size, 5 to 7 cm (2–2.75 in.) long and wide, thin, glossy, dark green above, lighter below, glabrous on both sides. Lobes broad, very rounded. Margins particularly toothed and slightly wavy. Petiole 4 to 5 cm (1.5–2 in.) long, sometimes reddish.

This very old hybrid is also very rare. An attractive specimen grows in the Arboretum National des Barres. The parentage of this maple seems well established, or rather has never been contested, but its propagation trials are few and seldom fruitful. Hardy to zone 5. The parentage implies this hybrid is closely related to *Acer ×coriaceum* and *A. ×durettii.*

	habit (Kew)
trunk (Kew)	leaves°

Acer rubrum

Linnaeus (1753)

Section: *Rubra.*

Epithet: *Ruber,* red, referring to the fall color.

Common name: Red maple.

Origin: Eastern North America, in the Great Lakes and Arcadian forest. Limited in the West by the Great Plains region and in the North by the boreal forest. In the South, it may be found from Florida to New Mexico. Introduced to Europe in 1656 by John Tradescant Jr.

General appearance: A large tree, 30 m (100 ft.) tall, with a broad, dense, oval crown formed by upright branches.

Trunk: Similar to that of *Acer saccharinum,* but smaller and covered with scales, the edges of which are easily detached.

Branches: Brilliant red to gray-brown, smooth, rather vigorous growing.

Buds: Red, with four to seven pairs of scales.

Leaves: Three- to five-lobed, longer than broad, 5 to 12 cm (2–4.75 in.) , dark green and glabrous above, blue-green below and more or less downy mostly along the ribs and on the young leaves. Central lobe longer than the others, which sometimes are very small. Margins roughly and irregularly toothed, teeth sharply pointed.

Flowers: Small, with red petals, on red peduncles, 6 to 8 cm (2.4–3 in.) long, growing at the axil of the new branches or on spurs on the older branches. Inflorescences are single-sexed, with male and female flowers growing in separate clusters, on the same tree or on separate trees. Appearing in March, well before the leaves. Pollination is by insects.

Fruits: Ripening around the end of May. Wings of samaras scarlet red, about 2 cm (0.75 in.) long, forming an angle of 60 degrees.

Propagation: By seed, cuttings, or grafting. Seed is collected at the end of May and must be sown immediately, since its viability decreases rapidly; it germinates quickly, and young seedlings are ready in October. *Acer rubrum* may be used as rootstock for all maples in its section, and may itself be grafted on *A. saccharinum.*

Acer rubrum, trunk°

leaves	flowering treetop
flowers	
flowers, young fruits	fruits+
young fruits	leaves in autumn

Acer rubrum in autumn (Connecticut)*

Acer rubrum, trunk (Winkworth)

*A*cer rubrum corresponds to *A. pycnanthum,* of Asiatic origin, which is smaller and has less distinct leaf lobes. It also resembles *A. saccharinum* by its early flowering, but the size of the fruits is very different.

Acer rubrum prefers moist, acidic soils bordering marshes, which is why it has a well-developed superficial root system. It nevertheless may adapt to dry and even rocky soils and to sites in shade. This very beautiful tree is suitable for large parks, planted near moist areas or on the edge of a pond. Individuals growing in cultivation are not as colorful as those growing in their natural habitat. European gardeners should select varieties suited to their climates. The wood is light brown, of average resistance and strength, and is not much used in North American industry.

A hybrid exists, *Acer ×freemanii* (*A. rubrum* × *A. saccharinum*), and is described elsewhere in this work.

Acer rubrum in autumn (New Jersey)

Cultivars of *Acer rubrum* are as demanding as the species. Even if they can very well withstand drought, they prefer moist, acidic soils. The height and size of many of them is compatible with urban settings, but their resistance to pollution is rather limited. The varieties have been selected for their flamboyant fall colors.

Acer rubrum var. *drummondii*

(Nuttall) Sargent (1884)

Endemic in the central and southern United States, in Arkansas, Texas, and even the Mississippi basin, this variety grows into a very bushy tree that is smaller than the species. The leaves have three lobes, with a cordate or rounded base, and a tough texture; they are glossy, dark green above and glaucous and very light-colored below. The flower is larger than that of the species, and the fruits have bright red wings.

This attractive variety is difficult to cultivate and only prospers in particular soil and climate conditions. Because it originates in southern climates, it only rarely takes on fall colors in Europe.

A. rubrum var. *drummondii*, leaves	*A. rubrum* var. *drummondii*, in autumn
A. rubrum var. *drummondii*, flowers (Herkenrode)	*A. rubrum* var. *drummondii*, on unfurling

A. *rubrum* var. *trilobum*, leaves	A. *rubrum* var. *trilobum*, branch (Hemelrijk)
A. *rubrum* var. *tomentosum*, leaves	

Acer rubrum var. *tomentosum*

Taush (1829)

This variety has a cultivar with the same name. As the name indicates, the leaf backside is tomentose. This variety is famous for its red fall color.

Acer rubrum var. *trilobum*

Torrey & Gray ex Koch (1853)

This variety originates in the southern United States. It is an average-sized tree. The leaves generally are three-lobed, sometimes with two very small lateral lobes, and usually considered as teeth. The young leaves are bright glossy red initially, turning green later but retaining their glossiness.

331

CULTIVARS

Acer rubrum 'Bowhall'

Scanlon (1951). United States.

Very well-known, in the United States and in Europe, this columnar cultivar grows up to 12 to 15 m (39–50 ft.) tall and has a compact crown 3 to 4 m (10–13 ft.) wide. The leaves are similar in size and shape to those of the species. In summer, they are a rather light green, turning orange-red to purple-red in fall. This maple is very much used in parks and gardens. It grows best in acidic soil.

Acer rubrum 'Columnare'

Rehder (1900). Germany.

An old columnar cultivar, with a tendency to broaden out when mature. Reaches 20 m (66 ft.) tall. Leaves are large, and growth rate is rapid. In autumn, the color varies between orange-red to crimson-red. Today this selection is replaced by 'Armstrong' or 'Bowhall', which are more attractive than 'Columnare' when young and have fall colors that are more brilliant.

Acer rubrum 'Globosum' (Lovenjoel, Belgium)*

Acer rubrum 'Bowhall' in autumn*

Acer rubrum 'Columnare' (Hillier)

Acer rubrum 'Columnare' in autumn (Arnold Arboretum)*

Acer rubrum 'Globosum'

Parons & Company (1887). United States.

This cultivar is very rare; just a few specimens are available in Europe. The branching is dense and the habit rounder than that of the species. This slow grower maintains good proportions and has attractive fall color. The modest plant size earns this cultivar a place in small gardens.

Acer rubrum 'October Glory'

Princeton University (1961). United States.

A medium-sized tree, with a broadly pyramidal crown, 5 to 6 m (16–20 ft.) wide at the base. The dark green leaf is similar in shape and size to that of the species but thicker. The leaves drop in late fall, giving more time to enjoy the orange to dark red hues. The color is more vivid on specimens growing in unfavorable conditions.

Acer rubrum 'Red Sunset'
in autumn (Hillier)

A. rubrum 'Red Sunset' in autumn	A. rubrum 'Sanguineum' in spring (Hemelrijk)
A. rubrum 'Sanguineum', leaves	

A. rubrum 'Sanguineum', early autumn
(Hemelrijk)

Acer rubrum 'Red Sunset'

Amfae Cole Nurseries (1966). United States.

A medium-sized tree with a broadly pyramidal crown. Leaves are rather large and growth
is rapid.

Acer rubrum 'Sanguineum'

Lavallée (1887). France.

A beautiful cultivar of French origin, which unfortunately is seldom cultivated. The habit
is similar to that of the species but smaller. The leaves are slightly different also: five-lobed,
with a cordate base and deeply cut lobes, the underside tomentose. Fall color is orange-red.

Acer rubrum 'Scanlon' in autumn°

Acer rubrum 'Scanlon'°

Acer rubrum 'Scanlon'

Scanlon (1956). United States.

A large columnar tree with dense branches, growing to 20 m (66 ft.) tall and 5 to 8 m (16–26 ft.) wide. Growth rate is average, but the tree is very robust and very tolerant of dry soil. Fall coloring comes early. The leaves turn color early in fall, becoming bright orange initially and later purple-red. This elegant cultivar is very well-known in the United States but not as common in Europe.

Acer rubrum 'Schlesingeri'

Schwerin (1896). Germany.

An old cultivar, seldom encountered in cultivation, although it was widely commercialized by the well-known Späth nurseries in Berlin. This medium-sized tree, with widely spaced, bare branches, sometimes has a shrublike form. The leaf is more wavy than that of the species and has a more toothed margin. The petiole is long and thin. This splendid cultivar is appreciated for its early fall color, which appears at the end of August. It is dark ruby red, shifting sometimes towards orange-red. This coloring progresses slowly, but the leaves fall early. The original plant of this cultivar, selected by Charles S. Sargent, grows at the Arnold Arboretum, in the United States (see photograph on p. 337).

A. rubrum 'Schlesingeri' in autumn
(the original plant at Arnold Arboretum)★

A. rubrum 'Schlesingeri' in autumn	*A. rubrum* 'Schlesingeri' in autumn

Acer rubrum 'Schlesingeri', a group of young trees in autumn (Hillier)

Acer rubrum 'Sunshine'

A medium-sized, upright tree, reaching 15 m (50 ft.) tall at maturity. The branches are red-brown, remarkable in winter. The leaf is easy to recognize by its large acuminate central lobe with an orange-red petiole. This new, strong cultivar has light-colored summer foliage. Fall color is orange.

Acer rubrum 'Tilford'

Scanlon (1951). United States.

A large tree with a rounded crown, very broad, reaching more than 20 m (66 ft.) tall. The shape and size of the leaves are very similar to that of the species: five-lobed, with a dark green upper side and a glaucous underside. Fall color varies considerably according to the soil type. Widely encountered in the United States, this attractive cultivar is also available in many European countries due to good growth and adaptability to most soils.

A. rubrum 'Sunshine' (Hillier)	*A. rubrum* 'Wagneri'
A. rubrum 'Tilford', leaf upper side	*A. rubrum* 'Tilford', leaf underside

Acer rubrum 'Wagneri'

Koch (1869). Germany.

A tree with widely spreading, pendulous branches. Leaves are three-lobed, a glossy dark green above and light green below. This cultivar is similar to *Acer rubrum* var. *drummondii*. A large, rare tree, it displays attractive, long-lived fall color.

Acer rufinerve

Siebold & Zuccarini (1845)

Section: *Macrantha.*

Epithet: *Rufus,* russet red, referring to color of the hair on the leaves, flowers, and fruits.

Common name: Honshu maple.

Origin: Widespread in Japan, except on Hokkaido Island. Introduced in 1879 by Charles Maries for Veitch Nursery.

General appearance: A vigorous-growing, medium-sized tree, 10 to 15 m (33–50 ft.) tall, with a narrow, upright habit and a thin crown. An understory tree often growing in a copse. Pruinose branches distinguish this species from all others in section *Macrantha.*

Trunk: Outstanding for its vertical white streaks on a green background. Becomes a dull brown-gray with age.

Branches: Green. Young branches and young shoots are covered with a bluish bloom.

Buds: Green in winter like the branches, then pink-red, reaching 2 cm (0.75 in.) in diameter just before opening.

Leaves: Three- or five-lobed, broader than long, 15 to 18 cm (6–7 in.) wide, 10 to 17 cm (4–6.75 in.) long, slightly tough, dark green and smooth above, lighter colored below. A slight reddish down appears in the spring along the veins but disappears late. Central lobe larger than others and triangular, the two lateral lobes pointed and well directed towards the outside. Margins small toothed.

Flowers: Greenish yellow, on a short peduncle only 3 to 6 mm (ca. 0.2 in.) long, connected to a common stem covered with a reddish down, the whole forming an erect then drooping inflorescence 7 to 8 cm (2.75–3 in.) long.

Fruits: Samaras initially pubescent where they are thickest, covered with a russet-red down, the wings up to 2 cm (0.75 in.) long and forming an angle between 60 and 120 degrees.

Propagation: Very easy, by seed, which ripens in autumn.

This understory tree prefers full or part shade. In full sun, black-brown burn spots may appear on the thin, tender bark, as it does on the bark of other maples in section *Macrantha. Acer rufinerve* prefers moderately humid and cool soils, although it is drought tolerant. It is very resistant and may also be cultivated in containers. Juvenile growth rate is rather slow.

pruinose branch	unfurling
flowers (Lenoir)	fruits
habit (Lanhydrock)	leaves in autumn (BMP)
	leaves in autumn (Japan)*

The leaves are uniformly green in the summer but remarkably colored in fall—red, orange, yellow, and purple. The striated bark is ornamental in winter, as are the pruinose branches. Buds are grayish white in winter, turning reddish pink before opening. *Acer rufinerve* is an excellent specimen tree in a large site with flowering plants, where its narrow, erect silhouette provides light shade.

CULTIVARS

Acer rufinerve 'Albo-limbatum'
Hooker f. (1869). United States.

A tree 6 to 8 m (20–26 ft.) tall with broad, erect branching. Slightly smaller than the species, it grows more slowly and the trunk has far fewer white stripes. Its originality is in the foliage, irregularly spotted with white. Some leaves stay white. The size and shape of the leaf, however, differ strongly from the species; they are much smaller, with fewer lobes, and resemble those of *Acer davidii*. Fall color is similar to that of *A. rufinerve* and features the simultaneous presence of many hues, yellow to purple through red. It will also be noted that the white spots turn pink and that each group of leaves changes color at a different time. Plants grown from seed differ from the original cultivar; thus propagation is best by grafting on young *A. rufinerve* trees. 'Albo-limbatum' is easily cultivated and hardy to zone 5.

Acer rufinerve 'Erythrocladum'
Marshall ex Brimfield (1953). England.

This shrub, which should not be confused with *Acer pensylvanicum* 'Erythrocladum', also has colored branches: they are yellowish in winter and more reddish in summer. The leaf is also somewhat smaller than that of the species. Of average hardiness, this cultivar is sensitive to frost and excessive sun. Consequently, the selection of a suitable location is important for this fragile and slow-growing tree. The cultivar name refers to the red color of the branches.

Acer rufinerve in autumn, with *A. micranthum* in the background
at left (Lake Hibara, Honshu, Japan)*

| *A. rufinerve* (Hillier) | *A. rufinerve* 'Groenendael' (Rond-Chêne) |

A. rufinerve 'Albo-limbatum', flowers* | *A. rufinerve* 'Albo-limbatum', flowers (Hillier)
A. rufinerve 'Albo-limbatum', leaves in autumn° |

A. rufinerve 'Albo-limbatum' in autumn (Hillier)

Acer saccharinum in early autumn (New Jersey)

Acer saccharinum

Linnaeus (1753)

Section: *Rubra.*

Epithet: *Saccharinus,* sugary, referring to the sap.

Common name: Silver maple.

Origin: Central and eastern North America (from the forested Saint Lawrence region of Ontario and Quebec to New Brunswick and Florida), along lakes and river banks. Introduced in Europe in 1725 by Sir Charles Wager.

General appearance: A very large tree, more than 35 m (116 ft.) tall, with a short trunk, often covered with young branches, growing vertically. The crown is open, broad, and rounded.

Trunk: Light gray.

Branches: Glabrous, vigorous growing, erect at first, then bending over and falling until their tips straighten up again.

Buds: Twice as long as broad, red, smooth, glossy, and typically with four pairs of scales.

Leaves: Five-lobed, glabrous and light green above, silvery below with a slight down that disappears late. Lobes more or less deeply cut; sinuses separating the lobes have a rounded base. Leaf tip irregularly pointed and doubly toothed. Base cordate.

Flowers: Green-yellow, without petals, in dense clusters, on short lateral branches. Male and female flowers grow on the same tree or on separate trees. Appearing in February or March, well before the leaves. Distinguished from other maples by its clusters of flowers surrounding the branch.

Fruits: Borne on drooping peduncles, 3 to 5 cm (1–2 in.) long, rather broad at 5 to 8 cm (2–3 in.), glabrous, often very colorful, the wings rounded at the end and forming an obtuse angle.

Propagation: Because the tree flowers very early and seeds falling to the ground germinate rapidly, seed of this species can be collected at the end of April, sown immediately, and result in 40-cm (16-in.) tall young plants in the fall. Layering is also possible.

leaf underside	young leaf
flower+	fruits
large trunks (Berlière)	

A traditional plant for parks and gardens, *Acer saccharinum* grows into a very beautiful tree, either alone or in a group. It is often used in Europe in large parks or along roads, whereas in the United States it is considered undesirable. It is not adapted for use in urban surroundings, where its large branches are sometimes torn off by high winds and its abundant branching makes pruning difficult.

The wood is considered of minor quality and mostly used for pallets, crates, and panels. In nature, *Acer saccharinum* grows primarily in humid lowlands, very seldom at high altitudes. It prefers rich, cool soils; excess limestone in the soil may discolor the leaves. Because of its

Acer saccharinum, trunk circumference of 5.14 m (16.9 ft.) in 1997 (Arnold Arboretum)*

Acer saccharinum, trunk circumference of 6.95 m (22.8 ft., near Auburn, Illinois)

Acer saccharinum in autumn (Hillier)

extended, superficial root system and its adaptability to very humid soils, it is easily transplanted. Silver maple grows very rapidly, but is short-lived, approximately 100 years and to a maximum of 130 years.

This maple continues to be used in parks and gardens because of its autumn and early spring colors, as well as its rapid growth. It is a pleasing companion with other plants because of its silver-lined leaves.

CULTIVARS

Acer saccharinum has no subspecies. Many cultivars, however, have been selected. These are hardy to zone 4. They are easily propagated by layering or by grafting onto young *A. saccharinum* trees. Although the species is American, all the cultivars selected in the 19th century originated in Europe, primarily Germany. Most of these cultivars have disappeared, and only a few of them may be found in arboreta and fewer still in nurseries. In addition to their scarcity in the trade, they have a short lifetime.

Acer saccharinum 'Asplenifolium'
De Bie van Aalst (1925). Netherlands.

'Asplenifolium' is the original name of this large cultivar and refers to the leaf, which has narrower lobes and is less deeply cut than leaves of the species. When the De Bie nursery went out of business, the cultivar continued to be propagated but under the name of 'Laciniatum Wieri', a very similar cultivar.

Acer saccharinum 'Laciniatum Wieri'
Ellwanger & Barry (1875). England.

The original tree was selected by Wier and later propagated by Ellwanger & Barry. It is large and strong growing, with a broad, flattened crown and branches that are more pendulous than those of the species. The leaf differs from that of the species and may easily be recognized by its deeply cut, separated lobes. The only other cultivar with leaves so deeply cut is 'Schwerinii'. Incorrect synonyms for 'Laciniatum Wieri' include 'Wieri', 'Wageri', 'Wagneri', 'Asplenifolium', or 'Laciniatum'.

A. saccharinum 'Asplenifolium'	*A. saccharinum* 'Laciniatum Wieri' (Hillier)
A. saccharinum 'Laciniatum Wieri' (Von Gimborn)	*A. saccharinum* 'Laciniatum Wieri' on unfurling
	A. saccharinum 'Laciniatum Wieri' (BMP)

351

Acer saccharinum 'Lutescens'

Späth (1883). Germany.

An attractive tree, of respectable size, growing up to about 20 m (66 ft.) tall. It has an erect habit similar to that of the species but is slower growing because of its yellowish foliage. The leaves are very light green-yellow when they unfold and may keep that color until early summer or turn a soft green in summer. Fall color is golden yellow. The leaves are similar to those of the species, and the underside is also glaucous in summer. The midrib of the upper surface is red, as is the 15- to 18-cm (5- to 7-in.) long petiole. *Acer saccharinum* 'Golden', from Jewell Nurseries (1947), United States, is very similar to 'Lutescens' in both size and habit. It grows in the Arnold Arboretum.

Acer saccharinum 'Pyramidale'

Späth (1885). Germany.

An old cultivar, with a pyramid shape, showing strong growth and quickly reaching a height of 15 to 20 m (50–66 ft.). The branches are stiff and attached to the trunk at an angle of 45 degrees. The twigs are generally reddish brown in winter, while the young shoots are soft green in summer. Young leaves are orange in spring. This good cultivar is available in most nurseries.

Acer saccharinum 'Schwerinii'

Beissner (1902). England.

An interesting cultivar, of erect habit and average size. The leaves are deeply cut and similar to those of 'Asplenifolium', and the lateral lobes are more curved and more open on 'Schwerinii'. The inner margin of these lobes is entire for half their length and has shallower notches than those of 'Asplenifolium' or 'Laciniatum Wieri'. Although very similar to the latter two, with the same superb fall colors, 'Schwerinii' may only be found in a few collections and has disappeared from most nursery catalogs.

Acer saccharinum 'Lutescens'

A. saccharinum 'Lutescens' in spring (Bokrijk)

A. saccharinum 'Pyramidale' (Hillier)	*A. saccharinum* 'Schwerinii'

Acer saccharum
Marshall (1785)

Acer saccharum
in autumn°

Section: *Acer.*

Epithet: *Saccharum,* sugary, referring to the sap, a source of maple syrup and sugar.

Common name: Sugar maple.

Origin: North America (Great Lakes and Saint Lawrence region, Arcadian forest, and southern Ontario). Introduced in Europe around 1735. The sugar maple was designated as Canada's national tree in 1965, and its red leaf adorns that country's flag.

General appearance: In forests this large tree develops a trunk without branches for at least two-thirds of its height, topped by a dense, rounded crown. The tallest trees reach 30 m (100 ft.). When grown as a single tree, it is distinguished by its very thick branches that form a broad, rounded crown.

Trunk: Pale to dark gray, split in long irregular strips.

Branches: Brilliant reddish brown, not pubescent.

Buds: Very pointed and on each side of the branch.

Leaves: Five-lobed, sometimes three-lobed, palmate, 8 to 13 cm (3–5 in.) wide, yellowish green above, paler below, pubescent at the axils of the major veins. Lobes distinguished by two U-shaped teeth separating the lateral lobes from the central lobe. Lobe sides parallel.

Flowers: Greenish yellow, without petals, on thin downy peduncles, 5 cm (2 in.) long, in upright corymbs. Appearing before the leaves.

Fruits: Glabrous, 2 to 3 cm (0.75–1 in.) long, containing a large seed; the wings of the samaras parallel or slightly divergent.

Propagation: The fruits ripen in autumn, but in Europe do not produce seed easily as the climate is too cool. Layering gives good results. Grafting on *Acer saccharinum,* in September, is possible.

A. saccharum leaf	*A. saccharum*, spring flowering (Kew)
A. saccharum, unfurling (BMP)	
A. saccharum subsp. *grandidentatum*, flowers	leaves in autumn
trunk°	silhouette°

An exceptionally majestic tree, *Acer saccharum* attracts many tourists and visitors to North America because of its imposing size and spectacular fall colors. While it is glorious on that continent, it is not well adapted to Europe's maritime climate where it lacks the summer warmth needed to ripen, bear fruit, and acquire its most beautiful fall coloring.

Acer saccharum thrives best in deep, fertile, and moist but well-drained soils, mainly if the substrate is rich in limestone. It can grow in shade but remains small. Its roots go deeper than those of most maples; however, in cool climates, the roots have a tendency to grow horizontally, in quest of heat. This large tree is a good companion of conifers or deciduous trees, and is rather long-lived, up to 400 years.

Maple syrup, a product of *Acer saccharum,* was gathered by indigenous peoples in present-day eastern Canada long before the arrival of European colonists. The colonists improved production methods. Currently this well-developed industry manufactures a significant amount of syrup—about 17 million liters (ca. 4.5 million gallons) per year. The wood of this species is an important source of timber.

Acer saccharum in autumn
(Bartholomew's Cobble)*

Acer saccharum in autumn (Massachusetts)*

Acer saccharum, fall coloring (New Jersey)

Acer saccharum subsp. *floridanum*
(Chapman) Desmarais (1952)

Section: *Acer.*

Epithet: *Floridanus,* from Florida.

Synonym: *Acer barbatum* Michaux.

Origin: Southeastern United States (Florida coastal plain, Virginia, Texas).

General appearance: A small tree, 10 to 15 m (33–50 ft.) tall, with dense, erect or curved, irregular branching.

Trunk: Pale gray-brown.

Branches: Brownish. Young shoots green, turning brown as the seasons progress. Twigs covered with lenticels.

Buds: Dark brown, with eight pairs of scales.

Leaves: Five-lobed, variable in size, about 10 cm (4 in.) long, 12 cm (4.75 in.) wide, prostrate and often asymmetrical looking, dark green and smooth above, glaucous gray-green below. The three main lobes carry a pair of acuminate teeth. Base cordate or truncate. Rib yellow, with white hairs on the bottom veins. Margins entire and slightly wavy. Petiole 5 to 12 cm (2–4.75 in.) long, yellow-green, reddish on top. Young leaves coppery red to soft green, very prostrate.

Flowers: Yellowish, identical to the species.

Fruits: Samaras with one side atrophied, generally forming a U.

This slow-growing tree often produces branches at the base of the trunk. In fall, the leaves turn orange-brown for about 10 days, a short period during which this species is highly ornamental. The leaf stays on the tree a long time before dropping.

Acer saccharum subsp. *floridanum* (Hillier)

Acer saccharum subsp. *floridanum*

Acer saccharum subsp. *grandidentatum*

(Torrey & Gray) Desmarais (1952)

Section: *Acer.*

Epithet: *Grandidentatus,* having large teeth, referring to the leaf margin.

Common names: Big-toothed maple, canyon maple, hard maple.

Origin: Western North America, from the Rocky Mountains to Oklahoma, Montana, Arizona, New Mexico, and Texas. Introduced at the Royal Botanic Gardens, Kew, by Charles S. Sargent in 1885.

General appearance: A tree 10 to 15 m (33–50 ft.) tall, generally shrublike, dense, with erect branches and twigs.

Trunk: Gray-brown.

Branches: Reddish to light brown, lightly striated with green, glabrous. Twigs covered with orange lenticels.

Leaves: Five-lobed, broader than long, 10 to 12 cm (4–4.75 in.) wide, smooth and glossy green on both sides except for some white hairs on the axil and the base of the ribs. Lobes triangular or ovate, well separated, basal lobes small, central lobe larger and longer on terminal leaves. Base cordate. Petiole yellowish.

Flowers: Yellow, in hanging clusters with short peduncles. Appearing with the leaves.

Fruits: Samaras 2.5 to 3 cm (ca. 1 in.) long, the wings forming an angle of 60 degrees, the nutlets round and glabrous.

Propagation: By seed, or by grafting on *Acer saccharinum.*

The leaves of this medium-sized tree are dark green in summer and turn brilliant colors in fall, ranging from red to orange-yellow. The colors are most striking in large mountainous regions, generally on canyon borders. *Acer saccharum* subsp. *grandidentatum* prefers dry soil and a sunny locations. Most American botanists consider it a species distinct from *A. saccharum.* It resembles *A. hyrcanum,* but the latter's leaves are smaller, lighter in color, and not glossy. Subspecies *grandidentatum* is hardy to zone 5.

leaves and fruit	fruits in early autumn
trunk (Hillier)	in autumn

a wild tree (Guadalupe Mountains, New Mexico)

Acer saccharum subsp. *leucoderme*

(Small) Desmarais (1952)

Section: *Acer.*

Epithet: *Leucodermis,* with a white skin.

Common name: Chalk maple.

Origin: Southeastern United States (from North Carolina to Texas).

General appearance: A small tree, sometimes a large shrub, 6 to 8 m (20–26 ft.) tall, with a dense, rounded crown.

Trunk: Pale gray or grayish white.

Branches: Young shoots are thin and glabrous.

Leaves: Three- or five-lobed, 6 to 12 cm (2.4–4.75 in.), green above, yellowish white below and not glaucous but covered with a velvety down. Basal lobes very small. Base cordate or truncate. Petiole red.

Flowers: Yellow, on small umbels. Appearing in April.

Fruits: Samaras small, 2 cm (0.75 in.) long, the wings almost horizontal, the nuts hairy initially, becoming glabrous.

Propagation: By grafting on any member of the *Acer saccharum* group.

The magnificent specimen growing at Westonbirt (see photograph on opposite page) is exceptionally large, due to competition from the nearby very large trees. Most individuals are smaller, especially the shrublike forms normally encountered in cultivation. The whitish color of the leaves, also visible in the photograph, is due to hair on the underside of the leaves.

This tree is common in northern Georgia and Alabama.

Acer saccharum
subsp. *leucoderme*
(Westonbirt)

leaf underside

leaves in autumn

Acer saccharum subsp. *nigrum*

(Michaux f.) Desmarais (1952)

Section: *Acer.*

Epithet: *Niger,* black.

Common name: Black maple.

Origin: North America (central and western Ontario, Saint Lawrence valley towards Montreal island; also Ottawa valley).

General appearance: A tree 25 to 30 m (82–100 ft.) tall, similar to the species, with a trunk circumference of 1 m (3 ft.).

Trunk: Dark gray, with long vertical fissures, sometimes scaly.

Branches: Reddish, dull brown. Young shoots are more orange than the branches and tomentose.

Buds: Gray-brown, pointed, with dull, hairy pairs of scales.

Leaves: Five-lobed, 8 to 12 cm (3–4.75 in.), dark green above, yellow-green below, with a thick brownish velvety down extending to the petiole. Lobes not well defined, ends almost square, separated by a deep sinus rounded at the base. Margins irregularly toothed. The petiole has small stipules.

Flowers: Small, yellow-green, without petals, hanging in clusters on a reclining peduncle.

Fruits: Samaras 3 cm (ca. 1 in.) long, the wings parallel, as they are in *Acer saccharum,* the seed large, on a pedicel as long as the fruit.

Compared to the species, *Acer saccharum* subsp. *nigrum* prefers sites that are more humid. It is hardy to zone 4 and, because it tolerates shade, may be used as an understory tree. It also produces a syrup-yielding sap. Compared with the species, the subspecies has a slower growth rate, a generally darker color, a more striated trunk, lobes that are more rounded, and orange young shoots. Fall color is yellow to reddish brown but is not as spectacular as that of the sugar maple, and the leaves drop very early.

The wood is very heavy, hard, and strong. Colored pale yellow-brown, it is used in commerce for the same purposes as *Acer saccharum.*

flowers	fruits

in early autumn (Hillier)

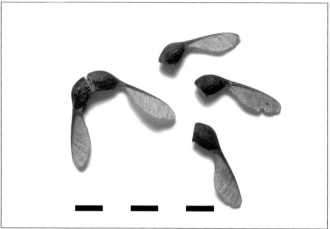

*A*cer saccharum is widely distributed in the United States. No fewer than six subspecies have been identified, indicating the species' adaptability to different soils and situations. Because of the climate, *A. saccharum* seldom bears fruit in Europe. Thus, all selected cultivars of the species are of American origin (going back to 1950). Many of them are not yet commercially available in Europe, excepting the great classics described hereafter.

Acer saccharum
'Brocade'

CULTIVARS

Acer saccharum 'Brocade'
Delendick (1983). United States.

A small tree, sometimes shrublike. Leaves with deeply cut lobes, down to the base. Of triangular shape, the leaves have a very narrow base and a broad point. They carry large lateral teeth, long and acuminate. The petiole is very long and bright red.

Acer saccharum 'Green Mountain'
Princeton Nurseries (1964). United States.

A medium-sized, pyramidal tree, 10 to 12 m (33–39 ft.) tall and 6 to 8 m (20–26 ft.) wide at the base. The leaves are rather large (15 cm or 6 in.) and tough, dark green above, glaucous below. Fall color is yellow to scarlet red. This cultivar is widely used in the United States for its average size, balanced shape, and good tolerance of urban pollution.

Acer saccharum 'Newton Sentry' (Hillier)

Acer saccharum 'Newton Sentry' in autumn (Hillier)

Acer saccharum 'Newton Sentry'

Harkness (1954). United States.

A fastigiate tree, about 15 m (50 ft.) tall, with a narrow silhouette. Each secondary branch also is fastigiate. This cultivar is very similar to 'Temple's Upright'. It has small twigs that keep the foliage close to the branches. Fall color tends towards yellow, as in the species. 'Newton Sentry' is also very similar to *Acer rubrum* 'Columnare', another large, fastigiate tree.

Acer saccharum
'Senecaensis'

Acer saccharum 'Senecaensis'

Slavin (1950). United States.

A large tree with a thick, broad, and rounded crown. The branches and twigs are very erect. The leaves are similar to those of the species, dark green above, a lighter, glossy green below. The petiole is long and thin.

Acer saccharum 'Sweet Shadow Cut-Leaf'

Powell Valley Nursery (1962). United States.

A small tree of nice proportions, with a broad, rounded crown. The "cut-leaf" appellation is appropriate, since the leaves have deep cuts, much deeper than those of 'Brocade'. The lobes overlap slightly. Leaf size is definitely smaller than that of the species. Fall color is an attractive orange-red.

Acer saccharum subsp. *nigrum* 'Temple's Upright'

Harkness (1954). United States.

A small columnar tree to 8 to 10 m (26–33 ft.) tall, with erect main branches. The secondary branches also are erect and lack horizontal branchlets. The leaves are slightly tough. Fall color ranges from orange-yellow to red.

'Sweet Shadow Cut-Leaf' in autumn (Oregon)°

'Senecaensis' in autumn (Hemelrijk)

'Temple's Upright' in autumn (Hillier)

Acer sempervirens

Linnaeus (1767)

Section: *Acer.*

Epithet: *Sempervirens,* evergreen.

Common name: Cretan maple.

Synonym: *Acer orientale* Linnaeus.

Origin: Countries bordered by the eastern Mediterranean Sea, western Turkey, Greece, and Lebanon. Introduced in Europe in 1752.

General appearance: A broad shrub 6 to 7 m (20–23 ft.) tall, evergreen or semi-evergreen, rarely a small tree. The form varies considerably depending on location and climate. Branching is dense and oval shaped.

Trunk: Gray-brown.

Branches: Sometimes (not always) downy.

Leaves: Unlobed or three-lobed, tough, base sometimes cordate, margins entire or superficially denticulate, sometimes with small teeth. Bright green, glabrous on both sides, small, 1 to 4 cm (0.4–1.5 in.) long, 1 to 2 cm (0.4–0.75 in.) wide. Young leaves brown-green. Petiole 3 to 10 mm (0.1 to 0.4 in.) long. Leaf form varies on the same tree (evident polymorphism). On trees, leaves are generally three-lobed, tough, semi-evergreen, borne on a 3- to 10-cm (1- to 4-in.) long petiole. On shrubs, leaves are often entire, yellowish green, few in number, borne on a 2-cm (0.75-in.) long petiole.

Flowers: Yellowish green, few, in corymbs.

Fruits: Samaras small, 1.5 to 2 cm (ca. 0.75 in.) long, glabrous, the wings parallel or forming an angle of 60 degrees, the nutlets almost round.

Propagation: By seed, or by grafting on *Acer pseudoplatanus.*

A typical plant of warm and dry climates, this dense shrub has adapted to tougher climates by developing very small leaves. In Europe, it has been observed to withstand very cold conditions, including the winter of 1996–1997, when temperatures dropped as low as –22°C (–8°F) and stayed below zero for seven weeks. Some specimens thrive in England in moderate climates and may reach above-average sizes, but growth will always be very slow. The main landscaping interest of this small tree resides in the blooming period. During these two weeks, the yellowish coloration is particularly noteworthy. The permanent leaves, a rare characteristic for maples, will earn this maple a special place in parks and gardens designed for winter conditions.

young leaves+	young plant (Rond-Chêne)
flowers	fruit (Kew)
in flower (Kew)	a wild tree (Crete, Mr. Charlier)

Acer shirasawanum

Koidzumi (1911)

Section: *Palmata.*

Epithet: *Shirasawanus,* after Japanese botanist Homi Shirasawa (1868–1947).

Common name: Shirasawa's maple.

Origin: Japan (Honshu and Shikoku islands). Introduced in Europe in 1826.

General appearance: A small tree or large shrub, with broad, dense branching, 6 to 8 m (20–26 ft.) wide in cultivation. Multitrunked with a rounded top. The main branches are very erect, the secondary twigs rather horizontal.

Trunk: Light brown, lightly striated with vertical gray-green stripes. The multiple trunks have no branches.

Branches: Sprinkled with small white spots, like the leaves.

Buds: Brown, with four pairs of scales.

Leaves: Nine- or eleven-lobed, green, glaucous, almost transparent due to its thinness, horizontal like a tray, with well-marked ribs below. Basal lobes cordate and very small, other lobes larger, strongly and doubly teethed, ending in long points. Margins often reddish. Petiole yellowish green, 3 to 5 cm (1–2 in.) long.

Flowers: Upright, with whitish petals and red sepals, in terminal inflorescences in upright umbels.

Fruits: In upright clusters, on very thin peduncles. Samaras up to 2 to 3 cm (0.75–1 in.) long, the wings reddish, upward-pointing, forming an obtuse angle, the seeds round and green.

Propagation: By seed, or if not available, by grafting on *Acer palmatum.*

This strong slow-growing small tree is well adapted to northern Europe, where it grows in part shade, in light, humic soils neither too alkaline nor too dry. It should be grown in shade, since the summer sun quickly burns its thin leaves. It is hardy to zone 5.

Acer shirasawanum has a very elegant shape, perfect for use in the landscape as a single, highly visible tree. Spring color is a spectacular lemon yellow. Leaves exposed to full sun may burn. The leaves are darker in summer, turning orange-yellow in the fall, sometimes with crimson-red margins.

Although this species is very similar to *Acer circinatum, A. japonicum, A. pseudosieboldianum,* and *A. sieboldianum,* it is distinguished by its upright flowers and fruits.

leaves (CECE)	flowers with fruits (CECE)
flowers (Hillier)	fruits in autumn (Hillier)
trunk (Hillier)	beginning of fall coloring
	fall coloring

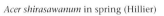

Acer shirasawanum in spring (Hillier)

Acer shirasawanum in autumn (Herkenrode)*

Acer shirasawanum 'Aureum' (Wakehurst Place)

Acer shirasawanum 'Aureum'°

CULTIVARS

Acer shirasawanum 'Aureum'

Siesmayer (1888). Germany.

A small compact thick tree, very slow growing at about 5 to 10 cm (2–4 in.) per year, although the young plant is very fast growing in its first year. The trunk is dark and smooth on young plants, light brown later, and in general slightly crooked. The leaves are very bright yellow-green in spring and remain that color on trees grown in shade. In summer, the leaves turn yellow and generally have sunburnt margins on trees grown in full sun. Fall color is a disappointing orange-yellow, turning rapidly to brown. This tree is more resistant to spring frosts than is the species. It should not be planted in soil that is too dry. Like the species, this cultivar produces upright flowers and fruits.

Acer shirasawanum 'Jūni hito e'

In general similar to the species, but some experts place it closer to 'Microphyllum' because of its small leaves.

Acer shirasawanum 'Aureum' in early autumn. The foliage at the top of the tree has been sunburnt (Lenoir).

A. *shirasawanum* 'Aureum', flowers★   A. *shirasawanum* 'Aureum' in spring

A. *shirasawanum* 'Aureum' in autumn   A. *shirasawanum* 'Aureum', trunk°

A. *shirasawanum* 'Jūni hito e' on unfurling   A. *shirasawanum* 'Jūni hito e' in autumn (Westonbirt)

Acer shirasawanum 'Microphyllum'

Siesmayer (1888). Germany.

A small shrublike bush, 5 m (16 ft.) tall, rather erect. The short, stiff branches result in a dense crown. The trunk is dark gray and smooth. The leaves have 11 lobes, sometimes only 9, and are short, ovate, and triangular, ending in a sharp point. Thick and dark green, the leaves are smaller than those of 'Aureum' at 6 to 8 cm (2.4–3 in.) long and 8 to 10 cm (3–4 in.) wide. Fall color is very beautiful and ranges from crimson-red to glossy yellow.

Acer shirasawanum 'Palmatifolium'

A thick, erect shrub, up to 8 m (26 ft.) tall. The trunk is dark green and the young shoots dull green. The leaves have 11 lobes, strongly cut down to at least two-thirds of their length, and are strongly toothed and acuminate. The leaves are slightly hanging, about 10 cm (4 in.) wide, and very thin, almost translucent, making them susceptible to sunburn. Protruding veins are visible on the leaf underside. Fall colors are superb and range from crimson-red to orange-yellow. The leaves drop rather early. Although it is available in specialized nurseries, this cultivar is seldom encountered and has not yet received the attention it deserves. It adapts to all soils and is hardy to zone 5. Propagation is by grafting on *Acer palmatum* or *A. sieboldianum*.

Acer shirasawanum var. tenuifolium

Koidzumi (1911). Japan.

Native to the mountains of central and southern Japan, this tree reaches 6 to 8 m (20–26 ft.) tall in habitat and is smaller than the species. The leaves have seven or nine lanceolate lobes, cut down to half the length of the leaf. They are doubly toothed and have margins with small silky hairs; the species is hairless. The leaves are light green, thin, pubescent below, and 4 to 6 cm (1.5–2.4 in.) long and 6 to 7 cm (2.4–2.75 in.) wide. The petiole is 3 to 5 cm (1–2 in.) long. The inflorescence is a terminal corymb, carrying yellow flowers with purple sepals. The samaras are 2.5 cm (1 in.) long and upright. Fall color is orange-red. Hardy to zone 5.

A. shirasawanum 'Microphyllum' in autumn	*A. shirasawanum* 'Microphyllum' in spring (Savill)
A. shirasawanum 'Palmatifolium'	*A. shirasawanum* 'Palmatifolium' in spring (Kalmthout, Belgium)
A. shirasawanum var. *tenuifolium* in autumn	*A. shirasawanum* var. *tenuifolium* in autumn (Herkenrode)

Acer sieboldianum

Miquel (1865)

Section: *Palmata.*

Epithet: *Sieboldianus,* after German botanist Philipp F. von Siebold (1796–1866).

Common name: Siebold's maple.

Origin: Japan (Hokkaido, Honshu, Kyushu islands, most abundantly on the latter). Imported in Europe around 1880.

General appearance: A small deciduous tree, 8 to 10 m (26–33 ft.) tall, shrubby, often multitrunked, and with a narrow, upright crown that broadens with age.

Trunk: Red-brown and smooth on young trees, becoming grayer with age.

Branches: Red-brown, rather thick, sprinkled with lenticels. Young shoots are dark red, covered with white hairs.

Buds: Small, triangular, red.

Leaves: Nine-lobed, sometimes seven- or eleven-lobed, green above, lighter green below, 6 to 10 cm (2.4–4 in.), covered with down on both sides, down remaining only on the underside in summer. Base cordate or truncate. Lobes divided half-way down the length of the leaf. Margins with pointed teeth. Petiole 2 to 4 cm (0.75–1.5 in.) long, reddish brown. Young leaves often orange-red, sometimes light pink.

Flowers: Small, with yellow petals and red sepals. Inflorescences terminal, recumbent umbels. Appearing after the leaves.

Fruits: On terminal peduncles 4 to 6 cm (1.5–2.4 in.) long, hairy. Samaras small, 1.5 to 2 cm (ca. 0.75 in.) long, the wings forming an obtuse angle.

Propagation: Easy, by seed. By grafting on *Acer palmatum* and vice versa; however, *A. sieboldianum* is indispensable as a rootstock because of its superior vegetative qualities and because its trunk has a larger diameter, making grafting easier. Like most maples, it is very sensitive to verticillium.

Acer sieboldianum,
young pubescent shoot

leaves (Hemelrijk)	young shoots in summer
on unfurling	flowers (Hemelrijk)
trunk°	fruits (Hillier)
	leaves in autumn

Acer sieboldianum on unfurling (Hillier)

Acer sieboldianum in autumn (Japan)*

Acer sieboldianum in autumn, as an understory tree (Hemelrijk)

With its very wide-spreading, shallow, evenly spaced roots, *Acer sieboldianum* is a robust and vigorous plant, easy to cultivate and even transplant. It is hardy to zone 4 and grows in any soil, except those that are very heavy and compacted. It does not tolerate full sun, growing only in the shade of other trees or buildings. Compared to *A. palmatum* or *A. japonicum, A. sieboldianum* has better resistance to spring frost, diseases, and transplanting problems.

Spring and summer colors of *Acer sieboldianum* are similar to those of *A. palmatum,* with a remarkable pink-red young leaf. In autumn, it is even superior with an earlier and more brilliant scarlet coloring.

Long underrated until the present, this species is now being promoted eagerly by some nurseries.

Acer sieboldianum
'Sode no uchi' in
spring (Savill)

CULTIVARS

Acer sieboldianum **'Kinugasa yama'**

A strong cultivar, well-built, rapidly yielding a small tree 6 to 8 m (20–26 ft.) tall. The leaf has seven lobes, each cut to half the length of the leaf and ending in an acute point. The petiole and young leaves are covered with minute red hairs, a distinguishing characteristic. Fall color is excellent. The tree is easy to cultivate, similar to the species in hardiness, and suitable for any garden. The Japanese name means "silky canopy" or "umbrella."

Acer sieboldianum **'Sode no uchi'**

A rare dwarf maple, becoming a rounded shrub 2 m (6.5 ft.) tall. Growth is slow, about 10 to 20 cm (4–8 in.) per year for young plants, and much less for older specimens. The small leaves have 11 lobes, sometimes 9, are ovate, and are 3 to 4 cm (1–1.5 in.) in size, even less on older branches. The petiole is short and stiff. This attractive plant fits well in small gardens. The leaves are soft green in summer, turning crimson-red to yellow in the fall. 'Sode no uchi' is very popular in Japan among all bonsai aficionados.

A. sieboldianum 'Kinugasa yama' in autumn*

A. sieboldianum 'Sode no uchi' | *A. sieboldianum* 'Sode no uchi'

Acer sikkimense subsp. *metcalfii*

(Rehder) de Jong (1994)

Section: *Macrantha.*

Epithet: *Sikkimense,* from Sikkim, a region in the Himalayas. *Metcalfii,* after U.S. botanist Franklin P. Metcalf (1892–1955).

Origin: China (Guangdong, Hunan, and Jiangxi provinces).

General appearance: An elegant small tree, 8 to 10 m (26–33 ft.) tall, with an upright habit.

Trunk: Brown-green, vertical white striation.

Branches: The young shoots are violet-brown and glabrous.

Leaves: Three- or five-lobed, 6 to 12 cm (2.4–4.75 in.) long, green above, lighter below. Lobes strongly acuminate, the two basal lobes absent or shallowly cut, the important central lobe triangular. Margins roughly and superficially toothed.

Flowers: In long racemes of 10 to 15 cm (4–6 in.).

Fruits: Samaras 3 to 4 cm (1–1.5 in.) long, the wings almost horizontal or forming an angle of 150 degrees.

The only observed specimen of this subspecies grows in the Hergest Croft Arboretum, where it prospers in the shade in cool soil in a wooded area. According to Alfred Rehder, this maple is related to *Acer davidii* subsp. *grosseri. Acer sikkimense* subsp. *metcalfii* is entirely different from the species, *A. sikkimense* Miquel (synonym *A. hookeri*), which grows at altitudes of 3000 m (9900 ft.) in the Himalayas of Sikkim. The species has dark green, entire, cordate, ovate, glossy leaves that tolerate strong sun, and its young leaves are a remarkable coppery red. In contrast, the subspecies is an understory plant, with leaves broader than those of the species, and of a fine texture. Furthermore, the leaves display no particular fall color.

leaves	fruits
trunk	habit (Hergest Croft)

Acer sinopurpurascens
Cheng (1931)

Section: *Lithocarpa.*

Epithet: *Sino,* Chinese, and *purpurascens,* purple, referring to the tree's origin and flower color.

Origin: Eastern China (Zhejiang province).

General appearance: A small, deciduous tree, 6 to 10 m (20–33 ft.) tall, with erect branching.

Trunk: Light gray-brown, rough.

Branches: Light brown. Young shoots have red-brown stripes and are covered with warts.

Buds: Three buds on each side, many scales.

Leaves: Three- or five-lobed, surface wavy, dark green above, green below, 8 to 15 cm (3–6 in.) long and wide. Lobes deeply cut, basal lobes very small, others ovate and ending in a point. Margins with widely spaced teeth. Petiole 8 to 13 cm (3–5 in.) long, yellow, glabrous, containing latex.

Flowers: Dioecious species. Red, with purple-red sepals, on long peduncles, in a large panicle.

Fruits: Samaras large, 3 to 6 cm (1–2.4 in.) long, the nutlets red and downy.

Propagation: Difficult by seed due to strong parthenocarpic tendency. By grafting on *Acer sterculiaceum.*

This species is very similar to *Acer diabolicum* in its magnificent flowering, but may be differentiated from that species by its smaller leaves, lobes that are deeply cut, reddish (not yellow) flowers, and fruits without horns. Fall color of *A. sinopurpurascens* is orange-red. It is the earliest flowering maple, and it bears flowers after only a few years, even if its height is barely 50 cm (20 in.). The spectacular flowers will earn it a highly visible location among smaller plants. Hardy to zone 5.

This species is very rare in cultivation. A beautiful specimen grows in the Trompenburg Arboretum, in Rotterdam, The Netherlands.

leaves with young shoot (Hillier)	flowers°
buds (Hillier)	early autumn (Batsford)
flowering in spring (Hillier)	

389

Acer spicatum

Lamarck (1786)

Section: *Parviflora.*

Epithet: *Spicatus,* carrying a spike, referring to the inflorescences.

Common name: Mountain maple.

Origin: North America (from the Great Lakes to the Saint Lawrence River, Arcadian forest, and southern boreal forest). Introduced in Europe in 1750 by the duke of Argyll.

General appearance: A deciduous shrub or bushy small tree, 8 m (26 ft.) tall, with a short trunk or several erect branches forming an open, irregular crown.

Trunk: Smooth or slightly furrowed, light gray especially in winter.

Branches: The young shoots are covered with a gray down, becoming glabrous later and turning vivid red in winter.

Leaves: Three-lobed, sometimes five-lobed, generally longer than broad, 8 to 13 cm (3–5 in.). Base more or less cordate. Lobes separated from the base by a wedge-shaped sinus. Margins coarsely toothed. Petiole reddish, long.

Flowers: Typical for section *Parviflora,* appearing later than the leaves and forming inflorescences in upright spikes at the ends of the branches. Greenish yellow, about 0.5 cm (0.2 in.) long, on small recumbent peduncles, connected to a central stalk. The male and female organs are on separate flowers, but usually present on the same spike. The male flowers disappear after pollination.

Fruits: Ripening in autumn, first red, then yellow or pinkish brown; some remaining on the tree during the winter. Seeds small. Wings of the samara 2 cm (0.75 in.) long, rounded, forming an angle of 90 degrees. Some seeds and winglets are atrophied, a characteristic of the species (see photograph on opposite page).

Propagation: Easy, by seed.

This maple is mostly an understory tree but withstands full sun without problem, as long as it has a good water supply. It favors the moist soil near a river, which is why most of the roots stay close to the surface of the ground. The leaves vary in width depending on their native habitat.

Acer spicatum is essentially a rather unobtrusive, background tree. The leaves unfold in spring and for a week are a unique reddish color and provide good contrast. The winter appearance of the tree should not be forgotten; its size and very red terminal shoots make it a good companion of other plants also possessing colored bark, like dogwoods or beeches. Fall color is a weak yellow or red. In the landscape, this tree is inconspicuous and barely visible.

leaves (BMP)	branches and trunk in winter (BMP)
flowers*	fruits (BMP)
flowering in spring (Hemelrijk)	

Acer stachyophyllum

Hiern (1875)

Section: *Glabra.*

Epithet: *Stachyophyllus,* having spiked (pointed) leaves.

Synonym: *Acer tetramerum* Pax (1889).

Origin: Himalayas (Sikkim) to central China (Hubei, Gansu, Shaanxi provinces), southeastern Tibet, and northern Myanmar, in mountain forests to an altitude of 1000 m (3300 ft.). Introduced by Ernest H. Wilson in 1901.

General appearance: A multistemmed shrub reaching 15 m (50 ft.) tall, with an erect, open silhouette, broadening at the top.

Trunk: Green, lightly striated in green-gray.

Branches: Reddish brown, even redder when less than one year old, drooping vertically sometimes.

Leaves: Unlobed or three-lobed, 6 to 12 cm (2.4–4.75 in.), pointed, silky above, rugged below. Margins roughly toothed, teeth forward-pointing, edges covered with tiny brown hairs, which are also present at the leaf base where the veins meet.

Flowers: Dioecious species. Yellowish. Female flowers on short lateral shoots, in short, pendent racemes. Male flowers at the axils of the leaves.

Fruits: Glabrous. Samaras 2 to 5 cm (0.75–2 in.) long, forming an obtuse angle, the seeds large, very distinctive for their striated and rifted exterior.

Propagation: Easy, by cuttings. No compatible rootstock is known.

This large, very strong shrub of insignificant ornamental value grows in the forest understory and looks like *Acer acuminatum*. It requires no particular soil but is sensitive to spring frosts and to verticillium wilt. Cankers on the branches weaken the wood.

Acer stachyophyllum is relatively rare in cultivation, seen only in selected collections. Fall color is of no particular interest.

Compared to the species, *Acer stachyophyllum* subsp. *betulifolium* has smaller leaves that turn an interesting orange color in fall.

young shoot (Hillier)	leaves (Hillier)
reddish branches	flowers
habit (Westonbirt)	fruits°
	dried fruits

Acer stachyophyllum subsp. *betulifolium*

(Maximowicz) de Jong (1994)

Section: *Glabra.*

Epithet: *Betulifolius,* having leaves like *Betula,* birch.

Synonym: *Acer betulifolium* Maximowicz (1889).

Origin: Central China.

General appearance: A large multistemmed shrub 12 m (39 ft.) tall, with fastigiate growth. Produces suckers.

Trunk: Green with large lenticels.

Branches: Brownish, very thin, and slightly drooping. Young shoots are reddish.

Leaves: Unlobed or three-lobed, elongated, very acuminate, 4 to 8 cm (1.4–3 in.) long. Edges irregular. Margins roughly toothed to lobed. Petiole scarlet red, very thin.

Flowers: Dioecious species. Yellowish in short, pendent racemes.

Fruits: Samaras 2 to 5 cm (0.75–2 in.) long, the wings forming an obtuse angle, the seeds smaller than those of the species.

Propagation: By cuttings, or by grafting on the species.

*A*cer stachyophyllum subsp. *betulifolium* is very similar to *A. stachyophyllum* to which it has been rightfully related. Indeed, the differences are minor, such as a smaller and more lightly colored leaf, a more rounded leaf margin, a shorter peduncle, leaf opening later in the season, and shorter plant height. Fall color varies from orange-yellow to peach-pink and is definitely more attractive than that of the type. Intensity of fall color depends on the nature of the soil.

Like the species, the subspecies is seldom encountered in Europe. The most beautiful specimen grows in the Hergest Croft Arboretum (see photograph of the trunk on the opposite page). A specimen growing in the CECE nurseries (Belgium) has reached 4 m (13 ft.) tall in 15 years and seems to withstand verticillium wilt better than *Acer stachyophyllum.*

Acer stachyophyllum var. *pentaneurum* Fang (1979) from China is very rare in cultivation (see photograph of flowers on opposite page). We have no information on this plant.

A. stachyophyllum var. *betulifolium,* young shoot	*A. stachyophyllum* var. *betulifolium,* flowers (Westonbirt)
A. stachyophyllum var. *betulifolium,* in autumn	*A. stachyophyllum* var. *betulifolium,* fruits (Hergest Croft)
A. stachyophyllum var. *pentaneurum,* flowers	*A. stachyophyllum* var. *betulifolium,* trunk (Hergest Croft)
A. stachyophyllum var. *pentaneurum* (Westonbirt)	

Acer sterculiaceum
Wallich (1830)

Section: *Lithocarpa.*

Epithet: *Sterculiaceus,* like *Sterculia,* a genus of tropical plants.

Synonym: *Acer villasum* Wallich (1830).

Origin: Western Himalayas, Kashmir, Nepal, and Bhutan, in mountains. Introduced to England in 1835.

General appearance: A deciduous tree, reaching 15 to 20 m (50–66 ft.) tall, erect, with a broad crown and strong branching.

Trunk: Gray-brown.

Branches: Gray-brown, vigorous growing, thick, and bearing reddish brown young shoots in clumps, alternating from one side of the branch to the other.

Buds: Reddish brown, with overlapping scales; lateral buds in groups of three, the central one containing a flower. Seven buds clustered at the branch tip, three opposite laterals and one terminal.

Leaves: Three- or five-lobed, large, 15 to 20 cm (6–8 in.), thick. Central lobe larger than the other lobes. Base cordate, sometimes asymmetrical. Margins roughly toothed. Petiole yellowish green, 7 to 15 cm (2.75–6 in.) long, slightly tomentose. Young leaves coppery green.

Flowers: Dioecious species. On pendent lateral inflorescences. Male flowers five to eight, in short racemes. Female flowers in panicles 10 to 15 cm (4–6 in.) long.

Fruits: Samaras 3.5 to 8 cm (2–3 in.) long, the wings forming an angle of 45 degrees or almost parallel, the nutlets round.

Propagation: By grafting on *Acer pseudoplatanus.* Difficult by seed due to strong parthenocarpic tendency.

Known in Europe for decades, *Acer sterculiaceum* is a collector's tree with no particular ornamental value. It is the type for section *Lithocarpa,* which includes only four species. *Acer sterculiaceum* is strong-growing tree and more resistant than subspecies *franchetii.* It is relatively hardy (zone 5).

young leaves (Hillier)	leaf
buds	trunk (Hillier)
branching	habit (Hillier)
flowers (Savill)	

Acer sterculiaceum, crown flowering in spring (Savill)

Acer sterculiaceum subsp. *franchetii*

(Pax) Murray (1969)

Section: *Lithocarpa.*

Epithet: *Franchetii,* after French botanist Adrien R. Franchet (1834–1900).

Origin: Central China and Tibet. Introduced in 1901 by Ernest H. Wilson for Veitch Nursery.

General appearance: A tree 20 m (66 ft.) tall, with upright, vigorous branching.

Trunk: Dark brown.

Branches: The young shoots are brownish green and glabrous.

Buds: Brown, with downy scales.

Leaves: Three-lobed, sometimes five-lobed with two small basal lobes, large, 10 to 15 cm (4–6 in.) long and broad, green, rough on both sides, the underside initially tomentose. Lobes triangular, irregular, not very distinct, with forward-pointing ends. Base slightly cordate. Margins roughly toothed. Petiole 15 cm (6 in.) long. Young leaves prostrate and recumbent.

Flowers: Greenish yellow, in recumbent racemes. The male and female flowers grow on the same tree, on lateral buds.

Fruits: Samaras large, 6 cm (2.4 in.) long, the wings forming a right angle, the nutlets rounded and tomentose.

Propagation: Difficult, as is true for all dioecious species. By grafting on *Acer sterculiaceum,* but this species is also rare.

An attractive medium-size tree, this maple was discovered by Adrien R. Franchet and is very rare in Europe. A good specimen, planted in 1980, grows in the Royal Botanic Garden, Edinburgh. The subject of the photographs (on p. 398) prospers at Westonbirt Arboretum, while another individual grows slowly in the shade of larger trees at Hemelrijk Arboretum in Belgium.

This subspecies is closely related to *Acer diabolicum* and *A. sinopurpurascens*. Its large leaves and its fruits resemble those of *A. pseudoplatanus.*

Hardy to zone 5. It prefers acid soils. The spring flowers appear with the opening of the buds and are this plant's most decorative feature. The large bunches of samaras display a most surprising contrast with the autumn leaves. Their size and abundance are reminiscent of those of *Acer macrophyllum.* Fall color is yellow.

A. sterculiaceum subsp. *franchetii*

(Westonbirt)

A. sterculiaceum subsp. *franchetii,* flowers

A. sterculiaceum subsp. *franchetii,* fruits

Acer tataricum

Linnaeus (1753)

Section: *Ginnala.*

Epithet: *Tataricus,* from Tartary, an old name for the region encompassing Central Asia and a part of Russia.

Common name: Tatarian maple.

Origin: Southeastern Europe, from Austria to Turkey, Asia Minor, Caucasus, and southern Russia. Introduced in northern Europe around 1759.

General appearance: A small deciduous tree, 10 m (33 ft.) tall, with a broad crown and numerous branches at the base and on the trunk.

Trunk: Light brown to gray-brown, vertically fissured. Smoother on young trees and striated in a lighter brown.

Branches: Often forked and twisted, bending down at the end under the weight of the fruit. Young shoots are light brown.

Buds: Thick, almost black, typically with eight scales.

Leaves: Unlobed, three- or five-lobed on young shoots, 10 cm (4 in.) long and almost as wide, ovate, rounded, green, glabrous, recumbent. Base cordate. The rib is strongly marked on the underside and slightly downy. Margins irregularly or doubly serrated. Petiole yellow or reddish, 5 to 8 cm (2–3 in.) long, and grooved at the top.

Flowers: Whitish, in upright terminal panicles, 3 to 5 cm (1–2 in.). Appearing in May or June.

Fruits: Rounded and slightly wrinkled. Samaras 2 to 3 cm (0.75–1 in.) long, red in early summer, then pink and finally brown in autumn, the wings parallel.

Propagation: Easy, by seed, which is abundant. Collect and sow seed in October for abundant germination the following spring.

on unfurling (Westonbirt)	flowers*
trunk°	fruits (BMP)

401

Acer tataricum in spring (Kew)

Acer tataricum bearing fruit (BMP)

Acer tataricum subsp. *aidzuense* (Les Barres)

Tatarian maple is appreciated for at least two reasons: its abundant display of reddish pink fruits in summer, and its good growth and robust constitution. It is hardy to zone 3. A well-shaped individual has a pleasing mushroom-shaped crown, but it is primarily in utilitarian groups—windbreakers, shields, roadsides, and ridges—that this thick, strong small tree is best used. It is a good companion of plants that feature autumn and winter colors, evergreen foliage, and so forth.

Acer tataricum subsp. *aidzuense*
(Franchet) de Jong (1996)

This subspecies is easy to identify by its upright samaras and a more prominent central lobe, dominating the other two lateral lobes. It is also smaller than the species and subsp. *ginnala*. Fall color is as deep as that of the species.

Acer tataricum subsp. *ginnala,* a very large specimen (Hørsholm, Denmark)°

Acer tataricum subsp. *ginnala*

(Maximowicz) Wesmael (1890)

Section: *Ginnala.*

Epithet: *Ginnala,* the vernacular name for this maple.

Common name: Amur maple.

Origin: Central China (Amur River region), Manchuria, Korea, and Japan. Initially shipped via train to Saint Petersburg by Carl Maximowicz, in 1857.

General appearance: A small multitrunked tree or large shrub, dense, easily reaching 8 to 10 m (26–33 ft.) tall, often broader than tall.

Trunk: Gray-brown, vertically fissured.

Branches: Red-brown, glabrous.

Buds: Small, dark brown, rounded.

Leaves: Three-lobed, 8 to 10 cm (3–4 in.) long, 3 to 6 cm (1–2.4 in.) wide, dark glossy green above, light green below, glabrous on both sides. Central lobe longer and more acuminate than the others. Base slightly cordate or truncate. Margins strongly toothed. Rib yellow. Petiole reddish.

Flowers: Creamy yellow-white, fragrant, growing in groups of five, on small panicles.

Fruits: Samaras 2.5 cm (1 in.) long, often red, glabrous, the wings almost parallel, the seeds small.

Propagation: Easy, by seed. Is a good rootstock for grafting other subspecies and the few cultivars of *Acer tataricum.*

A very resistant maple, *Acer tataricum* subsp. *ginnala* is well suited to urban settings, whether grown in containers on patios or alongside roads. It is also useful as a windbreaker in large or small gardens, as a focal point near flowering beds, or as a companion of larger trees to which it can provide color contrast in autumn. *Acer tataricum* subsp. *ginnala* is a strong plant and quickly becomes a thick dense shrub 5 m (16 ft.) wide. It may reach 12 m (39 ft.) tall in cultivation. Besides its many useful qualities, this subspecies is also beautiful: the leaf is dark green and pointed, turning purple-red in autumn. Hardy to zone 3.

on unfurling	flowers*
old trunk°	fruits°
leaves in autumn	leaves in autumn*
in autumn (Hemelrijk)	

Acer tataricum subsp. *semenovii*

(Regel & Herder) Murray (1982)

Section: *Ginnala.*

Epithet: *Semenovii,* after Russian botanist N. Z. Semenov (1806–1894).

Origin: Turkmenistan, Uzbekistan, northern Afghanistan, and Kazakhstan.

General appearance: A dense shrub 4 m (13 ft.) tall, with young branches often erect.

Trunk: Light brown-gray on the young shrubs.

Branches: The young shoots are brownish green, glabrous.

Buds: Small, pointed.

Leaves: Three- or five-lobed, smaller than those of *Acer tataricum* subsp. *ginnala,* 3 to 4 cm (1–1.5 in.) long, 2 cm (0.75 in.) wide. Base rather broad, central lobe longer than the others and with a narrow base. Margins strongly toothed. Young leaves often brown-red.

Flowers: Greenish, small, in terminal panicles. Appearing after the leaves.

Fruits: Samaras 2.5 cm (1 in.) long, set more widely apart than those of the type.

The small leaf indicates that the size of this thick bush will also be limited. This maple, nevertheless, is robust and very hardy. Its principal ornamental advantage is the pleasing bright yellow or sometimes orange spring color. It complements the species and subspecies *ginnala* in the landscape.

Acer tataricum subsp. *semenovii* in spring (Hemelrijk)

leaves (CECE)	leaves and young shoots
flowers (BMP)	leaves in autumn
	in autumn

Acer tataricum 'Erythrocarpum'°

CULTIVARS

Acer tataricum 'Erythrocarpum'

This cultivar resembles the species but has much redder fruits, hence the cultivar name.

Acer tataricum subsp. *ginnala* 'Durand Dwarf'

Harkness (1955). United States.

A very compact, dwarf shrub, not more than 50 cm (20 in.) tall. The leaves are smaller than those of the species, soft green in summer and scarlet red in fall. This cultivar has recently started to appear in the catalogs of specialized British nurseries.

Acer tataricum subsp. *ginnala* 'Fire'

Esveld (1983). Netherlands.

A thick shrub, 3 to 4 m (10–13 ft.) tall, dense and very strong, carrying long recumbent branches. The leaves are three-lobed, the central lobe very large. The tough, dark green leaves turn scarlet red in the fall and remain that color for a while.

Acer tataricum subsp. *ginnala* 'Flame'

Esveld (1982). Netherlands.

A small tree or large shrub, with spreading branches. Very hardy, like the species. Not as strong as *Acer tataricum* subsp. *ginnala* 'Fire'. Fall color lasts only a short time.

Acer tataricum subsp. *ginnala* 'Mondy'

Monrovia Nurseries. United States.

A large shrub or small tree, very thick. The leaves have three lobes; they are tough and dark green. Fall color varies between orange-red and orange-yellow. This maple is often available in the trade under the name Red Rhapsody® Amur maple.

Acer tataricum var. *torminaloides* (Hillier)

Acer tataricum var. *torminaloides* in autumn

Acer tataricum 'Rubrum'

Van Houtte (1873). Belgium.

The young leaves of this very old cultivar are blood-red on unfolding, turning green later and reverting to red in the fall. This plant is still available from specialized nurseries.

A. tataricum var. torminaloides

Pax (1886)

Of Russian origin. Some specimens are still found in European arboreta. A dense shrub, 3 to 4 m (10–13 ft.) tall. The leaves have three lobes, the two basal lobes being very small. The glossy green leaves are similar to those of *Acer ginnala*.

Acer tegmentosum

Maximowicz (1857)

Section: *Macrantha.*

Epithet: *Tegmentosus,* covered, hidden.

Origin: Eastern Asia, Siberia, Korea, and Manchuria. Also in the Chinese forests of Mount Hanbai. Discovered in 1850 by Carl Maximowicz in the Amur region of China. Introduced in Europe in 1895.

General appearance: A small tree or large shrub, 4 to 6 m (13–20 ft.) tall, sparsely branched, pendulous.

Trunk: Light green to yellow green, with long white vertical stripes.

Branches: Young shoots have a thick whitish-blue bloom that sets this species apart from its American relative *Acer pensylvanicum.* The young shoots are very erect with few branches.

Buds: Square, with red bilobed scales.

Leaves: Three- or five-lobed, large, 12 to 15 cm (4.75–6 in.). Basal two lobes very small. Bumps may be noted on the axils of the lower ribs. Margins doubly and irregularly toothed.

Flowers: On short peduncles, forming pendent clusters, 7 to 10 cm (2.75–4 in.) long. Appearing in May.

Fruits: Samaras 3 cm (ca. 1 in.) long, the wings almost horizontal.

Propagation: By seed, or by grafting on *Acer pensylvanicum* or *A. rufinerve.*

*A*cer tegmentosum is the Asian equivalent of *A. pensylvanicum,* from which it differs by its very pruinose young shoot. It is hardy but sensitive to late spring frosts. It favors a slightly acidic soil and part shade.

Like *Acer pensylvanicum,* it sheds its leaves in early autumn, which by that time are a pleasing yellow color.

The elegant aspect and beautiful bark make this species suitable for use as a specimen tree, preferably in partly shaded clearings. The epithet (*tegmentosum*) is well chosen, since the leaves entirely cover the branches.

Acer tegmentosum growing in a copse (Les Barres)

leaves	pruinose branches*
flowers	fruits (Les Barres)
trunk°	in autumn (Herkenrode)*

Acer tenellum

Pax (1889)

Acer tenellum (Hillier)

Section: *Platanoidea.*

Epithet: *Tenellus,* delicate, of fine texture.

Origin: China (Yunnan, Sichuan, and Jiangxi provinces).

General appearance: A tree or large shrub, 8 m (26 ft.) tall.

Trunk: Rather lightly colored, smooth, similar to *Acer mono.*

Branches: Dark yellow-brown, rather thin.

Leaves: Three-lobed, the smallest leaves ovate, unlobed, and appearing later in the season. Thin, delicate, slightly broader than long. Lobes triangular, pointed or blunt, mainly at the base. Base truncate or cordate. Petiole reddish, 5 to 8 cm (2–3 in.) long, hanging.

Flowers and fruits: Not observed.

*A*cer tenellum is very rare in cultivation. Fall color is yellow. This species differs entirely from other members of the section by the strongly rounded leaf base and very thin leaf. Borne at the end of a long, slack petiole, the leaf rustles in the slightest breeze. Like *A. palmatum,* it is well suited for small gardens. Hardy to zone 6.

A. triflorum on unfurling
(Westonbirt)

Acer triflorum
Komarov (1901)

Section: *Trifoliata.*

Epithet: *Triflorus,* having three flowers (per inflorescence).

Common name: Three-flowered maple.

Origin: Northern China, Manchuria, and Korea. Introduced in Europe in 1923.

General appearance: A medium-sized, slow-growing tree, reaching 10 to 12 m (33–39 ft.) tall, with a relatively narrow habit and sparse branching.

Trunk: The mature trunk is reddish brown and vertically fissured, peeling off in small scales. Outstanding.

Branches: Slightly drooping. Young shoots are reddish brown and covered with white hairs.

Buds: Pointed, with overlapping scales.

Leaves: Consist of three leaflets, ovate to oval or oblong, lanceolate, 3 to 10 (1–4 in.) long and 3 cm (ca. 1 in.) wide, dark green above, lighter colored below. Center leaflet larger than others, borne on a small but clearly visible petiole. White hairs persist on the central rib of each leaflet, on the underside. Margins entire and not toothed. Petiole reddish, 6 to 8 cm (2.4–3 in.) long.

Flowers: Yellow, in groups of three.

Fruits: On hairy peduncles 2 cm (0.75 in.) long. Samaras 3 to 5 cm (1–2 in.) long, the wings forming an angle of 120 degrees, the nutlets large, 6 to 9 mm (ca. 0.25 in.) in diameter, and covered with pale hairs.

Propagation: Rather easy, by seed, which must be stratified for 2 years, sometimes only one.

*A*cer triflorum becomes a strong and hardy tree, even withstanding light spring frosts. It grows in ordinary garden soils, rich, moist, and not too calcareous. Its juvenile growth is rather rapid. The texture and coloring of the trunk are interesting, but not as spectacular as those of *A. griseum,* which also has trifoliate leaves.

Acer triflorum is generally used in the landscape as a solitary tree, but sometimes as a companion of other lightly colored woody trees, with which its dark foliage provides a nice contrast.

Dependable fall color remains the major trump card of this splendid small tree, which is worthy of decorating the most beautiful gardens.

leaves from Shanghai*	leaves with young shoots
flowers (Herkenrode)	flowers (Hemelrijk)
fruits*	fruits (Herkenrode)
trunk°	leaves in autumn

Acer triflorum in autumn (Hillier)

start of fall coloring | trunk in autumn
in autumn (Herkenrode)

Acer truncatum

Bunge (1833)

Section: *Platanoidea.*

Epithet: *Truncatus,* truncated, cut short obliquely, referring to the leaf base.

Common names: Purple-blow maple, Shantung maple.

Origin: Northern China, Korea, and Japan. The first seeds were shipped to the Royal Botanic Gardens, Kew, in autumn 1881 and planted the following spring.

General appearance: A medium-sized tree reaching 15 to 20 m (50–66 ft.) tall, with a rounded crown. The branching is dense, with branches often intertwined and pendulous.

Trunk: In general, light gray and rough.

Branches: Break off rather easily. Lower branches are very drooping, mainly on young trees.

Buds: Small, brown-black.

Leaves: Five- or seven-lobed, variable in shape, deep glossy green, smooth on both sides. Lobes triangular, the two basal lobes backwards-pointing, the three terminal lobes often have two large teeth. Petiole 5 to 8 cm (2–3 in.) long, containing a milky sap, the base often upright. Young leaves reddish brown when opening.

Flowers: Yellowish green, in umbels 6 to 8 cm (2.4–3 in.) long, first erect then reclining. Appearing with the young leaves.

Fruits: Samaras bronze-red, 3 to 4 cm (1–1.5 in.) long, glabrous, with crescent-shaped wings forming a right or obtuse angle.

Propagation: By grafting on *Acer platanoides.* Easy, by seed. It is the only maple characterized by hypogeal germination (the cotyledons remain underground).

*A*cer truncatum is hardy to zone 5 and grows in average soils. It is vigorous, but its apical growth may be hampered by frost on the immature branches in autumn and on the young shoots in spring. The plant must be well supported to compensate for this inconvenience.

leaves	young shoots in summer
flowers	
trunk (Kew)	in autumn (BMP)

Acer truncatum is very ornamental in all seasons, even in winter, thanks to its light-colored bark and interesting branches. It is a "must" for any park or garden and is best as a solitary specimen in an open site.

In China, this medium-sized maple is used in Beijing and in the province of Shaanxi as a street tree. It also grows in selected British arboreta, where the champion was 13.5 m (45 ft.) tall in 1981.

CULTIVAR

Acer truncatum 'Akikaze nishiki'

A large vigorous tree, with dense branching, growing to 4 to 6 m (13–20 ft.) tall. The leaves have five to seven lobes and are very irregular, each one different from the next. The white spots on the leaf are also very irregular, covering sometimes half the leaf. Relatively large, the leaves are sometimes more than 20 cm (8 in.) wide. The pinkish-red young leaves accentuate the unique appearance of this shrub. Fall color is orange-yellow with hints of red.

A. truncatum, in spring (Hillier)

A. truncatum 'Akikaze nishiki', in spring (Hillier)

A. truncatum 'Akikaze nishiki', leaves (CECE)	*A. truncatum* 'Akikaze nishiki', young shoots
A. truncatum 'Akikaze nishiki', flowers and young fruits	*A. truncatum* 'Akikaze nishiki', fruits (Hillier)

Acer tschonoskii

Maximowicz (1886)

Section: *Macrantha.*

Epithet: *Tschonoskii,* after Japanese botanist Tschonoski (1841–1925), who collected seeds for Carl Maximowicz.

Common name: Tschonoski's maple.

Origin: Japan (Honshu and Hokkaido islands). Introduced in Europe in 1902.

General appearance: A small deciduous tree, 7 to 10 m (23–33 ft.) tall, often shrublike. Graceful habit with curved branches.

Trunk: Dark green, with lighter green vertical striation.

Branches: The young branches are glabrous, glossy red, and drooping.

Buds: On peduncles (winter buds).

Leaves: Five-lobed, rarely seven-lobed, 5 to 10 cm (2–4 in.), glossy, dark green above, lighter colored below. Lobes triangular, ending in long point. Base cordate. Margins strongly and doubly toothed. Petiole 3 to 5 cm (1–2 in.) long, glabrous. Young leaves have red hairs along the main vein on the underside.

Flowers: Yellowish, in groups of 6 to 10, on a terminal raceme, 10 cm (4 in.) long. The peduncles are short and glabrous. Appearing with the leaves.

Fruits: Few in number, upright. Samaras 2 to 3 cm (0.75–1 in.) long, the wings curved, forming an obtuse angle, the hairs light brown.

Propagation: Generally by seed. May be grafted on any maple in section *Macrantha.*

Like most maples with striated bark, *Acer tschonoskii* belongs to section *Macrantha.* The tree is unobtrusive while remaining interesting for small gardens and lawns. Its charming silhouette and five-lobed leaves are reminiscent of *A. micranthum,* as is the beautiful coppery red fall color. The distinction between *A. micranthum* and *A. tschonoskii* is not easy to make. The latter has thicker, fewer fruits, while the former has smaller, more numerous flowers. *Acer tschonoskii* is hardy to zone 5, although sensitive to spring frosts. It is best used as a solitary plant in shade. The branches are red in winter.

flowers (Hillier) | fruits (Herkenrode)

in autumn (Savill)

leaves in autumn

Acer tschonoskii subsp. *koreanum*
Murray (1977)

Section: *Macrantha.*

Epithet: *Koreanus,* from Korea.

Origin: Manchuria and Korea.

General appearance: A small tree or large shrub with upright habit.

Trunk: Gray-brown with vertical striation.

Branches: Reddish with yellow-green stripes in summer, coral red in winter.

Leaves: Five-lobed, 5 to 15 cm (2–6 in.), and dark green. Lobes very acuminate, very long, more so than in subsp. *tschonoskii.* Petiole red.

Flowers: Yellowish, in terminal racemes.

Fruits: In racemes. Samaras 3 cm (ca. 1 in.) long, the wings forming an obtuse angle.

*A*cer tschonoskii subsp. *koreanum* is geographically distinct from *A. tschonoskii,* which is confined to Honshu and Hokkaido Islands in Japan. The subspecies is very hardy (zones 4 and 5). It also is very ornamental in the fall when the leaves turn yellow, but mainly in winter when its coral-red branches are bare.

The old botanical form known as *Acer tschonoskii* var. *rubripes* Komarov (1904) is native to the Sorak Mountains in northeastern South Korea. This variety is distinct from *A. tschonoskii* subsp. *koreanum,* which has narrower, more pointed leaves (see photographs of the leaves of both on the opposite page).

| *A. tschonoskii* subsp. *koreanum,* leaves in spring | *A. tschonoskii* subsp. *koreanum* |
| *A. tschonoskii* var. *rubripes* (Lenoir) | *A. tschonoskii* var. *rubripes* (Lenoir) |

Acer velutinum

Boissier (1846)

Section: *Acer.*

Epithet: *Velutinus,* velvety, referring to the leaves.

Common name: Velvet maple.

Origin: Caucasus and mountains of northern Iran. Introduced in Europe by G. van Volxem.

General appearance: A large tree, to 25 m (82 ft.) tall.

Trunk: Light gray, very smooth, similar to *Betula* (birch).

Branches: Gray-brown, strong. Young twigs are reddish green and glabrous.

Buds: Thick, with overlapping scales. The scales at the tip of a branch are covered with a whitish gray down.

Leaves: Usually five-lobed, sometimes three-lobed, very large, 15 to 25 cm (6–10 in.), dark green, covered below with a velvet-thick light brown down, rib also has brown hairs at the base. Lobes rounded. Base slightly cordate. Margins with large blunt teeth. Petioles long, those downward-growing and bearing a terminal leaf up to 40 cm (16 in.) long. Young leaves have a more tender coloring, sometimes light brown as when unfurling.

Flowers: Yellowish green, forming inflorescences in erect corymbs, 8 to 12 cm (3–4.75 in.) long, at the end of the branches. Appearing after the leaves.

Fruits: Samaras 3 to 6 cm (1–2.4 in.) long, the wings downy and forming an angle between 90 and 120 degrees, the nuts small, downy.

Propagation: By seed, collected and sown in September or October. Germination is easy and plentiful. By grafting on *Acer pseudoplatanus,* but only a few grafts take.

Though hardy to zone 5, *Acer velutinum* needs warmth and a rich soil. It grows rapidly, as the leaf size, which is similar to that of *A. macrophyllum,* indicates.

It hybridizes spontaneously with *Acer pseudoplatanus,* another member of section *Acer.* The two species have similar leaves but different inflorescences.

Acer velutinum grows in large parks in Europe and in some Russian cities is used as a street tree. Its green color is rather commonplace. Fall color is yellow.

young shoots (Westonbirt)	young tree in early autumn (Westonbirt)
young trunk (BMP)	flowers (Kew)
	fruits

Acer velutinum (Westonbirt)

Acer velutinum, flowering in spring (Kew)

Acer velutinum (Everberg, Belgium)*

VARIETIES

Acer velutinum var. *glabrescens*

(Boissier & Bushe) Murray (1969)

As the epithet indicates, the leaves of this variety are glabrous from the time they unfold. They are also smaller than those of the species.

Acer velutinum var. *vanvolxemii*

(Masters) Rehder (1933)

Native to the western Caucasus, this variety grows in wooded mountain valleys. The first seeds were collected and sent to the Royal Botanic Gardens, Kew, by G. van Volxem, hence the epithet. The trunk has a lighter color and is smoother than the trunk of the species. The semi-lobed leaves are slightly glossy green above. The bases of the yellow ribs carry little or no down on the leaf underside. The petiole is yellow and at most 30 cm (12 in.) long. The photographs comparing this variety with the type (see p. 431) show that the latter's leaves are larger but less glossy than those of the variety.

A. velutinum / *A. velutinum* var. *vanvolxemii* (upper side / underside)	
	A. velutinum var. *vanvolxemii*, flowers+
A. velutinum, trunk (Westonbirt)	*A. velutinum* var. *vanvolxemii*, trunk°

Acer ×zoeschense

Pax (1886)

Epithet: *Zoeschensis,* after Zoeschen nurseries, near Berlin.

Origin: Garden. A hybrid of *Acer campestre* × *A. cappadocicum* subsp. *lobelii.*

General appearance: A medium-sized tree, 15 to 20 m (50–66 ft.) tall. Strong branches, slightly fastigiate, forming a broad, airy crown.

Trunk: Light gray-brown, slightly less corky than *Acer campestre.*

Branches: Gray-brown. Young twigs are red-brown, downy, and later glabrous. Older twigs gray-brown.

Leaves: Five- or seven-lobed, 8 to 20 cm (3–8 in.) long, glossy, dark green above, paler and downy below, later glabrous except for some tufts of hair at the axils of the clearly visible red ribs. Lobes pointed, the three main ones having a pair of teeth. Base cordate. Petiole 8 to 10 cm (3–4 in.) long, slightly pubescent, recumbent.

Flowers: Yellow-green, in erect in panicles, 5 to 10 cm (2–4 in.). Appearing after the leaves.

Fruits: Samaras 3 to 5 cm (1–2 in.) long, the wings almost horizontal, the nutlets flattened and downy.

This tree is hardy to zone 5. It can be used as a solitary specimen in the landscape, in small or large parks, or along streets. It has pleasing yellow flowers in the fall. *Acer ×zoeschense* resembles its parents, with minor differences. The leaves are larger and more pointed than those of *A. campestre,* and the angle of the lobes is more defined. The petiole also contains a milky sap and the samaras are horizontal. *Acer ×zoeschense* retains the erect character of the branches of *A. cappadocicum* subsp. *lobelii.*

The Zoeschen nurseries were owned by Count Graf von Schwerin, an eminent specialist in his time, who also selected three cultivars of this maple. The manager and head gardener of the nursery was G. Dieck (1847–1925), creator of the hybrid *Acer ×dieckii,* described earlier.

young shoots	leaves
flowers	flowers
branch with fruits (Dunlow Castle)*	fruits (Hemelrijk)
leaves in autumn (Hemelrijk)	

433

A. ×*zoeschense*, tree (Dunlow Castle)*	*A.* ×*zoeschense*, large trunk (Westonbirt)
A. ×*zoeschense* in autumn (Westonbirt)	*A.* ×*zoeschense* in autumn (Hemelrijk)

Acer ×zoeschense 'Annae'
Schwerin (1911)

Acer ×zoeschense 'Annae' in autumn

General appearance: A medium-sized tree with a rounded, spreading crown.

Branches: The young twigs are brilliant brown-red.

Leaves: Five-lobed, large, 8 to 12 cm (3–4.75 in.), thick, somewhat tough, almost glossy purple-red on opening, then green with a dark red sheen in the summer. The upper surface retains its brilliant aspect, the under surface is downy. Edges slightly wavy.

Flowers: Yellow, in upright spikes.

Fruits: Samaras horizontal, like those of *Acer campestre.*

Propagation: Easy, by layering, or by grafting on *Acer campestre* or *A. platanoides.*

An old, medium-sized cultivar, currently very popular as it is well suited to urban settings. It tolerates pollution and can be used in place of the American *Acer platanoides* cultivars, since the width of its crown is in proportion to the height of the tree.

This maple is very appreciated in the landscape for its dark red leaves, which are followed by abundant yellow flowers.

Fall color is a pleasing orange.

A. ×zoeschense in spring | *A. ×zoeschense*, leaves

A. ×zoeschense 'Annae' (Bokrijk)

437

Korean forest in autumn (Fotostock photograph)

MAPLES IN THE LANDSCAPE

The diversity of sizes, shapes, and colors among maples is such that an infinite number of landscape designs is possible; in fact, it is possible to use these plants exclusively for the creation of a garden (Carpenter et al. 1975). Such is the place that maples have in the landscape. Indeed, the family Aceraceae includes some 750 taxa, grouped in species, subspecies, and cultivars, widely distributed in the Northern Hemisphere.

IN NATURE

The flora of Asia is the richest and the most diversified flora of the Northern Hemisphere, as is well supported by the numerous maple species native to this continent.

The mountains of China are native to many species of trees, shrubs, conifers, and perennials. At least half the *Acer* species are dispersed among species of *Aralia, Camellia, Cornus* (dogwood), *Larix* (larch), *Osmanthus* (Chinese holly), *Picea* (spruce), *Pinus* (pine), *Rhododendron, Viburnum* (arrow-wood), and other genera.

The numerous volcanic islands of Japan are inhabited by groups of maple species scattered among the mountains. Among them are *Acer japonicum, A. palmatum, A. rufinerve,* and *A. sieboldianum*—all easily recognizable in autumn. Venerated by the Japanese, maples may also be found in every public or private garden.

In the United States, large areas of forest, which include maple trees interspersed with species of *Betula* (birch), *Liriodendron* (tulip tree), and *Quercus* (oak), display flamboyant colors during Indian summer. These forests are currently being monitored closely, since they are threatened by industrial pollution. They constitute a timber reserve and, occasionally, provide a source of maple syrup, but they also serve as a reminder of the area's heritage and attract large numbers of enthusiastic tourists each autumn. In other parts of the United States, the fall colors of *Acer negundo* and *A. saccharinum* may be admired, along with *A. circinatum,* vine maple, a small spectacular tree generally found on riverbanks in the wild.

In Europe, the maple forests no longer exist, except for a few populations of *Acer cappadocicum* in the Caucasus and in Turkey. The dominant species in large forests are big conifers or hardwood trees, such as *Quercus, Fagus* (beech), and *Fraxinus* (ash). *Acer platanoides* and *A. pseudoplatanus* are widely scattered and few in number. They are infrequent in the landscape, even if some beautiful specimens are very ornamental in spring and fall.

Japanese maples unfolding in spring, accompanied by flowering magnolias (Savill)

IN CULTIVATION

PARKS AND GARDENS

The primary inspiration in designing a garden derives from the desire to reproduce plant associations encountered in nature or to create particular settings, such as are often encountered in English parks. Parks and arboreta also serve as sources of inspiration for combining plants in various ways, whether by collection or by theme. The large number of maple species and cultivars allows us to create elaborate landscapes, by selecting from a wide choice of plants available commercially. This selection must, of course, be made in accordance with a given plant's soil and climatic requirements. Finally, the overall harmony of the planting should take precedence over the rarity or beauty of individual plants.

Large Parks and Gardens

Large maples are best suited in a typical English park along with other, large classical trees, such as *Betula, Castanea* (chestnut), *Quercus, Tilia* (linden), and conifers. The latter are often numerous in the landscape and sited in the background to provide contrast with plants in the foreground. Each season brings its parade of new colors, and a judicious selection of plants will allow a landscaper to optimize their ornamental potential.

Spring color associations of large trees are more complex than appears at first thought. In fact, the flowering and leaf unfolding periods of the selected plants must overlap. Among the trees generally associated with maples, those with spectacular new leaf color include *Cercidiphyllum japonicum* (Katsura tree), *Quercus phellos* (willow oak), *Q. ludoviciana*, *Q. warburgii* (Cambridge oak), and *Magnolia* and *Castanea* species. "Must-have" maples, such as *Acer shirasawanum* 'Aureum', *A. pseudoplatanus* 'Brillantissimum', and *A. palmatum* 'Deshōjō', deserve a well-thought-out location.

The summer color of most trees used in large parks is often very uniform and rather dark, especially at the end of the season. All-purple varieties are overused today. A better option is to select maples of various sizes, displaying lighter and yellowish hues. Some possibilities are *Acer cappadocicum* 'Aureum', *A. saccharinum* 'Lutescens', and the large cultivars of *A. platanoides* and *A. pseudoplatanus*. Likewise, the gray glaucous leaf underside of *A. rubrum*, *A. saccharinum*, or *A. pycnanthum* will accentuate color contrasts while remaining inconspicuous.

In autumn, the succession of coloring periods must be considered carefully to retain bright colors until winter. The earliest fall color can be obtained from *Acer rubrum* 'Schlesingeri', the latest from *A. saccharum* subsp. *floridanum* and *A. maximowiczianum*.

In general, maples provide a succession of colors by themselves, but they also are good companions for other large, colorful plants, such as *Liquidambar* (sweet gum), *Nyssa sylvatica* (black gum), *Quercus shumardii* (Shumard oak), and *Fraxinus excelsior* 'Jaspidea' (common European ash), or even the more colorful *Taxodium distichum* (swamp cypress), *Metasequoia glyptostroboides* (dawn redwood), and *Zelkova serrata* (Japanese zelkova). The yellower tones of *Fagus*, *Larix*, and *Nothofagus* (southern beech) or the pink hue of *Cecidiphyllum japonicum* fill in agreeably.

As is true for any planting, the largest trees should be sited first. Large maples can be used in a large park, among them *Acer cappadocicum*, *A. platanoides*, *A. pseudoplatanus*, and *A. saccharum*. Others, such as *A. rubrum* and *A. saccharinum*, can be placed close to a body of water, by themselves, or in small groups. Medium-sized trees and large shrubs from 4 to 12 m (13–39 ft.) tall are very often under-represented or even absent in large, old parks. Yet, this category of plants includes numerous species of *Acer* as well as *Carpinus* (hornbeam), *Castanea*, *Corylus avellana* (hazelnut), *Fagus*, *Magnolia*, *Quercus*, and *Prunus* (cherry). These are too seldom encountered, although they complement maples with their bark or foliage color, and contrast well with large background trees. Among medium-sized maples are *A. cissifolium*, *A. japonicum*, *A. sieboldianum*, *A. triflorum*, and *A. truncatum*, all of which can be used as isolated specimens or in groups.

In Thematic Compositions

Maples are useful in theme gardens. The "flower" theme is too often neglected. Many maple species, however, have very interesting flowers in spring. The earliest to bloom are members of section *Rubra;* the last to bloom is *Acer nipponicum.* Late-blooming *Hamamelis* ×*intermedia* 'Primavera' (witch-hazel), *Cornus mas* (Cornelian cherry), *Parrotia persica* (ironwood), *Corylus sieboldiana* and 'Contorta' (Japanese hazel), and *Forsythia suspensa* are excellent companions of early-blooming maples. Later in the season, the members of section *Platanoides* produce abundant flowers, especially *A. opalus* and *A. dieckii,* whose yellowish flowers appear just before the leaves unfold. In April, the elegant flowers of *Carpinus betulus* (common hornbeam) harmonize beautifully with those of *A. japonicum* and its varieties, while most other maples of section *Palmata* go best with *Rhododendron* and *Camellia* species.

The "bark" theme is suited to certain maples. Good companions for these include *Arbutus unedo* (strawberry tree), *Cornus, Fagus, Pinus, Prunus* (cherry), *Salix* (willow), and *Stewartia.* The bark of some maple species changes color in winter. For instance, the branches of

Acer palmatum 'Ōsakazuki' and *Hamamelis* (witch-hazel) in autumn (Savill)

Acer palmatum 'Sango kaku' with other fall-coloring foliage, including *Hydrangea paniculata* at the lower right (Savill)

Acer pensylvanicum, A. mono, and *A. argutum* become bright red in winter. Similarly, *A. griseum* and the snake bark maples have particularly unique bark. They are especially useful for brightening a garden in winter, since the vivid, contrasting colors of their bark and branches light up at the first appearance of the sun.

Maples also have a place in gardens with a "permanent plant" theme, such as those made up of bamboos, *Camellia,* conifers, *Ilex* (holly), *Laurus nobilis* (laurel), *Quercus, Taxus* (yew), and *Rhododendron.* Here maples with pale or colored bark, such as *Acer truncatum* or *A. caesium,* are recommended, and especially those of section *Macrantha—A. rufinerve, A. davidii* and its cultivars, *A. pensylvanicum,* or *A. ×conspicuum* 'Phoenix'. The green monotony of evergreen plants can be alleviated by selecting maples with colored bark or flamboyant fall color, such as is provided by the varieties of *A. palmatum.*

The "berry" theme is suited to maples with remarkable fruit production. For example, *Acer cappadocicum* subsp. *sinicum* produces splendid fruit in May, and *A. tataricum* in July. Generally, however, fall is the time of year that maples with colored fruit are most appreciated as companions to *Euonymus europaeus* (spindle tree), *Photinia* (Christmas berry), and *Viburnum.* Maples with colorful fall fruit include *A. capillipes, A. cissifolium, A. negundo* 'Kelly's Gold', and *A. palmatum* 'Bloodgood' and 'Ōsakazuki'. Even fairly large maples can be used for this purpose, including *A. heldreichii* subsp. *trautvetteri* and *A. pseudoplatanus* 'Erythrocarpum'.

Acer platanoides in fall colors (Fotostock)

Average-sized Parks and Gardens

In classical English gardens, only a few large maple trees are planted in the average-sized landscape, and these are preferably very ornamental or rare, such as *Acer diabolicum, A. mono,* or *A. pensylvanicum.* In more formal gardens, the best maples are slow-growing trees, such as *A. griseum* or *A. triflorum.* The columnar habit of *A. saccharum* 'Temple's Upright' or the rounded habit of *A. platanoides* 'Globosum' offers interesting possibilities for a medium-sized landscape, where these maples are planted along a path or road.

Small Gardens

A small garden is generally defined as one with an area of less than 250 square meters, although there is no definite rule in this matter. Because the primary limiting factor in such a garden is available room, it is indispensable to select plants judiciously for their erect, upright, narrow, dwarf, or globe-shaped habit. Many cultivars of *Acer palmatum* are perfectly suited for this purpose, such as 'Dissectum Garnet', 'Filigree', 'Inaba shidare', 'Nicholsonii', or 'Shishi gashira'. Other possibilities are *A. carpinifolium* 'Esveld Select', *A. circinatum* 'Little Gem', *A. distylum,* and *A. micranthum.* Slow-growing maples, such as *A. griseum, A. mandshuricum, A. monspessulanum, A. shirasawanum,* or *A. triflorum,* are best reserved for privileged locations, where their silhouette is displayed to advantage and accompanied by perennials or ground-covering plants. Finally, maples are an integral part of small gardens and with time grow into very characteristic, lovable shapes. Two such maples are *A. palmatum* 'Dissectum Ornatum' and 'Shishi gashira'.

SPECIAL USES

URBAN SITES

Pollution remains the major threat to plants in city gardens, whether large or small. Maples are fairly resistant to urban pollution, due to the thin protective layer that covers their leaves. Few maples, however, tolerate the compacted soil in which many street trees are grown. Some selections of *Acer rubrum* are more tolerant of such conditions; among them are 'October Glory'

Maples in autumn in an American forest (Fotostock)

and 'Scanlon'. Two other factors that limit the selection of street trees are the need for a narrow, compact silhouette and for a color that is harmonious with neighboring buildings. Among maples most suited for such conditions are *A. campestre, A. negundo* 'Auratum' or 'Aureomarginatum', and *A. platanoides* 'Crimson Sentry'.

Utilitarian Applications

Some maples have specific traits that make them useful for particular functions. *Acer campestre* has running roots, which make it suitable for planting in embankments alongside roads. *Acer stachyophyllum,* which produces suckers, can be used for the same purpose. *Acer circinatum* is useful for holding riverbanks or lake shores, while *A. rubrum* and *A. saccharinum* are suitable for very humid areas.

In Large or Small Containers

The growing of small maples is generally reserved for specialists or very sophisticated amateurs. Like other woody plants, maples can be kept quite small using very specialized techniques described in the literature on bonsai.

Cultivating maples in large or small pots is based on the same principle followed in bonsai, namely, limiting and shaping plant growth by interventions on the roots and the branches. The selection of a given species is determined by the rigor of the surrounding conditions, generally characterized by important temperature variations and drafts. Few maples withstand these conditions. *Acer tataricum* subsp. *ginnala, A. campestre* and its cultivars, and *A. monspessulanum* are exceptions.

In less humid or less exposed environments, most cultivars of *Acer palmatum* may be grown in containers, together with certain dwarf maples, such as *A. circinatum* 'Little Gem' or *A. campestre* 'Nanum'. The dwarfing tendency of the last two maples is emphasized in container culture. For *A. palmatum,* a definite natural equilibrium must be maintained between the volume of the available substrate and the desired adult size.

Bonsai in autumn (CECE)

Maples displaying fall colors in Japan (Lake Hibara)*

This substrate will have to be enriched, but in a measured amount, without excess, to control plant growth. Otherwise, frost, which is a greater problem for container-grown plants than for their in-ground counterparts, may destroy the young unripe shoots.

ON GOLF COURSES

By their very sophisticated nature, certain maples are perfectly suited as accents in public places where a special plant is required. A golf course is made more attractive when the beautiful, varied, and large cultivars of *Acer palmatum,* such as 'Elegans', 'Heptalobum', 'Katsura', 'Koreanum', and 'Linearilobum', are planted inside or on its boundary. If the course needs protection from wind, effective windbreakers may be provided by large, strong shrubs such as *A. campestre, A. tataricum,* and *A. tataricum* subsp. *ginnala.* Interplanting these last three with *Amelanchier* (serviceberry), *Crataegus* (hawthorn), *Euonymus, Hydrangea, Photinia,* or *Viburnum* also provides excellent fall color. Moreover, some color spots on a golf course may constitute landmarks useful in determining distances and differentiating between the fairways. By selecting characteristic shapes, rounded as in *A. maximowiczianum, A. opalus, A. truncatum,* or *A. platanoides,* or fastigiate as in *A. saccharum* 'Temple's Upright' or *A. cappadocicum* subsp. *lobelii,* the landscaper can create interesting focal points at strategic locations.

In summary, maples may be integrated into any kind of landscape and provide a key element. Japanese, English, and American parks and arboreta would certainly not be as beautiful as they are if maples were absent. The same is true for continental Europe, where interest in maples is rightfully growing year after year.

GLOSSARY

Acuminate Tapering gradually to a point

Anther That part of the stamen carrying the pollen

Axil The angle formed on the upper side by the union of leaf stalk and stem, or by the chief veins and midrib

Axillary Springing from an axil. Usually applied to an inflorescence arising at the axil of a stem, as distinct from the end

Biserrate With a row of doubly serrate teeth

Bloom A waxy covering. See *pruinose*

Bract A leaflike organ or a degenerate leaf from whose axil the flower or inflorescence is produced

Bud (for grafting) An undeveloped shoot with some bark that is grafted on a rootstock to produce a new plant

Compound Having several parts

Copse A thicket of small trees originating from shoots or root suckers

Cordate (of leaf base) With two rounded lobes, separated by a sinus; heart-shaped

Corolla The inner envelope of the flower composed of petals

Corymb A flat-topped inflorescence in which the outer flowers open first

Crenate Scalloped

Cultivar A group of cultivated plants which are clearly distinguished by specific characters that are retained when the plants are reproduced

Cutting A branch or other plant section that is cut from a plant and grown into a new plant

Deciduous (leaves) Dropping in autumn

Dentate Prominently toothed, the teeth directed outwards, as on the margin of a leaf

Denticulate Minutely dentate

Dichogamy Producing male and female flowers at different times, thus preventing self-pollination

Dioecious Having male and female flowers on separate individuals. Compare *monoecious*

Entire (margin) Whole, neither toothed nor lobed

Evergreen (leaves) Remaining on a plant through winter

Fastigiate (habit) Having a sharply erect growth habit, with branches almost parallel to the main stem

Forma, formae A unit of taxonomy below a variety, with often one single distinctive character (abbr. f.)

Genus, genera A unit of taxonomy consisting of a group of species with common characteristics

Glabrous Smooth, without hair or down

Glaucous Covered with a white, blue-white, gray-blue, or silver-gray bloom

Hardy Able to withstand a cold climate

Hermaphrodite Bisexual, having male (stamens) and female (pistils) parts in the same flower

Hybrid A plant resulting from a cross between two genetically dissimilar plants, usually belonging to two different species

Hypogeal germination Germination in which the seed leaves (cotyledons) remain below ground.

In most maples, the cotyledons emerge from the ground and function as true leaves (known as epigeal germination)

Inflorescence A group of flowers

Lanceolate Lance-shaped; applied to leaves several times longer than wide and broadest below the middle

Layering A propagation method in which a new plant is created at the spot where a branch contacts the soil and takes root

Leaflet A division of a compound leaf

Lenticel A corky or wartlike spot on the surface of bark through which gases pass

Lobe A division of the leaf, separated from adjacent divisions by sinuses

Lobulate Faintly lobed

Lobule A small lobe

Midrib The primary or central vein of a leaf

Monoecious Having male and female flowers on the same individual. Compare *dioecious*

Nut, Nutlet A small one-seeded fruit

Obtuse Ending in a blunt or rounded point

Obtuse angle More than 90 degrees but less than 180 degrees

Opposite (leaves) Arranged on both sides of a stem in pairs

Ovary The part of the flower enclosing the ovules that ultimately develop into seeds; the lower part of the pistil, as distinct from the style or stigma

Ovate Egg-shaped in outline

Ovoid Resembling an egg in shape

Ovule The body in the ovary (usually one of many) that, after fertilization, develops into a seed

Palmate (leaves) With lobes or veins radiating from a common point, like fingers on a hand; palm-like

Panicle A branched inflorescence; strictly, a branched raceme, as distinct from a single raceme or spike

Parthenocarpic Developing fruit without fertilization, such fruits being seedless

Pedicel The stalk of an individual flower or fruit

Peduncle The stalk of an inflorescence; the portion of a stem that supports a solitary flower

Perianth The floral envelope

Pericarp The envelope of the seed

Petal A division (modified leaf) of the corolla

Petiole The stalk of a leaf, by which it is attached to the branch or twig

Pistil An ovary with its style(s) (if present) and stigma; the complete female organ of a flower

Pollen The powder (male cells) formed in the anthers

Polymorphic Variable in habit or botanical characters

Pruinose Covered with a waxlike substance. See *bloom*

Pubescent Covered with short, soft hairs

Raceme An inflorescence in which the flowers are about equally stalked, and borne on a more or less elongated axis; the oldest flowers at the base, the youngest at the top

Rib A vein, nerve

Rootstock The plant on which buds or grafts are inserted and the part providing the root system for the new plant

Running (roots) Roots growing horizontally, just below the surface

Samara, samaras The winged fruit of maple, consisting of a nutlet and a wing

Seedling A young plant grown from seed

Semi-evergreen (leaves) Having some leaves that fall in autumn, while others remain on the tree until the new leaves unfold

Sepal A division of the outer envelope of the flower, attached below the petals

Serrate Having large irregular teeth

Sessile Not stalked

Shrub A multitrunked woody plant, smaller than a tree (in general less than 4.5 m or 14.5 ft. tall)

Sinus The opening between two lobes or two teeth of a leaf

Species A unit of taxonomy consisting of a group of plants with common characteristics that are retained generation after generation (abbr. sp.)

Spike A simple inflorescence, formed by an axis carrying sessile flowers

Stamen The male organ of the flower

Stigma The opening at the end of the style

Stipule A bractlike growth at the base of a petiole

Stratify To arrange seeds in layers, alternating with sand or soil, so they remain viable until they are ready for planting

Striated Striped

Style A component of the pistil, the female organ of a flower

Subspecies A unit of taxonomy below species (abbr. subsp.)

Sucker A shoot issuing from the root of a tree, growing close to the original plant

Taxon, taxa A taxonomic group of any rank, such as a species, family, or class

Taxonomy The science of classifying living (or extinct) species

Tomentose Covered with down

Toothed Having teeth; applied to margins

Trifoliolate Composed of three leaflets

Truncate Abruptly terminated as if cut cleanly straight across

Type The typical representative of a taxon

Umbel An inflorescence in which several stalked flowers are clustered at the end of a common stalk

Unfurling Opening of the buds, followed by the development of the leaves

Variety A unit of taxonomy below a species; strictly, a natural variation within a species; broadly, a form produced by cultivation (abbr. var.)

BOTANICAL DRAWINGS

Leaves: leaflets

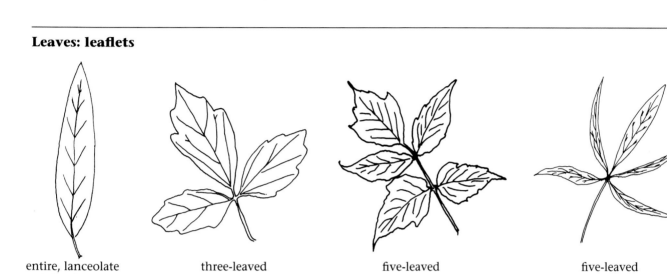

entire, lanceolate
A. laevigatum

three-leaved
A. griseum

five-leaved
A. negundo

five-leaved
A. pentaphyllum

Leaves: lobes

three-lobed
A. monspessulanum

five-lobed
A. platanoides

seven-lobed
A. sieboldianum

nine-lobed
A. circinatum

Leaves: margins

entire   ciliate   lobed   lobulate   dentate   denticulate

serrate   serrulate   biserrate   incised   crenate   crenulate

Flowers: cross section

Source: F. Pax, *Aceraceae*

A. saccharum, female flower

A. saccharum, male flower

Flowers

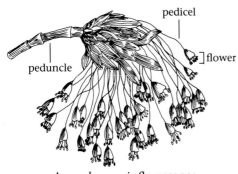

pedicel

peduncle

flower

A. saccharum, inflorescence

Source: F. Pax, *Aceraceae*

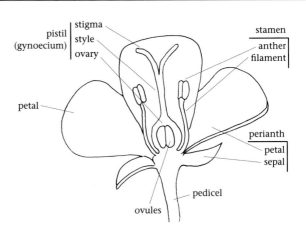

pistil
(gynoecium)

stigma

style

ovary

stamen

anther

filament

petal

perianth

petal

sepal

pedicel

ovules

Flowers: inflorescences

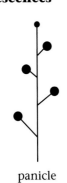

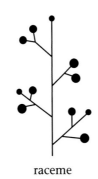

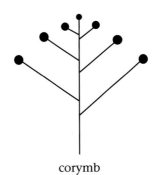

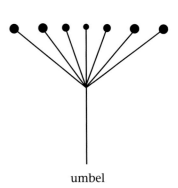

spike

panicle

raceme

corymb

umbel

Branch

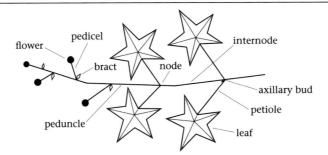

flower

pedicel

bract

peduncle

node

internode

axillary bud

petiole

leaf

452

DISCOVERERS AND BOTANISTS

Bean, William Jackson, 1863–1947.

English horticulturist and author. Worked at the Royal Botanic Gardens, Kew, for 46 years. A worldwide authority on plant adaptation and the cultivation of exotic plants and trees. Grew many Chinese plants from seed shipped to him by Augustine Henry, Francis Kingdon-Ward, and Ernest H. Wilson. Author of the four-volume *Trees and Shrubs Hardy in the British Isles*.

Carrière, Èlie Abel, 1818–1896.

Head gardener of nursery at the nursery of the Paris Museum, where many plants and seeds, brought back by missionaries, were cultivated. Afterwards, chief editor of the *Revue Horticole,* which published articles about the ornamental plants cultivated in the museum's gardens.

David, Jean Pierre Armand, 1826–1900.

French missionary and naturalist. Traveled through most of China, Mongolia, and Tibet from 1862 on. Tireless explorer and collector of zoological and botanical specimens. One of the principal suppliers of dry seeds to the Paris Museum.

Fang, Wen-pei, 1899–1983.

Chinese botanist. Collected more than 20,000 species, of which more than 100 were new. Specialized in Chinese maples and rhododendrons.

Feng, Kuo-mei, 1917– .

Botanist and plant collector. Developed a deep knowledge of Chinese plants and trees, particularly from the province of Yunnan.

Forrest, George, 1873–1932.

Scottish plant collector and traveler. One of the most astonishing plant collectors. Worked primarily in China, in the province of Yunnan, where he gathered an enormous quantity of plants and seeds. Introduced into Europe many plants and trees originally discovered by the French missionary Pierre Jean Marie Delavay.

Gagnepain, François, 1866–1952.

French botanist. Specialized in the Asiatic species at the Paris Museum.

Giraldi, Giuseppe, 1848–1901.

Italian missionary and plant collector. During the last 13 years of his life collected more than 5000 dried plants and seeds in the Chinese province of Shaanxi, including *Acer giraldii*, which he sent to the botanical garden of Florence.

Henry, Augustine, 1857–1930.

Irish physicist, plant collector, botanist, and author. Served in the Imperial Chinese Maritime Custom Service and reputedly sent from China more than 150,000 specimens of dried plants and seeds, including many new species and genera. Most of his major discoveries were introduced with success by Ernest H. Wilson.

Hers, Joseph, 1884–1965.
Belgian amateur dendrologist. Discovered *Acer hersii,* now known as *A. davidii* subsp. *grosseri.*

de Jong, Piet C.
Dutch taxonomist and dendrologist. In charge of the Experimental Research Center of Boskoop, Netherlands. Specialist of the genera *Acer, Betula, Euonymus,* and *Lilium.*

Kingdon-Ward, Francis, 1885–1958.
English plant collector, explorer, geographer, and author. Traveled extensively through China, Burma, Tibet, and Assam. Author of many books about his travels and a co-worker of George Forrest.

Komarov, Vladimir L., 1869–1945.
Russian explorer and botanist. Traveled through eastern Siberia, Manchuria, and North Korea. Collected more than 6000 dried plants and seeds, which he sent to the botanical gardens in Saint Petersburg.

Lancaster, Roy, 1937– .
English collector, author, and dendrologist. A world-renowned horticulturist. Author of *Travels in China: A Plantman's Paradise,* a chronicle of his botanical journeys, and other books such as *Hillier's Manual of Trees and Shrubs.*

Linnaeus, Carl, 1707–1778.
Swedish naturalist. Classified plants into 24 classes, now abandoned. His binomial nomenclature by genera and species is still in use.

Maries, Charles, 1851–1902.
English plant collector. Traveled in China, Taiwan, and Japan, from which he brought back many ornamental plants and trees, especially maples.

Maximowicz, Carl, 1827–1891.
Russian botanist. A worldwide authority on Asiatic flora. Successfully imported many dried specimens and seeds to the Saint Petersburg botanical garden. Became director of that garden.

Murray, Albert E., 1935– .
American botanist. Specialized in the genus *Acer.* Author of numerous publications on American maples, including "New Combinations of Asiatic species of *Acer*" published in the *Morris Arboretum Bulletin.*

Pax, Ferdinand A., 1858–1942.
German botanist and taxonomist.

Rehder, Alfred, 1863–1949.

American botanist. Professor of dendrology at Harvard University. The top authority on trees, particularly those of Chinese origin. Author of numerous publications, including important articles describing the collections of Ernest H. Wilson and Joseph Rock, and the book *Manual of Cultivated Trees and Shrubs*.

Sargent, Charles Sprague, 1841–1927.

American dendrologist, botanist, horticulturist, and plant collector. Founder and first director of the Arnold Arboretum. Wrote about collecting in North America in *Silva of North America*. Also traveled in China. Built Arnold Arboretum into one of the important arboreta of its period because of its diversity of plants, and particularly those from China.

Schwerin, Fritz Kurt Alexander von, 1856–1934.

German botanist and author of numerous publications on the genus *Acer*.

Veitch, Sir Harry James, 1840–1924.

English horticulturist and nurseryman. Sponsor of several expeditions to the Far East, including one by Ernest H. Wilson. Organized in 1912, with great success, the first Royal International Horticultural Exhibition.

Vilmorin, Auguste Louis Maurice Levêque de, 1849–1918.

French nurseryman. Founder of the Arboretum des Barres, south of Paris. Like Veitch in England, he is responsible for the diffusion in French gardens of exotic plants collected by French missionaries from around the world.

Wilson, Ernest Henry, 1876–1930.

English plant collector, traveler, and author. One of the most important plant collectors. First sent to China by Veitch. Director of the Arnold Arboretum. Introduced approximately 1000 new plants to Western gardens, some of which had been discovered by Augustine Henry.

HARDINESS ZONE MAPS

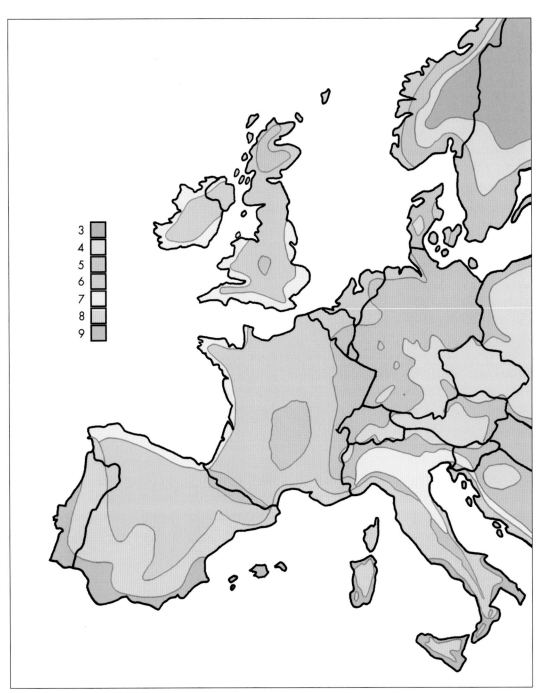

Map of European hardiness zones

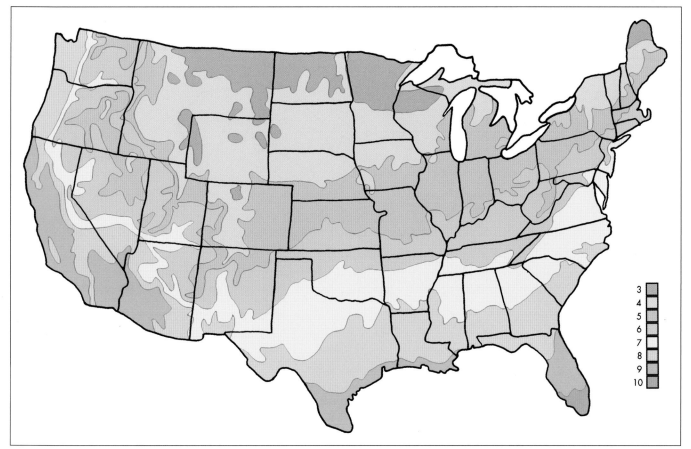

Map of U.S. hardiness zones

Hardiness zones are based on the minimum temperature for each area. The maps are derived from the U.S. Department of Agriculture (USDA) map, which defines 11 zones. This scale has also been adapted to the map of Europe.

Below −40°C	Zones 1 and 2	Below −40°F
−34 to −40°C	Zone 3	−40 to −30°F
−29 to −34°C	Zone 4	−30 to −20°F
−23 to −29°C	Zone 5	−20 to −10°F
−17 to −23°C	Zone 6	−10 to 0°F
−12 to −17°C	Zone 7	0 to 10°F
−7 to −12°C	Zone 8	10 to 20°F
−1 to −7°C	Zone 9	20 to 30°F
4 to −1°C	Zone 10	30 to 40°F

POLITICAL MAP OF CHINA

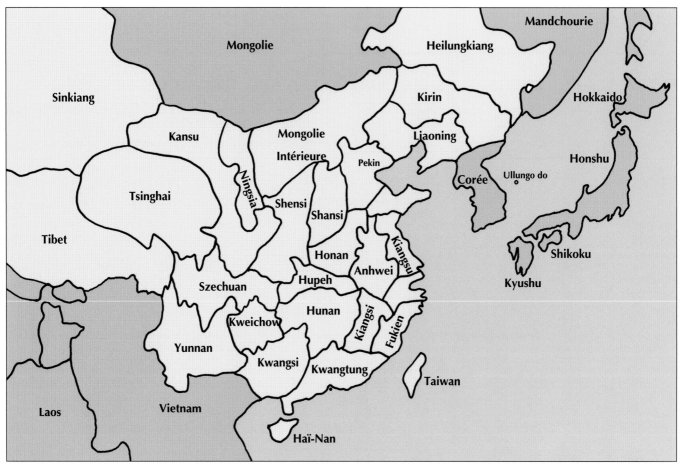

Chinese provinces

USEFUL ADDRESSES

AUSTRALIA

Gaibor's Nursery
Great Western Highway
Wentworth Falls, New South
Wales 2782
Tel: (047) 57 1223

Tristania Park Nurseries
28 Honour Avenue
Macedon, Victoria 3440
Tel: (03) 5426 1667

Yamina Rare Plants
25 Moores Road
Monbulk, Victoria 3793
Tel: (03) 9756 6535

BELGIUM

Pépinières BMP
Rue de Lens-St-Remy 5
B-4250 Geer
Tel: 32 (0) 19 58 88 64
Fax: 32 (0) 19 58 88 28

Pépinières CECE (Benoît Choteau) (Binche)
Avenue Leopold III 12
B-7130 Bray
Tel: 32 (0) 64 33 82 15
Fax: 32 (0) 64 36 94 62

Pépinières PAVIA
Roterijstraat 18
B-8540 Deerlijk
Tel & fax: 32 (0) 56 71 78 76

FRANCE

Association des Parcs Botaniques de France
15 bis, rue de Marignan
F-75008 Paris
Tel: 33 (0) 1 42 56 26 07
Fax: 33 (0) 1 42 22 54 56

GERMANY

Baumschule Schwendemann
77933 Lahr
Pestalozzistraße 1
Tel: 49 (89) 07821-32018
Fax: 49 (89) 07821-1867

ITALY

Nurseries Giraldi
I-20041 Agrate Brianza
Via delle Industrie, 21
Milan
Tel: 39 (0) 39 65 08 57
Fax: 39 (0) 39 65 38 26

NETHERLANDS

Firma C. Esveld
Rijneveld 72, NL-2771
XS Boskoop
Tel: 31 (0) 172 21 32 89
Fax: 31 (0) 172 21 57 14

NEW ZEALAND

Blue Mountain Nurseries
99 Bushy Hill Street
Tapanui
Tel: (03) 204 8250
Fax: (03) 204 8278

UNITED KINGDOM

Hillier Nurseries
Ampfield House
Ampfield, Romsey
Hampshire SO51 9PA
Tel: 44 (0) 1794 36 87 33
Fax: 44 (0) 1794 36 88 55

Mallet Court Nursery
Curry Mallet, Taunton
Somerset TA3 6SY
Tel: 44 (0) 1823 48 07 48
Fax: 44 (0) 1823 35 28 26

UNITED STATES

Boething Treeland Farms
2923 Alpine Road
Portola Valley, California
94028
Tel: (650) 851-4770
Fax: (650) 851-4252

Forestfarm Nursery
990 Tetherow Road
Williams, Oregon 97544
Tel: (541) 846-7269
Fax: (541) 846-6963

Mountain Maples
P.O. Box 1329
Laytonville, California 95454
Tel: (707) 984-6522
Fax: (707) 984-7433

PLANT LOCATIONS

BELGIUM
Arenberg Park, Brabant Province
Bokrijk Arboretum, Limburg Province
Domaine de la Berbère (private park), Hainaut Province
Fumal (private park)
Hemelrijk Arboretum (privately owned by Jelena de Belder), Antwerp Province
Herkenrode Gardens (privately owned by Philippe de Spoelberch), Brabant Province
Mariemont Arboretum, Hainaut Province
Pépinières BMP, Antoine le Hardÿ de Beaulieu, Liege Province
Pépinières CECE, Benoît Choteau, Hainaut Province
Ravenstein Golf Club, Brabant Province
Rendeux Arboretum, Luxembourg Province
Rond-Chêne Arboretum, Liege Province
Tervueren Arboretum, Brabant Province

ENGLAND
Batsford Arboretum, Moreton-in-Marsh, Gloucestershire
Great Park, Windsor, Berkshire
Hergest Croft Arboretum, Kington, Herefordshire
Sir Harold Hillier Gardens and Arboretum, Romsey, Hampshire
Lanhydrock Arboretum, Cornwall
Royal Botanic Gardens, Kew, Surrey
Savill and Valley Gardens, Windsor, Surrey
Sheffield Park, Uckfield, East Sussex
Wakehurst Place Garden, Ardingly, West Sussex
Westonbirt Arboretum, Tetbury, Gloucestershire
Winkworth Arboretum, Godalming, Surrey

FRANCE
Arboretum des Barres, Nogent-sur-Vernisson
Collège de la Berlière, Houtaing
Serre de la Madone garden, Menton

IRELAND
Dunlow Castle, Beaufort, Killarney

NETHERLANDS
Trompenburg Arboretum, Rotterdam
Von Gimborn Arboretum, Doorn

UNITED STATES
Bamboo Farm and Coastal Gardens, University of Georgia, Savannah
Bartholomew's Cobble, Ashley Falls, Sheffield, Massachusetts

BIBLIOGRAPHY

Baudouin, Jean-Claude, *Les arbres feuillus,* Ministère de la Région Wallonne, 1993.

Bean, William J., *Trees and Shrubs Hardy in the British Isles,* John Murray, 1996.

Burnie, David, *Les secrets de l'arbre,* Gallimard, 1996.

Carpenter, Philip L., Theodore D. Walker, and Frederick O. Lanphear, *Plants in the Landscape,* W. H. Freeman and Company, 1975.

de Belder, Jelena, and Xavier Misonne, *Arbres et arbustes pour parcs et jardins,* La Maison Rustique, 1994.

de Spoelberch, Philippe, and Jean-Claude Baudouin, *Arbres de Belgique, Inventaire dendrologique 1988–1992,* Fondation Spoelberch-Artois, 1992.

Hillier Nurseries, *The Hillier Manual of Trees and Shrubs,* 6th ed., David & Charles, 1991.

Keenan, J., "George Forrest, 1873–1932," *Journal of the Royal Horticultural Society* 98: 112–117, 1957.

Krüssmann, Gerd, *La pépinière, arbustes, arbres conifères et fruitiers,* La Maison Rustique, 1981.

Lancaster, Roy, *A Plantsman in Nepal,* Antique Collectors' Club, 1995.

Lancaster, Roy, *Travels in China: A Plantman's Paradise,* Antique Collectors' Club, 1993.

Lenoir, Robert, "Expérimentation à Rendeux d'érables exotiques," *Feuillets Dendrologiques* 3, 1971.

Lenoir, Robert, "La gelée tardive du 10 mai 1953 et les essences exotiques en Basse Ardenne," *Bulletin de la Société Royale Forestière de Belgique* (July), 1953.

Lenoir, Robert, "Les dégâts causés par l'hiver 1956 aux arbres et arbustes exotiques installés à Rendeux (Basse Ardenne)," *Bulletin de la Société Royale Forestière de Belgique* (March), 1959.

Phillips, Roger, *Les arbres,* Solar, 1978.

Rehder, Alfred, *Manual of Cultivated Trees and Shrubs,* Macmillan Company, 1947.

Stearn, William T., *Botanical Latin,* 4th ed., Timber Press and David & Charles, 1992.

van Gelderen, D. M., P. C. de Jong, and H. J. Oterdoom, *Maples of the World,* Timber Press, 1994.

Vertrees, J. D., *Japanese Maples,* 3rd ed., Timber Press, 2001.

World Conservation Monitoring Centre, *The World List of Threatened Trees,* World Conservation Press, 1998.

INDEX OF COMMON NAMES
AND SYNONYMS

INDEX OF PLANTS